INTERNATIONAL POLITICAL ECONOMY SERIES

General Editor: Timothy M. Shaw, Professor of Political Science and International Development Studies, and Director of the Centre for Foreign Policy Studies, Dalhousie University, Halifax, Nova Scotia

Recent titles include:

Pradeep Agrawal, Subir V. Gokarn, Veena Mishra, Kirit S. Parikh and Kunal Sen
ECONOMIC RESTRUCTURING IN EAST ASIA AND INDIA: Perspectives on Policy Reform

Gavin Cawthra
SECURING SOUTH AFRICA'S DEMOCRACY: Defence, Development and Security in Transition

Steve Chan (*editor*)
FOREIGN DIRECT INVESTMENT IN A CHANGING GLOBAL POLITICAL ECONOMY

Jennifer Clapp
ADJUSTMENT AND AGRICULTURE IN AFRICA: Farmers, the State and the World Bank in Guinea

Seamus Cleary
THE ROLE OF NGOs UNDER AUTHORITARIAN POLITICAL SYSTEMS

Robert W. Cox (*editor*)
THE NEW REALISM: Perspectives on Multilateralism and World Order

Diane Ethier
ECONOMIC ADJUSTMENT IN NEW DEMOCRACIES: Lessons from Southern Europe

Stephen Gill (*editor*)
GLOBALIZATION, DEMOCRATIZATION AND MULTILATERALISM

Jacques Hersh and Johannes Dragsbaek Schmidt (*editors*)
THE AFTERMATH OF 'REAL EXISTING SOCIALISM' IN EASTERN EUROPE, Volume 1: Between Western Europe and East Asia

David Hulme and Michael Edwards (*editors*)
NGOs, STATES AND DONORS: Too Close for Comfort?

Staffan Lindberg and Árni Sverrisson (*editors*)
SOCIAL MOVEMENTS IN DEVELOPMENT: The Challenge of Globalization and Democratization

Anne Lorentzen and Marianne Rostgaard (*editors*)
THE AFTERMATH OF 'REAL EXISTING SOCIALISM' IN EASTERN EUROPE, Volume 2: People and Technology in the Process of Transition

Laura Macdonald
SUPPORTING CIVIL SOCIETY: The Political Role of Non-Governmental
Organizations in Central America

Stephen D. McDowell
GLOBALIZATION, LIBERALIZATION AND POLICY CHANGE: A Political
Economy of India's Communications Sector

Juan Antonio Morales and Gary McMahon (*editors*)
ECONOMIC POLICY AND THE TRANSITION TO DEMOCRACY: The Latin
American Experience

Ted Schrecker (*editor*)
SURVIVING GLOBALISM: The Social and Environmental Challenges

Ann Seidman, Robert B. Seidman and Janice Payne (*editors*)
LEGISLATIVE DRAFTING FOR MARKET REFORM: Some Lessons from
China

Kenneth P. Thomas
CAPITAL BEYOND BORDERS: States and Firms in the Auto Industry,
1960–94

Caroline Thomas and Peter Wilkin (*editors*)
GLOBALIZATION AND THE SOUTH

Geoffrey R. D. Underhill (*editor*)
THE NEW WORLD ORDER IN INTERNATIONAL FINANCE

Henry Veltmeyer, James Petras and Steve Vieux
NEOLIBERALISM AND CLASS CONFLICT IN LATIN AMERICA: A
Comparative Perspective on the Political Economy of Structural Adjustment

Robert Wolfe
FARM WARS: The Political Economy of Agriculture and the International Trade
Regime

International Political Economy Series
Series Standing Order ISBN 0–333–71110–6
(*outside North America only*)

You can receive future titles in this series as they are published by placing a standing order.
Please contact your bookseller or, in case of difficulty, write to us at the address below with
your name and address, the title of the series and the ISBN quoted above.

Customer Services Department, Macmillan Distribution Ltd
Houndmills, Basingstoke, Hampshire RG21 6XS, England

Redefining the Third World

Edited by

Nana Poku
Senior United Nations Researcher
and
Lecturer in Security Studies
Department of Politics
The University of Southampton

and

Lloyd Pettiford
Lecturer in International Relations
Department of International Relations
The Nottingham Trent University

Foreword by Peter Vale
Professor of Southern African Studies
University of the Western Cape, South Africa

First published in Great Britain 1998 by
MACMILLAN PRESS LTD
Houndmills, Basingstoke, Hampshire RG21 6XS and London
Companies and representatives throughout the world

A catalogue record for this book is available from the British Library.

ISBN 0–333–71983–2

First published in the United States of America 1998 by
ST. MARTIN'S PRESS, INC.,
Scholarly and Reference Division,
175 Fifth Avenue, New York, N.Y. 10010

ISBN 0–312–21671–8

Library of Congress Cataloging-in-Publication Data
Redefining the third world / edited by Nana Poku and Lloyd Pettiford.
p.   cm. — (International political economy series)
Includes bibliographical references and index.
ISBN 0–312–21671–8 (cloth)
1. Developing countries—Economic conditions.   2. Developing
countries—Foreign economic relations.   3. Developing countries–
–Foreign relations.   4. Developing countries—Civilization.
I. Poku, Nana, 1971–   .   II. Pettiford, Lloyd.   III. Series.
HC59.7.R348   1998
37.1''172'4—dc21   98–19805
                                                                  CIP

This book is printed on paper suitable for recycling and made from fully managed and
sustained forest sources.

10   9   8   7   6   5   4   3   2   1
07   06   05   04   03   02   01   00   99   98

Printed and bound in Great Britain by
Antony Rowe Ltd, Chippenham, Wiltshire

Contents

List of Tables

Foreword

Why is the Third World always second? This deadly question hides within it the fact that, by any measure, more and more wealth, and consequently power, is concentrated in the hands of fewer and fewer people. Others have made the point, but 20 per cent of humanity controls 85 per cent of the world's wealth: the bottom 20 per cent must make do with 1.4 per cent of this wealth;[1] 'grinding poverty remains the most important characteristic of much of Third-World existence, where high infant mortality rates, chronic underemployment, and inadequate shelter and health care are the stuff of everyday life.'[2] In other words, it is the spectacles of sickness, ignorance and premature death, as well as the violence, ugliness and despair of daily life which distress most people about the Third World. The accompanying poverty and underemployment underline the perception of economic fatality. In this context, the critical theme of this book is crucial, and the observations offered here are centred around the notion of power and conceptions of powerlessness, subsequently addressed by the various contributors and in various ways. As a prelude to the reflections to follow in this book, it is crucial to understand the framing which shape both understandings and interpretations of international events.

THE CONSTRUCTION OF THE THIRD WORLD

In addition to methodological or theoretical considerations, this endeavour has a deep and abiding interest in real world problems, which explains why it is driven by questions that aim to unsettle the orthodoxy. The interest is in both explanation of the everyday conduct of international relationships and in enabling a process of transformation to take place; with Karl Marx therefore, this book is interested in interpreting the world *and* in changing it. All disciplines, including International Relations and Development Studies, for whose students this work may have particular appeal, are surrounded by myths that works such as this aim to debunk. Although attention is directed towards aspects of the relationship between etymology,[3] security, economics and the idea of the Third

World, the paradoxical nature of the use of words is highlighted; the world is not what words suggest it is.

An anglicised version of the French term, *Tiers Monde*, which was used by French writers in the 1950s, has been used as a 'portmanteau term for the states in Central and South America, Africa, the Middle East, Asia (excepting Japan) and the Pacific islands (excepting Australia and New Zealand) which have experienced decolonisation over the last two centuries'.[4] If, as some suggest, there was a 'three worlds' theory, it consisted of the comparative analyses of economic (and to some limited extent political) conditions of the three worlds, and to setting these within frames of 'ideal' types within which the dominant ones – capitalism and communism – were desired goals. This remains a powerful strain in discourses which include the idea of the Third World as a deprecating and pejorative term.

While its roots lie in a seemingly innocent moment of the immediate post-Second World War period, its ranking in the hierarchical patterns of analysis so popular at the time, suggest that to all intents and purposes it was to be no more than the third level in the real business of politics that were to be conducted between the self-styled First World and the appropriately-designated and suitably-distanced Second World. In its initial setting, it drew from the idea of the 'Third Estate' in pre-Revolutionary France. In passing, therefore, we should note its patronising tone, although it must be clear that the *tiers mondalists* were much more appreciative of, and sensitive to, the plight of colonial people that was to become increasingly associated with the term.

Located within these interpretations is the idea of the Third World. No small part of this is the notion of *civilisation* within the international system, who sets its terms and how it plays out. As Gerrit Gong writes, 'for many of these countries, part of their common experience with colonial patterns and the struggle for freedom was confrontation with the standard of civilisation'.[5] As Gong goes on to argue, it was a double standard having to be measured against a foreign standard of civilisation and to have mainly been found wanting; it was humiliating for non-European countries to have been declared 'uncivilised'. Further, it was even more agonising for them to have their traditional standards of 'civilisation' cast aside as being effete or inferior. The continued association of military and moral superiority, and of military and moral inferiority, linger on.[6]

The popularisation of the rankings (First, Second and Third) within the realm of discourse and politics followed logically. In a time when measurement meant everything in both science and social science, distance from centres of power (itself measured by the quantifiable damage of nuclear destruction) and the spatial under-standing of politics were strengthened by a processes of decolonisation in which measurement became a substitute for understanding and explanation.

Questions of identity, for example, appeared to be resolvable easily within the confines of a decolonisation discourse that invented nations-in-waiting which could move, or be moved, towards the most acceptable form of political organisation, the nation-state, that mainstay of modernisation and the discourses that so confidently drove it. The process of ranking them seemed as easy as accepting that, to all intents and purposes, they enjoyed what was un-problematically called state sovereignty.

Central theoretical points that need to be emphasised are the discourses which drove the understanding of relations between the First, Second and Third Worlds were framed in such a way as to place strong emphasis on the centrality of the state as the core actor of the international system and the emphasis on sovereignty as the key binding element in international relations. The impris-onment of the idea of the 'Third World' within predominant modes of theorising has wholly distorted the term's capacity as a point of mobilisation; hence the importance of this book.

Small wonder, then, the ease with which the term 'Third World' came to the fore within the security conscious debate that drove public and international relations at the height of the first Cold War. Newly homogenised societies, literally under the banner of newly invented nationalisms, were quickly captured by the near apocalyptic debates that drove all international crises, of which Berlin was the first (and Cuba the most dramatic) to enjoy the epithet.

But there is no finer example of the truly international nature of the discourses of the time than the events over the independence of the Belgian Congo in the early 1960s, which was also quickly called a full-blown 'crisis'.[7] Looking back, it quickly becomes clear that the essential issues were neither Congolese nor about the sep-arateness of the Third World, but the sense in which 'the Congo became a testing ground ... [regarding] the purpose of American power in the Third World'.[8] Not to put too fine a point upon it, the discourses that foregrounded the idea of the Third World were driven primarily by security considerations[9] of the powerful and those who controlled the discourses of social science.[10] These in turn were driven by experiences that derived from earlier understanding of international relationships. Of particular importance, both for analytical and heuristic reasons, was the US understanding of Latin America which, drawing on the Monroe Doctrine, continuously invoked the idea that sovereignty lay in Washington and not in the capitals of the individual nation-states.[11]

It was an easy step from here to the use of the term within the global politics that were playing out at the time. Never itself a subject within the great bipolar debate, the *Third* World was invariably the object of the attention of either the First or the Second. So Washington's policy was driven by the idea that by resisting change (in and towards the Third World), the USA would concede a strategic advantage to the Soviet Union.[12] In this framing of the world, 'the strategic balance between the two major power groups co-exist[ed] with and [was] affected by the economic, political and strategic problems of the Third World'.[13] As late as the mid-1980s, analysts were still categorising the relations between the USA and the Third World in terms of 'scorecards'.[14] The framing of Soviet policy remains, even at this late stage, a mystery, but here we accept the orthodoxy that, to a greater or lesser extent, it was a mirror image of US policy.[15]

So this naming of international names was a way of including the states designated as Third World within the unfolding geopolitics of the time while, at the same time, excluding them from the core; an agenda in which the self-styled great ideologies (capitalist or communist) were the true heirs of the Enlightenment tradition. Looking backwards with a quizzical eye, we are tempted to ask whether the term 'Between World' might have been a more apt description of a condition that existed from the mid-1950s until the collapse of the Berlin Wall.[16] But the limits of etymology, well illustrated in the foregoing paragraphs, are too well known to leave the analysis at this particular moment.

It was entirely doubtful that the states of the Third World enjoyed any of the trappings of statehood by which, all things being equal, they could be included in the state system. The most salient of these was, of course, sovereignty; who was to get it and who enjoyed it. The issue is crucial in explaining the idea of the Third World. The discredit into which the idea of colonialism fell during the Second World War opened the possibilities for the tide of 'independence' that was to follow. The problem was the structural inability of these 'new' states to follow through the undertakings that were inherent in their sovereignty; put quite simply, they are not sovereign states but quasi-states.[17] Invariably, this absence of the essential ingredient to conduct international relationships, the sovereignty element, weakened the capacity of the states of the Third World to operate within the international system, and even within the blanketing comfort of the idea of the Third World, they could never become more than bit players.

There seems no better example of this than the struggle over apartheid, always thought to be an issue that quintessentially engaged the Third World. Although invariably central to the concerns of Third-World countries, the capacity to influence directly the outcome in South Africa was hampered by the fact that apartheid South Africa, for strategic and economic reasons, enjoyed the protection of the richer and more powerful countries of the world, especially the USA and Great Britain. So, while the idea of emancipating South Africa's majority from the yoke of colonialism was a permanent feature of the concerns of the Third World, it was only possible to do so once the intense ideological divide that the Cold War provided was over.

If political power was limited and limiting, the power of the idea of progress that drove the great modernisation thrust of the 1960s envisaged endless vistas of progress within which, as if by their allotted destiny, the Third World could come to enjoy equality of status with the First or the Second. This introduces the development dimension of the term, Third World, and takes the discussion towards an endemic economic condition which, to all intents and purposes, has not changed. It was a blind faith in the ideology of progress that drove the debates around development with its end goal of a manqué Western state; a state which achieved self-sustaining economic growth over a sufficient period of time to show development in the primary, secondary and tertiary sectors of industry and to have achieved a consistent improvement in living standards for the population as a whole.

Here, too, the ideology rested on consideration of power and the power of ideas. The strongest motor force was the modernisation paradigm which is associated with Walt Rostow's stages of development with its emphasis on the propensities of people to engage successfully in economic development; that is, aptitudes to develop science, to apply science, to propagate and rear offspring, and to strive for material advancement.[18] But economic progress was, of course, as impossible to achieve as the analysis was impossible to defend in today's world. The economic setbacks of the 1970s and 1980s were to show that the idea of Third-World development was one of the more interesting oxymorons of International Relations scholarship. Tying this together with the idea of what true independence represented became a dominant theme in discourses around the Third World. And they came together, more in frustration than with a sense that anything substantial could change, in the 1975 Lima Declaration of the Non-Aligned Movement: 'The true meaning of independence must reflect unequivocally the common commitment to build the New International Economic Order.' While the 1980s were described as a decade of economic growth, the so-called 'trickle down' effect towards the Third World was minimal; per capital incomes declined in a range of countries in the South.

But such currents as outlined above have not been the only approach to explaining international relations. Arising from the work of Third-World writers, Dependency Theory was popularised by the work of Andre Gunder Frank.[19] Frank's starting point was imperialism, viewed as an amalgam of economic expansion and political domination. Under imperialism, capital accumulation is based on the export of capital from the advanced countries to underdeveloped areas. Political and military might is used to assert control over the means of production in foreign lands benefiting a segment of the citizenry in the advanced countries and their partners overseas. Thus dependency denotes the effects of imperialism on underdeveloped countries. A special form of domination and subordination, dependency's defining characteristic is vulnerability; the limits on a collectivity's ability to determine its own response to social forces within the world order. External forces – the economies of the 'core' (advanced capitalist nations) 'condition' the responses of the 'periphery' (Third-World countries) – narrowed the options for independent development. In this context, a country is dependent when the accumulation of capital cannot find its own dynamic within the national economy. By focusing on economic issues, the theory argued that relations benefited the developed countries and were injurious to those that were developing; capital, for example, was drained northwards, making the poor even poorer in absolute terms. The way to break out of the cycle of dependency was to overturn the trading system that sustained the disparities.

The major contribution of the dependency approach is to pin-point the process whereby imperialism has incorporated Third-World countries into global capitalism, thereby underdeveloping the internal socioeconomic structures within these countries. At a critical level, the dependency school mounted an effective critique of the modernisation thesis. For example, they helped to debunk the dualist thesis, which holds that Third-World economies are divided into a capitalist sector and a subsistence sector. On the contrary, commercialisation and accumulation do occur in peasant enterprises, and backward rural areas are yoked to the national economy as well as the world market. In practical terms, the dependency school helped to muster support for liberation struggles in Indo-China and Black Africa. Hence, during the 1960s and 1970s, dependency was the dominant approach to understanding the position of the Third World, especially Latin America, in international affairs.

The dependency movement's single greatest failure was not anticipating what Arie de Ruiter called the 'Anglo-American wind' – the free-market ideas that revolutionised both economics and politics in the late 1970s and the 1980s. So dependency theory has been unable to explain the success of the 'Asian Tigers'.[20] If trading relations between the First and Third Worlds were so harmful to the latter, how could dependency writers explain the apparent successes in Asia? For many, dependency theory is dead: it remains, however, a potent analytical force. As Steve Hobden has pointed out, it continues to draw attention to a number of factors when considering the international relations of Latin America; the significance of international economic relations, the relative poverty of the region and the importance of international factors in explaining that poverty, and the inequity in terms of power between different countries in the international system.

But what really changed the face of things was, if anything, always hidden from the public and political eye. The idea of a nationalism which resided in the comforting arms of a people and a state was based on interpretations of morality. Caught by Emile Durkheim as an example, societal cohesion was based on the solidarity between members of a society in which contractual bonding was essential in a pathway that led to modernisation. But such a nationalist focus has become increasingly anachronistic and identity is a much more blurred concern; multiple, evolving, transitory but difficult to impose. Accordingly, complexity in Third-World studies, as this book argues, is now essential.

CONCLUSION

However convenient and tidy the three-ringed circus of the Cold War appeared to be, it is no longer possible to confine the Third World 'to its assigned place' because it 'has penetrated the inner sanctum of the First World'.[21] The next step is hybridisation: a process through which it is no longer possible to see societies – local, state or international – as being settled by the boundaries they have, or that have been, drawn around them. Creolisation has come home to the metropole. Here the idea of 'Third World' has re-entered the discourses of International Relations. Whatever the misconstrued understanding of reality in the South, the countries of the North now face the same sets of societal and policy challenges – resource scarcities, over-population, under-development and environmental degradation[22] – that were once exclusively reserved for the Third World grouping of states. As Alain Geismar, a leader of the 1968 student uprising in France, has suggested, the Third World now starts in the suburbs – that is, the working-class districts around Paris. Geographical challenges to our understanding of the 'Third World' are an important element in this project.

However, this does not mean that the notion of the Third World is entirely devoid of content. The idea of the Third World (a construction of the power relations of the Cold War) is capable of doing more than merely reflecting the crude realist constructions of the early 1950s. There are important reasons to believe that, as the millennium draws to a close, the case for retaining the notion is stronger than ever. For one thing, the divide between rich and poor nations remains as much a feature of international relations as it has ever been. Efforts to supplant the notion of the Third World by replacing it with the idea of the global South have not been wholly successful, and, while admittedly diverse in their characteristics, especially when compared to the 1950s, the countries of the Third World continue to display common features. Finally, even within its highly discriminatory setting, it is important to keep alive the idea that the international system is still not one world, either in its workings or in the way people engage with it. It is still, borrowing Fantu Cheru's term, characterised by global apartheid. But the most compelling reason is that the idea of the 'Third World' still encapsulates a highly discriminatory world in which the majority of humankind continues to face hopelessness and daily struggle.

The world of Third World Studies is simply not recognisable from

that which went before and which encompassed some of the myths
to which I have alluded here. The challenge is to develop concepts
and ideas which bring the conditions on the ground and scholarship close together. This volume, with its collective commitment to
self-consciously reflecting on the idea of the 'Third World' and the
concomitant aim of developing a more satisfactory, and above all,
more sensitive, understanding of it, is highly significant for the push
it gives to International, Development and Third World Studies;
its legacy, it is to be hoped, should be complexity and reflexivity in
unravelling previous certainties. In adumbrating a historical narra-
tive as I have done, it is not my intention to write this book, but to
provide some background to it and commend it to you as an attempt to see how we might go beyond certain disciplinary myths.

PETER VALE

Notes and References

1. S. George, 'Why Stop Now?' in *The Right to Hope. Global Problems.
   Global Visions. Creative Responses to our World in Need* (London:
   Earthscan, 1995), p. 6.
2. J. George, *Discourses of Global Politics: A Critical (Re)Introduction to
   International Relations* (Boulder, Col.: Lynne Rienner, 1994), p. 2.
3. We consider etymology as the tracing of the origin and historical development of a linguistic form as shown by determining its basic elements, earliest known use, and changes in form and meaning, tracing
   its transmission from one language to another, identifying its cognates
   in other languages, and reconstructing its ancestral form where this is
   possible. See *The American Heritage Dictionary of the English Language, 3rd edn* (Boston, Mass.: Houghton Mifflin, 1992). Electronic
   version licensed from InfoSoft International, Inc. All rights reserved.
4. G. Evans and J. Newnham, *The Dictionary of World Politics* (Hemel
   Hempstead: Harvester Wheatsheaf, 1990), p. 317.
5. G. W. Gong, *The Standard of 'Civilization' in International Society* (Oxford: Clarendon Press, 1984), p. 12.
6. Ibid., p. 246.
7. One of the best discussions of this is C. C. O'Brien, *To Katanga and
   Back: A UN Case History* (New York: Simon & Schuster, 1962).
8. R. D. Mahoney, *JFK: Ordeal in Africa* (New York: Oxford University
   Press, 1983), p. 108.
9. M. Ayoob, *The Third World Security Predicament: State Making, Regional Conflict and the International System* (Boulder, Col.: Lynne
   Rienner, 1995), pp. 1–19.

10. As an example, in 1992 an entire edition of *The Annuals of the America Academy of Political and Social Science*, vol. 463, was devoted to international terrorism, with most case studies coming from the Third World.
11. I am grateful to Dr Steve Hobden for providing this insight in his draft paper provisionally entitled 'Latin America and IR Theory' (1997).
12. Ibid.
13. T. B. Millar, *The East–West Strategic Balance* (London: George Allen and Unwin), p. 161.
14. See J. Sewell (*et al.*), *US Foreign Policy and the Third World: Agenda 1985–86* (New Brunswick and Oxford: Transaction Books, 1985).
15. Gorbachev's 'new thinking' towards the Third World in foreign policy (in the late 1980s and early 1990s) says a lot about what the 'old thinking' was like.
16. Although 'Between World' might come similar to the meaning of China (Middle Kingdom as in 'central'), which certainly fails to encapsulate the idea of a periphery.
17. R. Jackson, *Quasi-States: Sovereignty, International Relations and the Third World* (New York: Cambridge University Press, 1990).
18. W. W. Rostow, *The Process of Economic Growth* (New York: W. W. Norton, 1952), ch. 2.
19. See A. G. Frank, *Capitalism and Underdevelopment in Latin America: Historical Studies of Chile and Brazil* (New York: Monthly Review Press, 1967); and *Dependent Accumulation and Underdevelopment* (New York: Monthly Review Press, 1979).
20. Although so too have conventional free-market analyses.
21. T. Ranger, 'Colonial and Postcolonial Identities', in R. Werbner and T. Ranger (eds), *Postcolonial Identities in Africa* (London: Zed Books, 1996), p. 271.
22. A. Acharya, 'The Periphery as Core: The Third World and Security Studies', in K. Krause and M. C. Williams (eds), *Critical Security Studies: Concepts and Cases* (Minneapolis: University of Minnesota Press, 1996), p. 304.

Acknowledgements

We wish to thank Professor Timothy M. Shaw for his help and encouragement throughout the project. Thanks are also due to our contributors for meeting deadlines and offering encouragement; we would particularly like to thank Professor Stephen Chan, Professor Peter Vale and Dr Pete Wilkin. Special mention must also be made of Aruna Vasudevan from Macmillan, and Soula Poku, for pushing us endlessly to meet our deadlines.

NANA POKU
LLOYD PETTIFORD

List of Abbreviations and Acronyms

AIDS	acquired immune deficiency syndrome
ASEAN	Association of Southeast Asian Nations
CBMs	Confidence-building measures
CIS	Commonwealth of Independent States (see FSU)
CSCAP	Council for Security and Co-operation in Asia Pacific
CWO	capitalist world order
ECOMOG	Economic Community of West African States Cease-Fire Monitoring Group
ECOWAS	Economic Community of West African States
EU	European Union
EIU	Economist Intelligence Unit
EPZ	export processing zone(s)
FDI	foreign direct investment
FNLA	National Front for the Liberation of Angola
FSU	Former Soviet Union
G7, G77 etc.	Group of 7 or 77 etc. countries
GDP	Gross domestic product
GNP	Gross national product
HQ	headquarters
IDA	International Development Association
IDB	International Development Bank
IFI	international financial institution
IMF	International Monetary Fund
IR	international relations
ISI	import substituting industry/industrialisation
KMT	Kuomintang (Taiwan)
LDCs	less developed countries
LLDCs	least developed countries
MERCOSUR	South American Common Market
MPLA	Popular Movement for the Liberation of Angola
NAFTA	North American Free Trade Agreement

NAM	Non-Aligned Movement
NATO	North Atlantic Treaty Organisation
NGO	non-governmental organisation
NIC	newly industrialising country
NIDL	new international division of labour
NIDP	new international division of power
NIT	new information technology
OAU	Organisation of African Unity
OECD	Organisation for Economic Cooporation and Development
OPEC	Organisation of Petroleum Exporting Countries
PAP	Peoples Action Party (Singapore)
PRC	Peoples' Republic of China
SAARC	South Asian Association for Regional Cooperation
SWAPO	South West African People's Organisation
TNC	transnational corporation
UMNO	United Malays National Organisation (Malaysia)
UN	United Nations
UNDP	United Nations Development Programme
UNITA	National Union for the Total Independence of Angola

Notes on the Contributors

Stephen Chan is a Professor of International Relations and Ethics at the Nottingham Trent University, UK.

Björn Hettne is Professor of International Relations at the University of Göteborg (PADRIGU), Sweden.

Karl Kaltenthaler is Assistant Professor of International Relations at Rhodes College, Memphis, USA.

Mehran Kamrava is Assistant Professor of Political Science at California State University, USA.

Norman Lewis is a PhD candidate at the University of Sussex, UK.

Frank O. Mora is Assistant Professor of International Relations at Rhodes College, Memphis, USA.

Giok-Ling Ooi is Senior Research Fellow at the Institute of Policy Studies, Singapore.

Lloyd Pettiford is a Lecturer in International Relations at the Nottingham Trent University, UK.

Nana Poku is a Senior United Nations Researcher and Lecturer at the University of Southampton, UK.

Fahimul Quadir is a PhD candidate at Dalhousie University, Canada.

Timothy M. Shaw is a Professor of Political Science and International Development Studies at Dalhousie University, Halifax, Nova Scotia.

Georg Sørensen is Senior Lecturer at the University of Aarhus, Denmark.

Peter Vale is Professor of Southern African Studies, University of the Western Cape, and Visiting Professor in Political Science, University of Stellenbosch, South Africa.

Peter Wilkin is a Lecturer in International Relations at Lancaster University, UK.

1 Introduction: Redefining the Third World?

Georg Sørensen with Nana Poku and Lloyd Pettiford[1]

During the Cold War years, no term appeared to achieve greater clarity and simplicity than that of the 'Third World': whether in the political writings of Fidel Castro, the poetry of Ame Cesaire, or the economic analysis of Mahub ul-Haq, the term came to represent an ideology of its own. More than merely a socioeconomic designation, it indicated (and constructed) a psychological condition, a state of mind encompassing the hopes and aspirations of three-quarters of humanity.

Outside the Third World, and intuitively perhaps, it created (and many people feel they *still* have) a clear idea of what constitutes the Third World. It is one of a whole series of pejorative terms, including 'underdeveloped', 'developing state', 'emerging nation' and so on, with implicit notions of inferiority or backwardness when compared with 'developed', 'industrialised' or 'First World', which suggest civilisation and superiority. Accordingly, people have an idea of the countries considered to be Third World; for example, India, Chad and Nicaragua; and those that are not, such as Japan, Italy or the United States of America.

Despite such – we would argue *misplaced* – intuition, many students and scholars have come to question this dichotomous understanding in which *states* fit into one category or the other and where very occasionally a state might justify reclassification. Questioning and rejection come from a variety of sources; empirically, there are a number of reasons why we need to re-examine and redefine the concept Castro once described as 'an affirmation of Afro-Asian unity'. Fundamentally this book is an examination of some crucial questions which as a whole challenge the certainty of the 'Third World' as an organising concept for study and for policy orientation in world politics. These questions stem from a number of sources: rejection of the simplicity of the idea and of the categories (First and Third Worlds) themselves; caution, doubt and tentativeness

1

regarding modernisation (the idea that states *will* or can develop along a path that moves from Third to First World); and a discomfort with the ethnocentrism inherent in this whole modernisation (development) discourse (the inferiority/superiority idea is hard to sustain when it is evident that traditional wisdom has been destroyed by so-called civilisation).

Accordingly, this book aims to capture the creative tension between the need to engage critically with the concept at the theoretical level and the reality of what it denotes for the 'majority world'. Predicated on the Cold War, the book offers a detailed analysis of the rise and contemporary significance of the 'Third World'. There are a variety of reasons why now may be seen as a useful time to re-examine the idea of the Third World as well as a number a objections to the very term which are implicit in its existence and usage, in International Relations especially. These practical problems and inherent criticisms are outlined below and will, it is hoped, lead to an awareness of the potentiality of multiple meanings.

In order to begin a reconsideration of the Third World it is a worthwhile foundation to look briefly at the evolution of the term. Here it is interesting to note that its origins in French, while still implying notions of superiority, mean that the 'third' of Third World is from the French for 'third' as a fraction, rather than 'third' as in position, place or order. Its translation into an inferior positional attribute is therefore significant and is tied in with the whole modernisation thesis.

Credit for the introduction of the term 'Third World' is usually given to the French demographer and economist Alfred Sauvy following an article in *France Observateur*. The term alludes to the French term of *le Tiers État*, the label identifying the large group of underprivileged in preindustrial society. The popularity the term has subsequently achieved is linked to the process of decolonisation as well as to the Cold War. In the early years of Development Studies, 'backward regions' were thought to be on the verge of a rapid process of development in the image of the modernising, capitalist countries in Europe and North America; or, alternatively, destined to remain as they were because the preconditions were simply too adverse. Whichever view was subscribed to, 'Third World' is connected with a certain common background of emerging states, namely that of colonialism, and with economic and political features that set Third World countries apart from the industrialised West.

Having thus outlined the term and its origins, we are now in a position to undertake a more thorough-going analysis of what this book is about: the empirical and theoretical necessity of redefining the Third World.

THE NEED TO REDEFINE THE THIRD WORLD?

One obvious criticism aimed at the idea of the Third World is that since the end of the Cold War the 'Second World' has ceased to exist. The collapse of the system of 'socialist' states set up in Eastern Europe after the Second World War on the periphery of the Soviet Union, and the subsequent collapse of that system, have done away with the 'Second World' as a separate entity; and they have entirely removed the Cold War as a defining feature of global politics. As we have seen above, 'Third World' itself has travelled the road from *Tiers Etat* meaning 'a third of the world' to Third World meaning 'the world in third place'; the pejorative implications of this latter meaning could only be reinforced by simply promoting the 'Third World' into second place, but the non-existence of a Second World does at least present an opportunity to question the whole idea of a global pecking order based on gross national product (GNP) per capita.

Despite problems with the 'ordering' of countries, and the tendency to do this on the basis of GNP, some argue that the vast differentiation among countries of the Third World means that, rather than reject a hierarchical ordering of states, more categories are called for. The varying trajectories to appropriate modernisation discourse of different countries and regions within the 'Third World' since the 1940s have called into question the usefulness of the blanket term 'Third World' to cover developing nations, especially if they are assumed to be *uniformly* poor and underdeveloped.

Exactly how many categories might be needed is debated, and some literature already makes effective distinctions between LDCs and LLDCs (Less Developed and Least Developed Countries). A variety of countries present problems to the would-be categoriser. There are also a whole series of NICs (Newly Industrialising Countries) which have enormously varying GNPs, including on a per capita basis; and vast accumulations of wealth have been made in a limited number of oil states. Some Third World countries, such as China, India or Brazil, have weight, influence or presence in international politics by virtue of their size, while others have been so dominated by foreign powers throughout their history as to have little influence – for example, Nicaragua. Some states have fallen or are in the process of falling apart, such as Sierra Leone. How are we to classify all these different states? Should we attempt to? And what about nominal players in the international system, such as Chad, where the state has virtually or actually ceased to exist in any meaningful sense?

Clearly, an important basis of 'Third World' and some proposed revisions of a classificatory system is the method of measuring where a state belongs to a category on the basis of per capita GNP. In thinking about redefining the Third World, this idea itself is in need of questioning, for a variety of reasons. Does it really represent the most appropriate way to classify states? Since GNP includes destruction and depletion of assets as well as production, is it an accurate or desirable method of measurement, either economically or environmentally? One wonders, furthermore, if, given examples such as South Korea and Portugal, it really is helping to break down imaginings of what constitute the First and Third Worlds?

Perhaps the most serious objection to the idea of GNP is its underpinning of modernisation. Modernisation represents ultimate faith in development wherein 'development' is the destination and all states are on the road to it. Some may not be doing terribly well, but 'developed' is where all states are heading. In order to judge just how far down the road any given Third-World state is we need only look at its figures for GNP. There are some very practical ecological reasons for being unhappy with this way of thinking; and there are also some moral objections to supposing that there is only one way to do things. Furthermore, empirical observation just does not bear out the optimism of development; George Rist compares it to a religion whose practitioners continue to believe because of miracles such as South Korea, despite the social and ecological consequences and despite some of the heretical methods used along the way.[2]

GNP is also unsatisfactory, and this relates directly to debates over the usefulness of the Third World as an idea, because it is based on states. The changing nature and spatial distribution of poverty under pressure from the forces of globalisation must surely challenge a state-based, geographical notion of the Third World. If we look at China, we surely see many different worlds, some characterised by growth, dynamism and conspicuous consumption, others by environmental nightmare and grinding poverty. Similarly, in all countries of the world we can see huge disparities of wealth. As mobile capital chases the cheapest labour, living in the so-called First World and being unskilled is not a comfortable position to be in, and it is characterised increasingly by the hopelessness and despair associated with the idea of a 'Third World'. Of course, the linkages and divisions between the worlds of the rich and the poor are definable, but how can we draw lines around countries and allocate Third-World status if the structurally rich and poor are neighbours in many global cities?

While some of the contributors to a lively debate (encapsulated in this book) disagree, what the above suggests to us is not the need for a new group of categories by which the third, fourth . . . ninth, tenth, etc. worlds may be delineated, nor for some more sophisticated colouring scheme whereby the interior of China is a different colour from the condominiums of Rio and perhaps the same colour as the *favelas* of Rio and areas of Liverpool, Athens or Madrid. What it does suggest is coming to terms with a changing pattern of international relations and adapting our thinking accordingly towards the Third World.

In this sense, whether and how to redefine the Third World becomes not a task to be accomplished but an open ended question and site for academic debate. In a broader sense, academic study becomes, we suggest, not just a question of exposing the reasons why Third-World states have been excluded from much of International Relations, and then trying to include them, but thinking about who and what else is excluded and how this might be included. The Third World, despite the problems with it and its pejorative connotations, remains a potent symbol of the marginalised and oppressed; however, to the extent that it has frequently been co-opted by those doing the oppression it needs to be reclaimed.

Basically, the foregoing is a plea, made throughout this book, for greater complexity in Third-World studies and subjectivity for the Third World in international relations. In making our arguments here we think it useful to note that not everyone insists on rejecting the image of the Third World as a Weberian ideal type of poverty, political cleavages, low economic clout and poor political prestige. Accordingly, and before outlining the contributions to this volume, we adumbrate below arguments for regarding the 'Third World' as an 'ideal' type for use as a reference or point of comparison.

THE THIRD WORLD AS A USEFUL STEREOTYPE?

In this context it is helpful to treat the concept of the Third World as an ideal type in the Weberian sense. Max Weber defined the ideal type as follows:

> An ideal type is formed by the one-sided accentuation of one or more points of view and by the synthesis of a great many diffuse, discrete, more or less present and occasionally absent concrete individual phenomena, which are arranged according to those one-sidedly emphasised viewpoints into a unified analytical construct. In its conceptual purity, the mental construct cannot be found empirically anywhere in reality.[3]

This leads us to analyse what a Third World country would be in ideal type terms. First, it would be a country with a colonial past. The most important wave of decolonisation involving Africa, Asia and the Middle East came after the Second World War, although there were two earlier periods of decolonisation/creation of new states: in Latin America in the early nineteenth century, following the Napoleonic Wars and the demise of the Spanish and Portuguese empires; and in the Middle East after the First World War, following the demise of the Ottoman Empire. There has also been one later phase of state creation, in Central Asia after the end of the Cold War, following the demise of the Soviet Union. Decolonisation meant a significant break with the past in two ways: first, new local rulers had a much higher degree of autonomy than earlier; and, second, the international system granted membership to a new player.

Turning to the socioeconomic characteristics of a Third-World country, it would typically lack the socioeconomic capacity to secure a decent standard of living for the vast majority of its population. There are several ways of describing a Third-World economy. The best known is probably the World Bank classification according to gross domestic product (GDP) per capita, with LDCs at the lower end of the ladder and LLDCs at the bottom. Another approach is taken by the UNDP, which measures the degree of 'human development' on a Human Development Index, a composite measure of life expectancy, education and output per capita. Even though there are some interesting deviations between the two measures it is generally clear that there is a close relationship between a low level of economic capacity and human deprivation. Behind these measures are economies characterised by structural hetero-geneity and external dependence. Heterogeneity denotes the simul-taneous coexistence of several forms of production, each with specific features: there are sectors with modern industry and service in the cities while the countryside displays a mixture of capitalist, feudal and semi-feudal forms of production. These latter forms are found within a large, informal sector which is only partly integrated in the formal economy. Dependency denotes the fact that Third-World economies are not self-centred; they are heavily dependent on a large number of inputs from the world market, be it in the form of production technology, semi-finished goods, know-how, or fertilis-ers. In return, Third-World countries export raw materials, agri-cultural produce and non-sophisticated industrial mass products. In sum, the typical Third World economy is characterised by struc-tural heterogeneity and world market dependence, combined with a low standard of living for the bulk of the population.

The other main characteristic of a Third-World country concerns political institutions and their relations to society. The typical Third-World country is a weak state in political-institutional terms. Weak states are not fully capable of performing those core functions that we expect from effective states: the preservation of domestic order and security from external threat; justice in the sense of maintain-ing the rule of law and equality before the law; and personal free-dom, including basic civil and political rights. Weakness in these respects is connected with institutions that are insufficiently devel-oped, lacking in resources, and with a staff that is largely incompe-tent and corrupt. In sum, the state lacks what Michael Mann has called 'infrastructural power', defined as 'the capacity of the state actually to penetrate civil society and to implement logistically political decisions throughout the realm.'[4]

Colonial past, structurally dependent economy and an institu-tionally weak state; does this characterisation of a Weberian ideal type retain analytical value? For some authors it does and it is to this question that we now turn.

THE IMPORTANCE OF BEING THE THIRD WORLD

By looking at the role of Third-World states in the international system and the factors of weak economies and political institutions, the following sections aims to make the case for a continuing validity in the use of the term 'Third World' by highlighting peculiar and distinct characteristics.

A Weak Player in the International System

In contrast to European experience, the Third-World state is created primarily from the outside and not from the inside. Colonial powers drew up the borders and organised the economies and polities of those states. The colonisers were not preoccupied with the long-term viability of would-be independent states. They were concerned about their own short-term economic and political interests. Consequently, colonial areas had little in terms of substantial statehood around the time of independence. Decolonisation marked a new development in international society because a group of weak players were now given independence irrespective of their lack of substantial statehood. In earlier days, such weak would-be entities would have been swallowed up by stronger competitors seeking to expand their domains. Decolonisation meant quite the opposite, in that international society agreed to respect the borders of weak ex-colonies. In that sense, international society guaranteed the existence of the ex-colonies, irrespective of the fact that many of the new states were so weak that they could not survive without outside help.

The Third-World state is also the basis for international aid regime providing bi- and multilateral assistance to Third-World countries. Before the arrival of Third-World states, international society did not have an aid regime. States were supposed to take care of themselves, to fend for themselves in a competitive international order. However, the typical Third-World state cannot play that competitive game. Given their vulnerability, the most important protection they have is the international norm that respects the borders and the formal sovereignty of Third-World states.[5] All this does not mean that the international system suddenly presents only gifts and no demands on Third-World members. Weak statehood means a high level of susceptibility to outside pressure and influence. The situation is one of secure insecurity. That is the peculiar security dilemma or paradox of the typical Third-World state. On the one hand, it is guaranteed survival by the international system and no matter how deficient it is in substantial terms, its continued legal existence is secure. On the other hand, the external guarantee takes on the role of an insecurity container, because Third-World populations are open to the manipulations not only of strong outside forces, but also of their own state elites.

This paradoxical situation compels Third-World countries to make highly conflicting demands on the international system. On the one hand, Third-World countries demand to be treated as equals in the international system – that is, to have sovereignty in the form of freedom from outside intervention and the same legal rights as any other independent state. Yet on the other hand, Third-World states demand to be treated as unequal in the international system – that is, as weaker units that need to develop quickly and therefore qualify for aid. Third-World countries want external aid without external interference. Following this logic, developed states have an obligation to help Third-World states, but 'no corresponding rights to ensure that their assistance is properly and efficiently used'[16] by recipient governments.

This is a precarious situation peculiar to Third-World states. Another aspect of this unique position of Third-World states in the international system concerns the Third World's simultaneous struggle to maintain the status quo and for change. The commitment to the status quo concerns Third-World support for sovereignty and non-intervention. The Third-World backing of these institutions is even said to be 'stronger than that of the developed states of the West, which were initially responsible for the formulation and global dissemination of these governing principles of the international system'.[7] At the same time, Third-World countries seek to create a much redefined international order which will provide more aid, more international governance and thus eventually a better position for all the Third-World countries in the system. This simultaneous commitment to entrenched stability and drastic change of the rules of the game in the international system is another peculiar consequence of the distinct characteristics of Third-World states.

A Weak Player in the Global Economy

The economic success of some Southeast Asian countries, notably the four tigers of South Korea, Taiwan, Hong Kong and Singapore, has led some observers to argue that this means the end of the Third World because now a group of Third-World countries has demonstrated that it is possible to break out from underdevelopment and have set an example for others to follow.[8] This reasoning is misleading in several respects. First, the concept of the Third-World is not tied to any deterministic notion about Third-World countries having to remain in economic underdevelopment forever. It is true that some development theorists from the dependency school argued that Third-World economic development is blocked as long as these countries remain integrated in the capitalist world economy,[9] but the concept of the Third-World does not stand or fall with that theory. Second, the idea that Southeast Asian success stories set an example that others can pick up and follow with similar success is not convincing. The unique features of the city-states of Singapore and Hong Kong are easily established. But even when it comes to Taiwan and South Korea these countries stand out as being unique historically when looked at from a comparative perspective. Beginning with the distinctive traits of Japanese colonisation, the specific features of divided countries with a front-line status during the Cold War, and therefore candidates for special preferential treatment from the United States, and the unique situation of domestic developmental elites with an extraordinarily high degree of autonomy from society, these countries display a pattern of development-conducive factors that are not easily replicated elsewhere.[10]

Current debate based on the ideology of developmentalism is dominated by the notion that by applying the correct strategy all countries can be successful in economic development. Currently in vogue, a liberal market economy strategy combined with social welfare state regulations is in many ways a sympathetic development strategy, a significant distance from the neoliberal market-mania of the 1980s. But the important point in the present context is that development strategies alone, no matter how congenial they may be, cannot guarantee a development success. Such a success depends in no small measure on the structural preconditions for development in each case. This means that we all need to ask, can all countries develop no matter how adverse the structural preconditions may be? Of course, we cannot be certain, but can say that while Third-World countries are not doomed to economic underdevelopment, neither are they predestined to achieve economic development. Some Third-World countries *have* had some success in this area, often displaying a unique set of preconditions, but, regardless of this, it must be assumed that economic development will remain a problem for most Third-World countries.

A Weak Player at Domestic Politics

With the end of the Cold War, the problem of state failure has grown dramatically. State failure is an accentuation of the problems inherent in weak states; and the situation is frequently accompanied by violent conflict that affects the civilian population. William Zartman has described state failure as follows:

> As the decision-making centre of government, the state is paralysed and inoperative; laws are not made, order is not preserved, and societal cohesion is not enhanced. As a symbol of identity, it has lost its power of conferring a name on its people and a meaning to their social action. As a territory, it is no longer assured security by a central sovereign organization. As the authoritative political institution, it has lost its legitimacy... As a system of socio-economic organization, its functional balance of inputs and outputs is destroyed.[11]

The accentuation of weak state problems inherent in state failure can take place in several ways and some sort a categorisation of types of state failure would be helpful at this point. A first attempt in this direction has been made by Jean-Germain Gros.[12] He makes a distinction between five different types of failed state:

1. 'Anarchic states' with no centralised government (for example, Somalia, Liberia).
2. 'Phantom or mirage states' with 'a semblance of authority that exhibits its efficacy in certain limited areas' (for example, Zaire).
3. 'Anaemic states' which are 'able to fulfil some of [their] functions, however locally, niggardly and sporadically, whereas the phantom state does not even attempt to do anything beyond protecting the maximum leader' (for example, Haiti).
4. 'Captured states' that have 'a strong centralised authority but one that is captured by members of insecure elites to frustrate, and in the extreme eradicate, rival elites' (for example, Rwanda).
5. 'Aborted states', states that 'experienced state failure even before the process of state formation was consolidated' (for example, Angola, Mozambique).

Suggested remedies for this problem seem to hold further problems within them. On redrawing boundaries, David Fromkin suggests that 'there is a strong case to be made that Africa should be totally restructured along tribal lines. But tens of millions of people would have to be killed'.[13] Similarly, increased democracy seems to create more, rather than less, violent conflict in weak states and sometimes leads to state collapse. In fact, there is no smooth and easy pathway from being a weak to a strong state, although a number of states in Latin America and Asia appear to be moving in that direction. For the large number of very weak states in Sub-Saharan Africa and elsewhere, advice on creating strong states has been offered for many years with little effect. The weak Third-World state is the basis for a distinctive set of problems concerned with state breakdown and failure.

OBJECTIONS OVERRULED!

In making a case for continuing use or validity of the term 'Third World', the foregoing has sought to outline a distinctive set of problems. Having allowed this case to speak, two obvious objections spring to mind, the first of which we have mentioned in more detail above. One could be called the differentiation argument based on the heterogeneity within the group of Third-World states, from oil-rich Gulf states to Sub-Saharan Africa, from Latin America to Southeast Asia, and so on. However, if it is clear that the colonial experience varies dramatically between Latin America, Asia and Africa, and that the regions demonstrate dramatic differences in levels of economic and political development and/or decay, such variations, it could be argued, are precisely part of the usefulness of the ideal type. By identifying empirical deviation from the ideal type we can, so the argument goes, develop hypotheses concerning deviations in development trajectories in various regions and countries.

The second objection (precisely *not* the basis of this book's more substantive challenges), is not so much to the idea of an all-embracing concept but to the term itself. That is, in speaking about whether 'Third World' should be replaced by another term such as 'South' or 'Developing Countries' or 'Emerging Areas', even if we are using an ideal type? Some are clear that it should:

Three and a half billion people, three quarters of all humanity live in the developing countries . . . Together the developing countries, accounting for more than two thirds of the earth's land surface area, are often called the Third-World. We refer to them as the South.[14]

However, the problem with 'developing countries' is the misleading indication that these countries are all undergoing a constructive process of development and that this process leads to some preordained goal called 'developed'. This might not be the case. The problem with the 'South' is first that it is more neutral geographically, and therefore a less analytical term. Second, it implies that all countries in the South (including, for example, Japan) are of the Third-World variety, and that all countries in the North are of the developed variety (including, for example, Haiti). Accordingly, it is quite possible to argue that the analytically most fitting term remains 'Third-World'.

The ideal type then expresses some core features, rebuffs some obvious objections and allows argument in favour of the validity of the term 'Third-World'. However, despite the defence presented here, a changing global agenda presents us with further objections, not necessarily regarding the term but critically concerning the ways in which it is studied and the way we are to think about it in the future. While we may have some common ground with those preferring the 'ideal type' argument, in that we too are continuing to use the term as our point of departure, this book has, since conception, been predicated on the idea that serious and fundamental engagement with the idea of the 'Third World' is possible.

OBJECTIONS SUSTAINED? THE BOOK

In talking about objections, then, we are not specifically talking about objections to the label 'Third World', or even to its use. More, the objections come from the way the Third-World is thought about and analysed. This book, therefore, is asking for conscious reflection on an idea that has become normalised; in their different ways, that is what the contributors to this volume have attempted.

In seeking not simply the (re-)creation of a new name or new geographical area(s) the current volume begins with some chapters seeking to offer insights into more satisfactory methodologies with which to pursue a late 1990s agenda. Stephen Chan's chapter is typically forthright in calling for a constructive debate between

historical sociology and international socialisation about the construction and interpretation of the 'other' in International Relations. Building on these arguments, Chapter 3 sees Nana Poku and
Lloyd Pettiford argue against unicausal parsimony and in favour of
complexity in Third-World research. This is a theme also advanced
by Mehran Kamrava in Chapter 4, where he seeks an extension of,
and greater sophistication by the 'state-in-society' approach to cover
other factors: namely, political economy, political culture and the
idea of 'randomness'.

Moving specifically to the arena of changing global agendas, Björn
Hettne (Chapter 5) offers the idea of a 'new Third World' and
urges its occupants to adopt a policy of 'regionness' in an effort to
avoid, or escape from, peripheralisation. In Chapter 6 Norman Lewis
engages with the effects of globalisation on Third-World states,
arguing for a more critical reading than is the norm. Meanwhile,
in his wide-ranging essay about World Cities (Chapter 7), Peter
Wilkin also deals with globalisation and highlights some problems
of geographically delineating a Third World in this latest phase of
the capitalist world order. Fundamentally, he demonstrates how
World Cities are of central concern in understanding a redefined
Third World, precisely because they illustrate the difficulties and
complexities of the idea of Core–Periphery.

In the first of four chapters, with a more traditional area studies
focus, Giok-Ling Ooi (Chapter 8) puts much of Wilkin's complex
analysis in a concrete context by looking at the multiple problems
involved in planning Third World urbanisation. Her concerns are
global, but her rich empirical research has been conducted in an
Asian context and this is reflected in the range of examples offered. In Chapter 9, Frank O. Mora and Karl Kaltenthaler consider the record of neo-liberalism in Latin America. Looking at
the region's economic reforms of the past decade or more, which
have involved the dismantling of much state bureaucratic apparatus, they argue that only by remaking the state, albeit in new ways,
can this region of the Third World look forward to a revitalised
future; simply dismantling the state without providing a range of
new institutional safeguards, they argue, holds the seeds of future
disaster. Focusing on Southeast Asia in Chapter 10, in Fahimul
Quadir and Timothy Shaw also consider the consequences of neo-
liberalism and crises of government legitimacy. However, their approach is somewhat different; again warning of potential future
problems, they look at the nature of security and military–civil re-

lations. In the final chapter, Nana Poku engages with Africa's turbulent post-colonial history and outlines the continent's security predicament at the end of the Cold War.

Notes and References

1. The core theoretical points of this introduction were provided by Georg Sørensen and put into an introductory framework by the editors.
2. G. Rist, *The History of Development: From Western Origins to Global Faith* (London: Zed Books, 1997).
3. M. Weber, *The Methodology of the Social Sciences* (translated and edited by Edward A. Shils and Henry A. Finch) (New York: The Free Press of Glencoe, 1949), p. 90.
4. M. Mann, 'The Autonomous Power of the State: Its Origins, Mechanisms, and Results', in J. Hall (ed.), *States in History* (New York: Basil Blackwell, 1986), p. 113.
5. See also G. Sørensen, 'Individual Security and National Security. The State Remains the Principal Problem', *Security Dialogue*, vol. 27, no. 4, December (1996), pp. 371–86.
6. R. H. Jackson, *Quasi-states: Sovereignty, International Relations and the Third World* (Cambridge: Cambridge University Press, 1990), p. 44.
7. M. Ayoob, *The Third-World Security Predicament. State Making, Regional Conflict, and the International System* (Boulder, Col.: Lynne Rienner, 1995), p. 3.
8. N. Harris, *The End of the Third World* (Harmondsworth: Penguin, 1986).
9. S. Amin, *Unequal Development: An Essay on the Social Formation of Peripheral Capitalism* (New York: Monthly Review Press, 1976); also, A. G. Frank, 'The Development of Underdevelopment', in R. I. Rhodes (ed.), *Imperialism and Underdevelopment: A Reader* (New York: Monthly Review Press, 1970).
10. G. Sørensen, *Democracy, Dictatorship and Development. Economic Development in Selected Regimes of the Third World* (London: Macmillan, 1991).
11. I. W. Zartman (ed.), *Collapsed States. The Disintegration and Restoration of Legitimate Authority* (Boulder, Col.: Lynne Rienner, 1995), p. 5.
12. Gros, J. G. 'Towards a Taxonomy of Failed States in the New World Order: Decaying Somalia, Liberia, Rwanda and Haiti', *Third World Quarterly*, vol. 17, no. 3 (1996), pp. 455–71.
13. D. Fromkin, *Newsweek*, 27 November (1995), p. 23.
14. The South Commission, *The Challenge to the South* (Oxford: Oxford University Press, 1990), p. 1.

2 Redefining the Third World for a New Millennium: An Aching Towards Subjectivity

Stephen Chan

How might we redefine the Third World? Of French origin, the term was probably adapted from the class order of pre-revolutionary France. The Third Estate rose and overthrew the monarchical, aristocratic and clerical order. In such parliaments as the French king convened, the Third Estate sat to the far left. Thus, even today, the terms 'left wing' and 'Third World' depict those who maintain an agenda of victimisation, and rebellion to the point of revolution. For a time in the post-Second World War years, revolutions swept over the Third World. Now, in the later decades of the century, with the exception of the Iranian revolution, the image is one largely of victimisation – what dependency theorists have called immiseration of the Third World. It is an object in someone else's grander command of the world as a whole; it is deprived of initiative; it is not the free subject that might claim its due, after first having conceived freely what its due might be. This, however, is more resonant of a reductionism than a general truth. The Third World – if such a term, although in general usage, can be accepted at all – is multifarious. Taking the general usage at face value, and looking at the Third World as something 'found' – that is, able to be discerned by artefacts and their measurements, we find not one Third World but, in the most basic taxonomies, five:

1. The world of aching poverty in which, despite a small, wealthy elite, the majority of people are in an international category of least income, and there is *no resource base* that can, in the near or medium future, alleviate this; example are countries such as Mali.

2. The world of tolerable poverty in which, despite a larger elite, there is the assumption that an existing resource base could be better used for the majority, and *sometimes is*, if only to manipulate the population's political sensibilities; examples are countries such as Kenneth Kaunda's Zambia; and in a less manipulable way, many Caribbean and island Pacific states.
3. The world of extremes of poverty and wealth, in which both segments are large, coexisting sometimes uneasily, and in which the poor are marginalised in political life and catered for by means other than mere redistribution; here, it is accepted that capital investment, technology, and industrial production are normal and desirable – *even for those for whom it is out of reach*; examples are countries such as Brazil, India, and the future South Africa; probably also the future China.
4. The world of a highly wealthy elite but sufficient wealth distribution overall to engender what may be called a 'satisficing' of the population – not full but enough satisfaction of needs and wants, even technological commodity wants – to command stability and the prolongation of elite control based on the economic manipulation of a reliable resource base; examples are countries such as the Arab 'rentier' states,[1] and Indonesia.
5. The world which is no longer a Third World at all, and which can only with a modest degree of irony be called a 'newly industrialised state', since Malaysia, Singapore, and South Korea are well-developed and their investments often the medicine for Britain's own underdeveloped regional economies.

With problematic exceptions, such as North Korea and Cuba, such a taxonomy suffices for a descriptive, materially-based view (the problem being that the Bretton Woods institutions use formalised data, based on no more sophisticated a view, for prescriptive purposes). In this taxonomy, the 'Third World' of general usage is really only the first three, sometimes only the first. Description, certainly limited description, does not necessarily imply understanding. For this, other instruments are needed. One attempt at constructing an instrument (but literally for instrumental purposes, unfortunately) was the Chinese attempt at a Three World Theory in the 1970s.

In a very real sense, the Chinese Three World Theory was an attempt to understand a world of power relationships. In terms of International Relations theory, it was 'realist', although with a twist, based as it was on forms of antique Chinese military theory with a dose of thirteenth-century folklore and literature.[2] It divided the contemporary world into three: the first world was a combined pole of imperial power, grouping together the United States and the Soviet Union (an unusual, even radical view in the 1970s); the third world was the 'Third World' of general usage, but with the important addition of China as champion of Third-World interests, as knight gallant in the first rank of the struggle against imperial adventurists and hegemonists; while the second world was all that lay between first and third – particularly Europe – and which could be won over by one side or the other. International relations was thus a battle for alliances, in which the proletariat sought to win over the bourgeoisie. What Mao Tse Tung borrowed from antique Chinese Theory, he brought into guerrilla struggle nationally, and then sought to bring into international struggle. Here, the Third World was not one-dimensionally a victim, but fought back – perhaps, if conditions and alliances were right, even triumphed. The Third World had agency, had subjectivity, moved towards its own freedom – or rather, China did on its behalf, with Mao still viewing China chauvinistically as the middle kingdom, the central kingdom of old.

There is a view of historical sociology here. If that case may be made of China's world view and intellectual history, why not then of any number of actors in international relations? Why may there not be said to be a multiplicity of historically and culturally-induced views of the world and, within them, views from all actors in all taxonomies of the Third World?

TOWARDS A DEBATE

There is a meeting point of historical sociologies on the one hand, and the international socialisation which the Western state system assumes to be hegemonic to the point of subsuming within it all possibilities of normative value. The amazing thing is how the academic discipline of International Relations has so easily accepted this assumption – to the point of adding its own weight to it. Thus, normative debate may be subsumed under renditions of Immanuel Kant or Friedrich Hegel; but not under Sun Tzu (an origin for Mao's thought, above), or Averroes or Maimonides (two twelfth-century thinkers, one Mohammedan, one Jewish, but both repre-

senting a 'non-Western' inheritance of Aristotle), still less those
thinkers who have sought to refute all that is Western. (Averroes
had a hermeneutic methodology at least as sophisticated as Gadamer's. In fact, arguing by analogy, and Maimonides allows this,
Averroes and Maimonides may be seen as not unlike Gadamer and
Ricoeur. So why adopt a particular post-positivist stance, as some
daring hermeneuticians within International Relations do, by reference only to Gadamer and Ricoeur? This surely, to turn tables,
is the Hegelian empire of habit, which enslaves and does not, because it cannot, emancipate.)

The argument here is not an opposing assumption: that historical sociologies triumph over international socialisation. They meet.
The dynamics of the meeting point – how each meets its Other
and absorbs from the Other to the point where it becomes just
another in a widened different frame of reference – is absent from
International Relations and its view of the 'Third World'. The point
here is a widened frame of reference. In particular, international
socialisation cannot assume it *excludes*, just like that, all that existed
outside socialisation. The debate, should it begin in earnest, cannot have an easy vocabulary – precisely because it will be about
vocabula*ries*. The 'Third World' does this better than the 'First'. In
Brazil, for example, the syncretic religions of slum populations –
those for whom commodified development is out of reach in the
third of our five categories, above – are marvels of widened frames
of reference and compression once again, in which what came from
the developed world has been socialised by the poor of another
world. Who socialises with whom, and who socialises what, and
what allows socialisation of any sort, and how and when, are con-
stituents of an international view in which subjectivities, even if
finally anchored (and not always in a predictable or readily ascer-
tainable manner), have their moments of cool or frenzied freedom.

WHAT DOES IT MEAN TO HAVE A FREE
SUBJECTIVITY?

Precisely because it is the slum dwellers of São Paolo and Rio de
Janeiro, unaided by academicians and, in particular, abandoned by
formal government, who compose their own syncretic world views,
and not the nation-state of Brazil that does this, we are not only
talking of the subjectivities of the 'Third World', but of a Third

World *of* subjectivities. This is the pluralism that International Relations, as an academic discipline, has shirked.

The direct implication here is that neither in economic and material measures, nor in terms of cultural foundations, are there excuses for dictatorships. The unhegemonised world begins from the unhegemonised slum or, in Rajni Kothari's writing, the unhegmonised village.[3] Paolo Friere, in seeking a pedagogy for the poor oppressed, established his practice on the idea that literacy was an instrument of emancipation because it allowed each person, anew and fresh, to name the world.[4] In that brief luminescent moment of free subjectivity, the foundation analogy for a multicultural, pluralist International Relations has been laid. When *you* name the world, you begin to change the idea that your only place within it is as a victim.

In less poetic terms, it means that the democratic agenda, particularly to do with free expression, is important, not because it is Western and imposed, but because it emancipates thought and ultimately challenges the West, or at least its assumptions that its own thought is securely more than habitual. The Zimbabwean trade union leader, Morgan Tsvangirai, wrote in 1990, at the height of a political struggle to consolidate multi-party democracy in his country, that all too often intellectuals had decried democratic institutions merely because they had a Western form, proposed the workable form of no alternatives, and seemed merely aloof within their own social privileges.[5] Zimbabwean intellectuals were naming a world of sorts, Tsvangirai seemed to be saying – a very safe world – but were condescending and paternalist to those who would name nothing or little.

There is thus an irony here: to speak truths to the West in international relations form must be borrowed from the West so that truth might be spoken within national relations. If scholars do not speak with the people (*with*, not for), they are like International Relations academicians who do not speak with the full world in their view. In national relations, a free subjectivity depends upon all citizens being able to speak, name and compose national as well as international views, to draw limits to the world's socialisation at various points, provided the democratic freedoms of pluralism are not themselves limited.

To take, then, a conspicuously bold type of example: what is free in international relations – unhegemonised, culturally independent, but socialised for all points of practical association within the world – would be a democratic Islamic state in which debate flourished and rights were safeguarded.

Now there are dangers in this sort of composition. The actualities of what currently call themselves Islamic states, or – as with Singapore – what call themselves Confucian states, is that the cultural label is a disguise for lack of freedom. So we are talking of ideal types here: of the possibility of a *normative typology* of the Third World, rather than the typology with which this essay began. Below, we look at a typology that has normative characteristics.

FOR HEURISTIC PURPOSES, A TYPOLOGY

What is offered here is an heuristic exercise; and it is capable of significant sub-divisions, especially that part to do with Islam. Moreover, as it stands, reflecting to its own extent the world that is 'found', it includes no ideally democratic state: there is no syncretic culture of the Brazilian shanties that is yet the Brazilian state. Even so, the typology assumes the existence of states and even, conditionally, of nations that suggest general belief systems associated with their states. So we move from the ideal realm to the generalised, but even so, this is not a usual exercise for the discipline of International Relations.

1. The world where historical motifs are generalised, if not related, to underpin authoritarian regimes; for example, countries such as Zaire.
2. The world where historical and philosophical 'stories' are generalised, if not recreated, to underpin regimes that are to an extent authoritarian but, simultaneously, beneficent; for example, countries such as Zambia.[6]
3. The world of chauvinism, accurate to an extent in itself, but adapted to direct modern government and its policies; for example, countries such as Mao's China or Lee's Singapore.
4. The world of text-based normativities – which may be given interpretation on literal and exegetic grounds; for example, various Islamic countries.
5. The world that is text-based but given interpretation on a sectarian – even minor sectarian – basis; for example, countries such as Libya with its almost totally unremarked Sanusi inheritance.[7]

6. The world that is text-based but given opportunistic interpretation for a clan or family purpose; for example, countries such as Saddam Hussein's Iraq.
7. The world of successful revolution which has lost its text: perhaps in action and struggle transcended it, and has engendered its own peculiar idealism; for example, countries such as Eritrea.
8. The world of successful revolution that long ago transcended or distorted its text and adopted an idealism that exercises an expunging cruelty towards the reality it encounters; for example, Cambodia under the Khmer Rouge.
9. That future volatile world of revolution in which texts collide and the syncretic belief systems, lately compounded to resist oppression, overthrow it and enter an international relations helpless before it; for example, countries such as Mexico under the Zapatistas.

Each such world, imperfectly certainly, is a world aching towards subjectivity in international relations. So, what does this mean for us who have viewed this 'Third World' – materially and otherwise many worlds – in such a limited fashion? It means a view not of victimhood but a recognition of self-conception, of bodies – eventually, at least – of free citizens; of those who, impatient with our own slowness of redefinition, have begun a history of autochthonous redefinition. We should view this with understanding and sympathy, if the new millennium is not to belong, in a way that excludes us, to subjective 'Others'.

Notes and References

1. 'Rentier' is a term referring to a state that lives off its 'rent', in this case the ownership of all natural resources. See H. Beblawi, 'The Rentier State in the Arab World', in G. Lucani (ed.), *The Arab State* (London: Routledge, 1990).
2. See S. Chan, 'Revolution, Culture and the Foreign Policy of China', in S. Chan and A. J. Williams (eds), *Renegade States: The Evolution of Revolutionary Foreign Policy* (Manchester: Manchester University Press, 1994).
3. See, *inter alia*, R. Kothari, 'Communication for Alternative Development: Towards a Paradigm', *Development Dialogue*, vol. 1, no. 2 (1984).
4. P. Freire, *Pedagogy of the Oppressed* (New York: Seabury Press, 1970).

5. Reported in *Southern African Review of Books*, vol. 5, no. 1, January/February (1993), p. 19.
6. For a deconstruction of Kaunda's 'historically-derived' philosophy, see S. Chan, *Kaunda and Southern Africa: Image and Reality in Foreign Policy* (London: I. B. Tauris, 1992), ch. 5.
7. For a most sensitive treatment, see J. Davis, *Libyan Politics: Tribe and Revolution – An Account of the Zuwaya and their Government* (London: I. B. Tauris, 1987), chs 4 and 5.

3 A Call for Complexity in Third-World Research: Challenging the False God of Theoretical Parsimony

Nana Poku and Lloyd Pettiford

The definition of the universal is a particular definition of the particular system and, within that system, the definition of the particular has no particularities but is a universal of that system. As long as that system is functioning reasonably well, the debate about the relationship between the particular and the universal is not only academic, but the very terrain and process of the debate tends to reinforce the structure of the cultural hierarchy and oppression internal to that system. It is only when the system itself comes into crisis (in this case with the ending of the Cold War) that we have real options and the possibility of real debate.[1] Such a systemic crisis now exists and we argue here that we can, and should, engage in such a debate.

The French author who coined the term the Third World meant specific strata not belonging to either of the most privileged groups of the day: the nobility and the clergy. During the Cold War years, the concept both reflected the objective reality of a bipolar world and served as a vehicle for political expression and action by a multiplicity of states attempting to enhance their own status and influence within that bipolar context. In common usage, the term encapsulated all countries not included in the First and Second Worlds. The First World alludes to the Western capitalist countries plus Japan, Australia and New Zealand, and this grouping often found room for Israel and South Africa as well. Until the demise of the Soviet Union and its ideological allies in Europe, the Second World consisted of the socialist countries of the East. Robert Pinkney[2] suggests that the Third World was broadly delineated at the point where the First and Second Worlds ended, while Sheikh Ali contends that 'the appellation Third World refers to a non-cohesive group of economically underdeveloped countries located in Asia, Africa, and Latin America'. Membership of this 'Third World' was loosely based on a familiar list of characteristics: relatively low per capita income, high rates of illiteracy, agriculturally-based economies, short life expectancies, low degrees of mobility, strong attachment to tradition, and a shared historical tragedy in the history of colonial and imperial subjugation.

Never without its critics, today the notion of a Third World is even more highly contested. Some assert that three worlds are too many; that ultimately all human beings live in and experience the same single reality, and the term is frequently challenged for over-simplicity in its geographical ring-fencing. Others take a recursive view, arguing that a global socioeconomic stratification scheme with only three categories is a far too simplistic and generalised model to reflect the great diversity of cultures, economies and values across the globe, and within nation states. Shiva Naipaul, for example, in one of the last essays of a brilliant but tragically short career, claimed that so great was the internal diversity of the Third World that its existence could be no more than mythical; that 'there is no such thing as the Third World'.[3] Much like a star, the concept should be studied obliquely, since under direct observation it appears to dissolve so readily that one questions whether it was ever really there.[4]

In what is to follow, we shall explore and distinguish between the difficulties that were always present in the term, and those that have arisen as circumstances have changed.

Specifically, the chapter is in two halves. The first half covers some necessary but relatively familiar territory, considering a changing world and a transformed global economy. The purpose of this section is to examine some core ideas and to lay out the skeleton of the argument. Following this, the second half of the chapter argues for complexity in Third World research. That is, the questions about the structure and functioning of the Third World (like World Politics in general) that beg for answers today are inherently complex. They involve the interactive effects of the polity and the larger society of which the polity is but a part. They involve feedback relationships between the world political system and the world economic system, and various sub-systems of the world polity and the world economy: countries, intergovernmental organisations and regimes, transnational associations, corporations, interests groups, political parties, social movements, and influential individuals. There is no presumption that the way the world polity works is determined by material factors more than by ideational factors.

In this context, the quest for parsimonious explanation – for the single *dominant* variable or condition – to which most of the behaviour we are interested in can be attributed, is not really appropriate to the complexities of contemporary Third-World politics. As will be argued in the second section of this chapter, there is no compelling reason, either in logic or in considerations of usefulness, for the continual restriction of Third-World studies to a particular unit or level of analysis. Drawing specifically on the ontological reasoning of critical international theory, this section eschews unicausal parsimony and contends that a complex array of social forces crucially conditions any set of outcomes, and that any event or series of events emerge out of the totality of social life.[6] Before returning to such considerations, we are at the point where we need to contextualise the debate.

TRANSFORMATION AND DIFFERENTIATION IN WORLD POLITICS

Kenneth Jowitt reminds us of how the Cold War provided a striking instance of a stereotyped political division of labour.[7] In each of the parallel universes (West and East), one country patriarchally monopolised political decisions through coercion, inducement and, occasionally, force. As a result, for the most part, the behaviour of any member of either universe (Liberal or Leninist) could be predicted by knowing the camp to which it belonged. Mutual fear of ideological contamination manifested itself as murderous hysteria in the Soviet Union and gratuitous hysteria in the United States of America, and this mutual fear was exacerbated by efforts of each to disrupt the other's camp. Ideally, the members of each camp, world, or bloc were unidimensional entities who defined themselves exclusively in terms of membership in their respective political and military organisations; they had one dominant referent, the leader of their respective camps, and one identity, the ideology that formally distinguished one camp from the other. Thus entities as different as Mozambique, Nicaragua and Romania were viewed as Communist, while South Africa, Guatemala and Greece were viewed uni-dimensionally as free world or imperialist countries.

This was the pervasive dichotomy that characterised world politics until the late 1980s, a decade which began with the onset of the second Cold War and ended with unparalleled co-operation between the superpowers. In 1980, the Soviet Union had just invaded Afghanistan, communism had arrived on the USA's doorstep in Nicaragua,[8] and many in the West feared these events to be a reflection of Moscow's heightened global ambitions. Furthermore, the US military establishment had become gravely concerned over the USSR's first-strike nuclear capabilities, and urged the American president to take urgent counter-measures. The two superpowers appeared to be locked in a newly heightened relationship of tension and danger from which there was no escape. Yet, by the end of the decade, the Cold War was officially declared to be over; Moscow had pulled its troops out of Afghanistan, the Sandinistas were ousted democratically in Nicaragua, and the old communist elites in Eastern Europe had been toppled by popular revolutions. Even the USSR itself had begun the process of disintegration. Both superpowers were cutting their nuclear arsenals, while all the time calling for bigger reductions and new initiatives. The USA and the Soviet Union no longer saw each other as enemies. The Cold War system, with which the world had grown so familiar since its evolution in the late 1940s, had suddenly collapsed.

Without wishing to traverse the corpus of literature surrounding the specific factors leading to the demise of the Cold War, Francis Fukuyama's neo-Hegelian interpretation of its significance for World Politics is interesting. The central thesis of Fukuyama's *The End of History and the Last Man* is not the literal and rather absurd one that time has stopped, nor that historical events have ceased to happen. Rather, the end of the Cold War is seen to have given rise to the hope that the international system is at last ripe for a complete overhaul; the time has indeed come to change its organisational principles and ground rules. According to Fukuyama, the end of the Cold War signalled that certain historical alternatives – socialist central planning and authoritarian governments – have become irretrievably discredited. Liberal democracy (allied with free-market economics) was left without any competition, as the only remaining ideology of potential universal validity. The future could consist only of the continued spread of liberal democracy, albeit with an occasional temporary regression to one or other of the discarded and discredited alternatives. But, in the (undefined) longer run, there was a fundamental process at work that dictated a common evolutionary pattern for all human society, something like a Universal History of Humankind in the direction of liberal democracy.[9]

Unfortunately, this Kantian vision, liberally sprinkled with references to the Enlightenment, has had to contend with international realities that stubbornly refuse to fit into any teleological scheme. For want of a new international order, what we have today is not 'disorder', a necessarily relative and mainly descriptive term, but the growing tension within the dynamics of power between the dominant players in the international system. In other words, the Cold War was a 'Joshua' period, one of dogmatically centralised boundaries and identities. In contrast to the Biblical sequence, the post-Cold War era has moved from a Joshua period to a Genesis environment; from a world centrally organised, rigidly bounded, and hysterically concerned with impenetrable boundaries, to one in which territorial, ideological and issue boundaries are attenuated, unclear and confusing.[10] We now inhabit a world that appears to be transient, fragmented and increasingly polarised, lacking in Fukuyama certainty.

The changes that are occurring are compounding and exposing the ambiguities associated with the orthodoxy of dividing the world into three. In viewing these transformations, the question appears simple; if the Second World of state socialism has indeed vanished into historical limbo, what meaning or purpose can now be attributed to a Third World, defined in contrast to it? None, certainly, if the Third World had been nothing more than the creation of Cold War politics. In reality, however, this was simply not the case, with the term 'Third World' acquiring meaning and significance separate from its association with First and Second Worlds.[11]

From the perspective of developing countries, the idea of a *strategically* bipolar world was always a distortion. The influence of the Chinese revolution was extremely powerful, particularly in East and Southeast Asia, and although it has evolved, and perhaps fundamentally mutated in character, Communist China has survived the Soviet and East European collapse. In retrospect, the distortion is even more apparent when one looks at the global influence of the Soviet Union. For the great majority of Third-World states, the issue was never one of finding a third way between the houses of communism and capitalism, but to find a 'second way' that preserved some independence from the dominant capitalist economies of the developed world. It was the collective experience of colonialism, and a reasonable fear of neo-colonialism,[12] that newly

independent countries were determined to keep at bay. As Nigel
Harris has rightly noted, the Third World 'identified not just a group
of new states joined later by the older states of Latin America, nor
the majority of the world of the poor, but a political alternative
other than that presented by Washington and Moscow, the First
and Second Worlds'.[13] Kwame Nkrumah, in characteristically flam-
boyant style, pursues this theme further, suggesting that the 'Third
World is neither a practical political concept nor a reality'. To
Nkrumah, the term was a misused expression that came to mean
'everything and nothing'. The differentiation was ideological, tied
to capitalism and scientific socialism.

To an extent, then, Naipaul is certainly right – the Third World
was always mythical, in the sense that it was never real, but rather
an abstraction, a mental construction, an idea. It is in this way
similar to numbers: 'extremely useful figments of the human imagin-
ation'.[14] The concept was at once intellectual, metaphysical and
experiential; it was much more than merely a helpful but fundamentally trivial – or even non-existent – idea. It was in this sense a
mental region – an image, if you wish – but a tremendously profound and vital one. We might liken it to Macondo, the mythical
Colombian town of Gabriel Garcia Marquez' epic novel *One Hundred Years of Solitude*. Macondo, as a town, does not exist – because it exists everywhere; it is a part of the consciousness of South
America.[15] Equally, the 'Third World' has never existed; yet it con-
notes the psychological condition referred to above, encompassing
the hopes and aspirations of the vast majority.

In this sense, Nigel Harris's assertion that the Third World is
disappearing is based not on the notion – less still on the countries
or their inhabitants – but rather on the argument itself. Harris
suggests, quite rightly, that a new set of economic determinisms
have created a complex modern global politico-economic system
that supersedes and problematises the old simplicities of 'First and
Third world, rich and poor, haves and have-not, industrialised and
non-industrialised'.[16] Central to this analysis are the observable
changes in the global economy during the period since the 1960s.
Here we find that during the 1970s and into the first half of the
1980s, unemployment in the Western industrialised countries soared
to levels unknown since the world depression of the 1930s. During
this same period, crippling financial debts became apparent within
the global economy, threatening not only to abort embryonic economic developments in certain regions but also to stretch to breaking

point the political and social cohesion of entire continents. At the same time, trade tensions re-emerged as a prominent destabilising force within the global economy.

Within the Third World, these changes in the international economy had both positive and negative impacts. Table 3.1 indicates the growth in per capita GNP for selected groups of countries during the period 1965–89. While the figures for OECD and 'Third World' countries are the same across the entire period, these figures hide some striking differences. Although economic performance varied within the industrialised countries and difficulties were experienced, in general they achieved good growth in GNP per head of population, not only in the 1960s and 1970s but also into the 1980s. Meanwhile, during this latter period, economic retrogression extended itself via the debt crisis and falling oil prices to Central and Latin America and the OPEC countries. Economies least affected by the recession of this period were those, particularly East Asian economies, that not only had already impressive growth but were achieving this through investment in industries that could produce manufacturing exports. Additionally, India and China, who were following an inward looking strategy of industrialisation, fared relatively well. However, in Africa south of the Sahara, after initial positive figures, the 1970s saw stagnation set in and the 1980s were a period of drastic setbacks, as the annual figures show. While the population of Sub-Saharan Africa increased by 118 million in the years 1980–92 (that is, by 32.4 per cent), its GDP (at 1980 prices) fell by almost 27 per cent during the same period.

Thus, what has happened since the 1960s has not been the uncomplicated succession of economic take-offs that modernisation theory had predicted.[17] Neither has there been a continuously growing gap in income and welfare between the rich countries and the poor countries predicted by the dependency schools, witnessed by better *aggregate* statistics in the 1980–90 period for Third World *as a whole* as opposed to the OECD countries. Instead, there has been a combination of some apparent take-offs, mainly in East Asia, and some severe cases of economic retrogression, mainly in Sub-Saharan Africa. It is a situation where universalising ideas of development seem entirely inappropriate and where, despite the gloating optimism of Fukuyama, imaginative and flexible policy responses are needed in the face of a difficult and varied set of problems. In this sense, the debate about redefining the Third World is not based on the concept itself nor, indeed, or the need to find new labels. Rather, the

Table 3.1   GNP per capita annual growth rates in Third-World regions, 1985–90

Regions	1965–80	1980–90	1965–89
Sub-Saharan Africa	1.5	–1.7	0.3
South Asia	1.4	2.9	1.8
East and Southeast Asia (excluding China)	3.9	3.3	3.7
China	4.1	8.2	5.7
Arab states	3.0	0.5	2.1
OECD countries	4.4	3.0	3.1
Latin American and the Caribbean	3.8	–0.4	1.9
Third World	2.9	3.4	3.1

Source: UNDP, *Human Development Report 1992* (Oxford University Press, 1992), p. 37; and World Bank, *World Development Report 1990* (Washington, DC: World Bank, 1990), p. 192.

debate is about the most appropriate way to study the changing nature of the Third World.

THE CASE FOR COMPLEXITY IN THIRD WORLD ANALYSIS

In other words, the debate is centred at the cognitive stage of research. With the exception of the gifted few, the starting point for most Western academic research into Third World issues has traditionally been classical theoretical models. Only after a model has been chosen does a search begin for appropriate field sites to test hypotheses derived from a grand theory. When most Western scholars select a dozen indicators connected with an abstract model and proceed to collect information from a dozen countries, the objective may be to get hold of an elusive reality; it may involve very complex computer operations and result in a generalisation that constitutes a refinement over earlier applications of the model.

However, the whole enterprise may contribute very little to the understanding of what is going on in the Third World. In the literature, the most extensive work deals with economic conditions and tendencies, theorised across social formations at a very high level of abstraction. The fatalist twists so often imbedded in these works are now, rightly, regarded as contentious and problematical.

In the words of Paul Streeton, 'There is something, if not illegitimate, at any rate distasteful, in people from safe and comfortable
positions recommending revolutions, or painful reforms or, for that
matter, the maintenance of the *status quo*, to others'.[18] More importantly, however, to force reality into a mould by selecting only
those aspects that are suitable for the systemic needs of a paradigm is to forget that the objective of research is not illumination
of a theory but the illumination of the real world or worlds. It is
also to disregard the Marxist insight that the test of theory is practice; that in the last analysis the purpose of the theory is not a
controlled experiment in which 'all things are held equal', but rather
effective action in the real world where all things hang together.[19]
It is in this respect that Albert Hirschman put forward the idea
that the uncritical use of paradigms may become a hindrance to
our understanding of reality.

In the above context, the debate is about the most appropriate
method for studying the noted polarisation within and between Third-
World societies and their developed counterparts. Elsewhere in this
volume, Mehran Kamrava calls for a 'new conception of Third World
politics': one that can be conceptualised via a typology of state–
society relations, or what he calls 'the State-in-Society Approach'.
He calls for socioeconomic factors to be included in the analysis of
societies and draws our attention to the linkages of property rights
and capitalism to political sovereignty. Thus, rather than emphasising
unicausal parsimony in conformity, he contends that a complex array
of social forces crucially condition any set of outcomes, and that
any event or series of events emerge out of the totality of social
life.[20] If this is accepted, then claims to social knowledge that pur-
port to stand apart from a prevailing order, or from history, must
be considered as being fundamentally misguided, whether advanced
in the form of instrumental rationalities focused on problem-solving (modernisation theories), or critical theories (dependency theories) proposing alternative and better worlds rationally available.

This conclusion leads students of poststructuralism to favour research strategies like the genealogical method of Friedrich Nietzsche
and Michel Foucault. These deconstruct forms of domination flow-
ing from the nexus of power and knowledge by examining the ways
discourses of knowledge and truth make possible particular power
relations, and vice versa.[21] Genealogy strives for the subversion of
all totalising claims grounded in foundations purporting to be outside history. Poststructuralism, however, contains its own founda-

tion principle in the view that we are always either within or outside history. Rather than emphasising the deconstructive aspects of Foucauldian-style genealogies, it might instead be enquired whether such revealing reconstructions of the constitution of the human subject might serve not only to subvert, but also to reconstruct, our understanding of subject–object relations and, in turn, social theory.[22]

This leads us to examine what the terms of such a reconstruction would be. We can confidently contend that it would not resort to empiricism, like the modernisation school. Empiricists have been widely attacked for their failure to demonstrate the cumulation of knowledge (see, for example, Stephen Chan's contribution to this volume). All too often, specific empirical findings are *not* integrated, comparable, or in any clear sense cumulative.[23] These problems have had multiple consequences but one has been a concerted effort to give more legitimacy to theory in general, and to theories of unobservable entities (such as structure) in particular, thereby enhancing both the cohesion of orthodox accounts and the authenticity of portrayals of the research process. This approach, known as scientific realism, has become increasingly fashionable across the spectrum of the social sciences. Scientific realists argue that theoretical terms referring to unobservable entities are not merely useful instruments for organising and predicting experience but can be regarded as real if the entity in question produces observable effects, or its manipulation permits us to intervene in the observable world.[24] Further, scientific realists contend that if we can explain the physical dispositions and causal processes of unobservable entities, then we can make legitimate inferences about naturally necessary relations between cause and effect and explain with far greater authority the constant conjunctions of temporally sequenced observations identified by empiricists.[25]

However subtle the scientific realist view, it merely extends both empiricist and realist arguments into a more sophisticated and wide-ranging account of orthodox scientific method. By contrast, the demands of reflexivity, particularly a claim as to the constitutive role of theory in both the understanding and shaping of social 're-ality', require movement beyond both empiricism and scientific realism towards a position generally termed 'constructivist'. Drawing on and extending Thomas Kuhn, constructivists contend that scientific method is so theory-dependent that it is a construction, and not a discovery procedure; that the world or reality examined is in a crucial way 'constructed' from the theoretical tradition within which the particular school of interpreters operate.[26]

One important aspect of the above process is the rhetorical dimension. Close inspection of argument and 'proof' in formal debates about the Third World, for example, reveals a vast store of rhetorical practices including metaphors and the use of irony and other tropes (whether discursively, statistically or mathematically rendered) which enjoy authority primarily because, by research tradition, and the subsequent development of modes of interpretation, it is agreed that they should do so in the relevant community of interpreters. Of course, mere recognition of the rhetorical aspects of knowledge formation does not lighten the burden of scholarly argumentation, or the need to provide the best (that is, the most persuasive) case in the light of internal criticism, but it does challenge, even more deeply, faith in the idea of cumulative empirically verifiable knowledge. Some of these contentions have already been incorporated into orthodox conceptions of method in the philosophy of social science and International Relations. They are reflected in the widespread appreciation of the hermeneutic/interpretative aspects of social science, particularly the role of competing paradigms, research programmes, research traditions and reflection thereon in the shaping of knowledge formation.[27]

Yet, as we have noted, for the most part these have merely been grafted on to essentially empiricist or scientific realist rationalisations of method that leave deductive hypotheses capable of definitive empirical 'proof'. By contrast, constructivism requires us to go further, embedding the positive or empirical moment of research more thoroughly in interpretative and critical moments. That is, it forces us to consider how research traditions, in part, constitute social reality (the interpretative moment) while also opening up the possibility of a reconstruction of social life by agents reconsidering that reality in the light of different traditions of understanding and the interplay between them (the critical moment). The following section expands on these ideas.

CONSTRUCTIVIST EPISTEMOLOGY AND THIRD-WORLD RESEARCH

We turn now to how this formulation might be spelled out and related to the need to redefine methodology in Third-World research. In the first instance, constructivists do not deny the existence of an independent phenomenal world. Indeed, they insist that each datum remains an intersubjectively discriminational aspect of the world. However, they do contend that we can never know all the features of the world independent of discourse about it. As Nicholas Onuf has succinctly noted, we 'construct worlds we know in a world we do not'.[28] Accordingly, constructivists view the relationship between the subject and the social world as being radically unstable and variable, and refuse to grant sovereignty to either. On this basis, Onuf has argued for a conception of world politics that regards human subjects and societies as, quite simply, constructing or constituting each other. From this perspective, poststructuralists are right to deconstruct the constitution of the subject in modernity and reject the subject–object dichotomy, but wrong not to simply transcend the duality. We do not have to accept that we are either within or outside history, for 'we are always within our constructions even as we choose to stand apart from them, condemn them, or reconstruct them'.[29]

The constructivist thus has it both ways, positing a foundation that the act of constitution (the co-constitution of people and society) makes history, while also asserting that social construction is 'a contingent effect of political practices within history'.[30] Such a claim can also be conceived as part of a wider effort to transcend the dichotomy between objectivism and relativism in contemporary social theory by developing a notion of human rationality as practical but critical reason or wisdom.[31] By rejecting the subject–object dichotomy and embedding the analyst, and indeed all human agents and subjects, in the co-constitution of history, constructivism opens up a rapprochement between philosophy and ontology or theories about the making of social worlds and histories, and with these the making of being-in-the-world.

Orthodox (positivist) views of ontology define it as consisting of 'things' and 'entities', and the relationships between them, imputed to the real world and invoked in a theory, research programme or discourse's explanations. A constructivist, by contrast, emphasises the plurality of the social worlds that human agents create (or, in the jargon, co-constitute), notwithstanding the existence of an independent phenomenal world. This then brings us to consider what an adequate social ontology would look like. One approach would point to the pervasive role of rules in bounding (although not governing) human conduct. This suggests a particular agent-structure or structurationist claim as to ontology where structure is understood as generative rules and resources. Significantly, recent work in social theory suggests the terms of a 'structurationist' claim in which action and structure are regarded as the complementary terms of a duality: the 'duality of structure'.[32] This notion, advanced by the leading exponent of 'structurationism', Anthony Giddens, conceives structure as both the medium and the outcome of the conduct it recursively (backwardly) organises.[33] It suggests that the structures which render an action possible are, in the performance of the action, reconstituted. It also suggests that 'structures' (or more precisely, the structural properties of social life) do not exist outside action, for it is only through the practices of agents that they are instantiated, reproduced and, potentially, transformed.[34] Agents, in Giddens' schema, are knowledgeable in that they are both capable of rationalising their actions and reflexively monitoring their locale and context through time. They enjoy discursive consciousness, and a wider 'practical consciousness' of things known and understood about the world, without being articulated as such. They also choose whether to follow a rule or not in the light of their assessment of the consequences of such conduct. More generally, Giddens affirms the centrality of agents when he emphasises that it is their very reflexivity that opens up the possibility of multiple motivations and interpretations of any situation, and with this the agent's ability to 'act otherwise', whether the specific agent is advantaged or disadvantaged in resource terms.[35]

This argument as to the transformative capability of agency and the possibility of doing 'otherwise' is the first face of power in 'structurationism'. Although we might suspect this represents a slide to voluntarism, Giddens contends not; he accepts a notion of structural constraint defined broadly as the setting of limits upon the feasible range of choices that an actor can follow. He also seeks not to equate social structure with practical knowledge, and hence elides the distinction between an analysis of the structural conditions of a certain kind of society, and a mere summary of what actors already know in 'knowing how to go on' in that society. Giddens contends, that the accounts agents are able to give of their actions, and are 'bounded' by both the unintended consequences of action and the unacknowledged conditions of action. The latter subsumes the former in so far as the unintended consequence of action is the reproduction of a structural property that renders further action possible. The inherent reflexivity of agents and the role of social science in elucidating structural conditions merely create the possibility of intentionally transforming practices, institutions and structural constraints.

It follows from this discussion that, while the structural properties of social life are constituted and reconstituted by agents, they are also constitutive of them in that they form sets of relations that 'mobilise bias' and help define the identities, powers and interests of agents that occupy social structural positions. A reference to 'social structural positions' is, however, somewhat misleading, as Giddens deems structures to have no descriptive qualities of their own in that they exist only as memory traces and as the instantiation of rules in the situated activities and practices of agents. Rather, 'structure' represents 'materials' in the form of rules and resources drawn upon and reproduced in action. For this reason, Giddens generically defines structure as generative rules and resources. Power in this context is defined not as a resource but as a distinct type of organisational power or generalised means drawn upon in action. Different types of social (organisational) power and knowledgeability generate particular logistical techniques which, in turn, are promiscuous in the sense that no single social group permanently controls such techniques. Giddens shares this 'organisational' or 'institutionalist' conception of power with other historical sociologists such as Mann.[36] It is now time to draw our argumentation together by offering a framework in which it might be understood.

CONCLUSIONS

Based on the above, we need now to look at the specifics of how such a framework might look. Table 3.2 contains a number of phenomena that may be important and inseparable aspects of a particular political scenario. As will become apparent in Mehran Kamrava's chapter, each of these phenomena may belong primarily in one of five areas: state, society, political-economy, political culture, and uncertain principles. As we have noted, however, many political phenomena traverse the original area from which they were generated; political development, for example, may be initiated by the state but also influences society and culture, and involves elements of political economy as well. If the researcher's job is to study political development in a given country, s/he needs to

Table 3.2   Areas of analytical focus in explaining various political phenomena

---

State
Fluctuations in degree of autonomy, internal paralysis, political institutionalisation, democratisation from above, political development, policy making and implementation, palace and military coups, international relations, wars, trade disputes.

Society
Social change, cleavages/cohesion, urbanisation, middle class growth in size and economic power, political mobilisation, population growth and shifts, interest groups and political parties.

Political culture
Chasm into political and regime orientations, hero worship, apathy and/ or cynicism, patriarchal tendencies, zero-sum nature, civil society.

Political economy
Industrialisation, economic nuances (inflation/recession), consumerism, foreign and domestic investment levels, dependence, foreign market orientation/export-led growth, interdependence, foreign aid, expansion of labour-intensive industry, infrastructural growth, proletarianisation, government social security net.

Uncertainty principle
Historical accidents, individual initiatives, unintended consequences.

---

determine what state factors were involved (for example, institutions and other policy-making mechanisms, intents and consequences) and how, if at all, such other areas as the political economy or political culture came into play or were influenced.

This is not to imply that comparative analysis has to always remain at the macro level. Micro level analysis of specific aspects of a particular phenomenon is possible under the same rubric, though the scope is much narrower and, naturally, more specialised. Instead of the larger processes and consequences involved in political development, for example, analysis would only focus on the highly specialised factors that are pertinent to the investigation. Nevertheless, the analyst must remain mindful of the fact that although a very specific phenomenon is being studied (in this case, a particular facet of political development), there are other forces and factors that *may potentially* be of significance to the subject of investigation as well. In other words, employing such an approach in Third-World studies will allow researchers both to draw on the recent trend to blend insights across traditions, and to extend it further, on the premise that a claim of complexity, not unicausality, is the preferred starting point for analysis.

There is already evidence of important work being done in this genre. Although this work has, predictably, had less impact on international development and development policy debates, it provides the basis for a theoretically informed historical perspective on 'development' that is global in its level of analysis. This work has sought to privilege the specific over the systemic. Dissatisfaction with the elite-orientated focus of much of the work on India, for example, has given rise to Subaltern Studies. Informed by Gramscian, and later, post-structural, theory, Subaltern approaches have focused on the peasantry and workers with particular concern to delineate structures and techniques of domination, strategies of resistance and the historical particularity and role of culture and religion. The concern here is to restore the subaltern class to history, and to provide the intellectual underpinning for a less elite-orientated politics. In general, these scholars aim to draw attention to the way in which the expanding world economy has neither historically nor currently levelled 'pre-capitalist' structures and discourses to the degree that many of the earlier theoretical models implied.

Again, using Latin America as a critical point of study, Steve J. Stern, for example, has shown how the central dynamics of the region's history since the colonial era have been the various approaches and popular resistance strategies of the inhabitants, the interests of mercantile and political elites (whose 'centres of gravity' were in the Americas), and the world-system. For our purpose, what is interesting is how Stern's methodology draws from Jean-François Bayart's *longue durée* thesis which attempts to historicise 'state' in Africa, rejects the state-society dichotomy and argues that colonial and post-colonial 'states' should be seen as historically rooted in particular social formations rather than regarded as alien institutions. This we might call a historicity claim implying an appreciation of the tension between 'structure' and history in the study of Third-World societies, while none the less giving priority to history and, in turn, to the historically constituted character of institutions and their endogeneity.[37] Such a claim contests the goal of general unified theory posited by established approaches to Development Studies, recent efforts to make such analyses more differentiated, conditional and context-specific notwithstanding.[38]

To sum up, then, what we have attempted to do in this chapter is to recognise by brief historical survey the enormous complexity within what has come to be known as the Third World. Acceptance of such complexity renders obsolete much previous work done in order to explain it, which, using an inadequate methodology, has concentrated on unicausal parsimony and has tended to over-emphasise the work and ideas of Western 'experts'. In making a counter-claim for complexity we have discussed competing conceptions of methodology and set out an alternative framework that seeks to provide a more satisfactory way forward in looking at a rapidly changing agenda.

Notes and References

1. I. Wallerstein, *Unthinking Social Science: The Limits of Nineteenth-Century Paradigms* (Oxford: Polity Press, 1991).
2. R. Pinkney, *Democracy in the Third World* (Milton Keynes: Open University Press, 1993).
3. S. Naipaul, 'A Thousand Million Invisible Men: the Myth of the Third World', *The Spectator*, 18 May (1985), pp. 9–11.
4. J. Norwine and A. Gonzalez (eds), *The Third World: States of Mind and Being* (London: Unwin Hyman, 1988), p. 2.
5. W. Haas, *The Destiny of the Mind: East and West* (London: Macmillan, 1956).
6. It follows that to insist on the primacy of any one 'factor' or 'dimension' in historical interpretation is to unleash a 'ritual without hope or an end' in which scholars seek fruitlessly to advance one view over another. See M. Mann, *The Sources of Social Power: The History of Power from the Beginning to 1760 AD Volume One* (Cambridge: Cambridge University Press, 1986), p. 19.
7. K. Jowitt, 'A World Without Leninism', in R. O. Slater (ed.), *Global Transformation and the Third World* (Boulder, Col.: Rienner and Adamantine, 1995).
8. The extent to which Nicaragua was a communist country, though disputed, is less important here than the fact that it was perceived as such by the vast majority of policy makers in the USA.
9. F. Fukuyama, *The End of History and the Last Man* (Ithaca, NY: Cornell University Press, 1992), p. 48.
10. K. Jowitt, 'A World Without Leninism', p. 10.
11. The term 'Third World' has often been criticised for having pejorative connotations, and certainly it is avoided in the names of certain groupings (for example the Non-Aligned Movement and Group of 77) but attempts to substitute other terms have encountered similar problems without achieving the same consensus and implicit understanding connoted by using the term 'Third World'.

12. The term neo-colonialism denotes a many-sided attempt by the former metropolitan powers to tie the new 'nation' closely to the interests and needs of their own economic growth. At times this is overt – for example, when France imposed military agreements on its former colonies such that many of them, when becoming independent, had still to accept the presence of French troops on their soil. It is rather the structural (or covert), economic relationship between former colonial powers and their colonies that has given content to neo-colonialism. The argument holds that colonialism fostered economic dependency through turning colonial economies into cash-crop economies. The post-colonial impact of this are twofold: first, it has rendered post-colonial regimes highly vulnerable to fluctuations in world market conditions that affect primary products. Second, the weakness of their economies has placed them at a disadvantage in their dealings with former colonial leaders at the global level.
13. N. Harris, *The End of the Third World* (Harmondsworth: Penguin, 1990), p. 18.
14. K. Boulding, 'Science: Our Common Heritage', Presidential address, annual meeting of the American Association for the Advancement of Science, San Francisco, California, 1980.
15. G. Garcia Marquez, *One Hundred Years of Solitude* (New York: Avon, 1971).
16. N. Harris, *The End of the Third World*.
17. See W. W. Rostow, *Stages of Economic Growth* (Cambridge: Cambridge University Press, 1960).
18. P. Streeton, *The Limits of Development Studies* (Leeds: Leeds University Press, 1975), p. 12.
19. J. A. Kahl, *Modernisation, Exploitation and Dependency in Latin America, Germani Gonzalez Casanova, and Cardoso* (New Brunswick, NJ: Transaction Books, 1976), p. 203.
20. See M. Mann *The Sources of Social Power*, p. 19.
21. For example, M. Gibbons, 'Interpretation, Genealogy, and Human Agency', in T. Ball (ed.), *Idioms of Inquiry: Critique and Renewal in Political Science* (Albany, NY: State University of New York Press, 1987).
22. W. Connolly, 'Identity and Difference in Global Politics', in J. Der Derian and M. Shapiro (eds), *International/Intertextual Relations* (Lexington, Mass.: Lexington Books, 1989), pp. 335–41.
23. D. Dessler, 'The Use and Abuse of Social Science for Policy', *SAIS Review*, vol. 9 (1989), pp. 209–12.
24. A. Wendt, 'The Agent–Structure Problem in International Relations', *International Organization*, vol. 41 (1987), pp. 335–70.
25. Ibid.
26. R. N. Boyd, 'The Current Status of Scientific Realism', in J. Leplin (ed.), *Scientific Realism* (Berkeley and Los Angeles, Calif.: University of California Press, 1984), pp. 51–2.
27. R. Bernstein, *Beyond Relativism and Objectivism: Science, Hermeneutics and Praxis* (Oxford: Basil Blackwell, 1983), pp. 30–4.
28. N. Onuf, *World of Our Making: Rules and Rule in Social Theory and*

International Relations (Columbia, SC.: University of South Carolina Press, 1989), p. 39.

29. Ibid., p. 43.
30. Ibid., pp. 42–3.
31. Bernstein defines objectivism as some permanent, ahistorical framework to which we can ultimately appeal in determining the nature of rationality, knowledge, truth, reality, goodness and rightness. Relativism, by contrast, he defines as the claim that there can be no higher appeal than to a given conceptual scheme, language game, set of social practices, or historical epoch (see R. Bernstein, *Beyond Relativism and Objectivism*, pp. 8–11).
32. This discussion of structurationism is focused principally on the work of its prime exponent, Anthony Giddens, general commentary thereupon, and recent discussion of theory in International Relations.
33. A. Giddens, *The Constitution of Society: Outline of a Theory of Structuration* (Oxford: Polity Press, 1984), p. 374.
34. In the light of the claim to reflexivity advanced above, one key question a discussion of structurationism prompts is that it has gained such prominence in current social theory. One answer is that it engages difficult and recurring questions in social ontology in novel ways. Central to this is the way structurationism reflects the influence of the current 'post' or 'late' modern mentality which accepts that there is no fixed reality, touchstone of truth, secure foundations or Archimedean point on which to ground an objective reason. Such a view embodies a new appreciation of the centrality of contingency in social life. Agnes Heller has expressed the sensibility thus: 'contingency is not a philosophical construct which could be replaced by any other constructs but the life experience of the modern individual, a vexing, threatening but also promising experience (termed by Kierkegaard the experience of possibility and anxiety)' in A. Heller, 'The Moral Situation in Modernity', *Social Research*, vol. 55 (1988), pp. 531–50. This notion of contingency implies not only the endogenity of all social institutions but also the contingent way the human subject's knowledge and identity are co-constituted with social reality. Such a conception of the reflexive agent's relationship with social institutions is central to structurationism which, in turn, can be understood as an ontology of contingency. An appreciation of this suggests, as Giddens himself has argued, a radical new phase of modernity in which all institutions come to be viewed as potentially revisable on a global scale.
35. Onuf has insightfully elaborated the point thus: 'human agents author rules and deploy resources in accordance with those rules so as to secure and ensconce advantages over other agents. Their differential success produces asymmetries in the ability of agents to control the actions of other agents in time and space as well as the possibility that disadvantaged but competent agents can subvert or reverse such asymmetries' (N. Onuf, *World of Our Making*, p. 60).
36. See M. Mann, *The Sources of Social Power*.
37. Rob Walker has expressed the rationale for such a claim well: 'To engage with the literature on the emergence and development of the

states-system is to be impressed by the transformative quality of both the state and the character of relations between states. States can then appear to us as historically constituted and always subject to change.' See R. B. J. Walker, 'History and Method in International Relations', *Millennium*, vol. 18 (1989), pp. 163–83.
38. See, for example, A. Escobar, *Encountering Development* (Princeton, NJ: Princeton University Press, 1995). See also D. Apter, *Rethinking Development: Modernisation, Dependency, and Postmodern Politics* (London: Sage, 1996).

4 Modifications to the State-in-Society Approach: A Sharper Focus
Mehran Kamrava

Comparative and Third-World studies have undergone significant paradigmatic changes in recent years, ranging from the ideologically laden poles of the dependency and modernisation approaches of the 1970s to the somewhat more neutral neo-statist perspective of the 1980s. Concurrent with this shift in analytical focus has been a zealous rediscovery of culture and its relevance, to political analysis.[1] Out of this intellectually enriching odyssey, and in fact as a synthesis of many of the previous paradigms, has grown a perspective best described as the 'state-in-society' paradigm.[2] Building such a perspective, this study presents a slightly modified methodology for conceptualising Third-World politics. More specifically, the arguments here seek to sharpen the approach's focus by pointing to several areas of analysis that the main proponents of the perspective have either completely ignored or have under-emphasised.

To adequately understand politics in the Third World, as well as elsewhere now that the 'Third World' no longer exists as it did previously,[3] analysis must go beyond the states and society and their mutual social and political interactions. There are three additional elements that must also be considered. They include the prevailing political culture; political economy, especially in relation to the economic causes and effects of the state–society interaction; and the grey area of uncertainty and unpredictability that is the inevitable outcome of historical accidents, individual initiatives, and unintended consequences. Before elaborating on the need for and merits of these modifications, some of the main premises of the state-in-society approach need to be highlighted.

THE STATE-IN-SOCIETY APPROACH

In the past few years, a number of scholars have tried to devise an explanatory paradigm for conceptualising comparative politics in general and Third-World studies in particular, in an attempt to address some of the glaring shortcomings of the dependency, modernisation, and neo-statist approaches. Enunciated in detail in only a handful of publications,[4] the new approach places the focus of analysis on state-society interactions. In a book published in 1988, Joel Migdal elaborated on the need to examine states and societies in tandem. He argued that:

> The model suggested here depicts society as a melange of social organizations than the dichotomous structure that practically all past models of macrolevel change have used (e.g., center–periphery, modern–traditional, great tradition–little tradition)... In this melange, the state has been one organization among many. These organizations – states, ethnic groups, the institutions of particular social classes, villages, and any others enforcing rules of the game – singly or in tandem with one another, have offered individuals the components for survival strategies.[5]

Later, in refining their arguments concerning the precise nature of the state's interactions with society, Migdal and his collaborators maintained that states are often constrained in their autonomy when it comes to dealing with society. Therefore, the relative 'weaknesses' and 'strengths' of the two entities must be analysed. Analysis also needs to be 'disaggregated', requiring the examiner to go beyond the surface tops of both state and society and to look at the more subtle give-and-take of state–society interactions. One must further realise that 'social forces, like states, are contingent on specific empirical conditions', meaning that 'the political action and influence of a social group are not wholly predictable from the relative position of that group within the social structure'. 'The political behavior of social groups,' in other words, 'tends to be context-specific.' Finally, states and social forces may be 'mutually empowering' and, in fact, seldom assume overtly hostile postures toward one another.' Migdal argues:

> The ability of any social force, including the state, to develop the cohesion and garner the material and symbolic resources to

project a meaningful presence at the society-wide level depends on its performance in more circumscribed arenas. In those arenas, it must dominate successfully enough (close to total transformation or, at least, incorporation of existing social forces) so as to be able to generate resources for application in other arena struggles and, ultimately, the society as a whole. Whether any social force, from social classes to the state, will succeed as the basis for integrated domination is far from a foregone conclusion.[6]

The analytical merits of this latest perspective seem quite impressive and the approach appears, at least initially, to have filled the gaps left by the previous paradigms. Significantly, the approach points to the common denominator that all political systems in some way or another share, the manner in which states and societies interrelate. Politics may be, and often is, influenced by a variety of factors and forces, but its simple essence is the relationships that exist between those in power and the people they seek to govern. At its core, politics is made up of a series of interactions that occur within the state, and within society, and between the state and society.[7]

Similarly, the new framework appears, by and large, to be value-free, reeking with neither the conservatism of modernisation theory nor the radicalism of the dependency approach.[8] It simply points to a number of structural and functional characteristics that it sees as being responsible for bestowing on national politics their unique characteristics.[9] It also makes sense of the confusing array of political oddities that have appeared since the demise of the Cold War.[10] States and societies may be 'weak' or 'strong' compared to each other, and their respective strengths and capabilities determine the nature and manner of their mutual interactions.[10]

Nevertheless, upon closer scrutiny, it becomes clear that the above approach also overlooks some of the basic premises of politics. It is unclear, for example, whether such factors as political and/or economic performance play any roles in shaping state–society relations, or in bestowing people with specific perceptions about themselves or their larger polity. In other words, does political culture play any role in determining the nature of state–society relations? Also, what about the economy? The economic agendas of the state, or of social actors, and the various consequences of the economic activities of both state and society (for example, industrialisation, consumerism, rising standards of living and so on) have a significant bearing on both domestic and international politics. Such economic factors cannot be ignored in any analytical formulations about the very nature of politics.

It is also relevant to ask whether there is not an underlying assumption of political and historical determinism in the state-in-society approach that points to a gradual evolution of political systems from one type to another. Can all of politics be explained through the mechanical interactions of state and society, or does the involvement of human agency introduce an inherent element of uncertainty into it? Social and political *actors*, we must remember, are *people* and *individuals* who do not always behave and react as expected. Thus, to assume that there are immutable 'political laws' that provide an analytical explanation for everything is at best optimistic. By nature, politics contains an element of randomness, one that is often overlooked by political scientists. Some of the proponents of the state-in-society approach have touched on this issue, though only briefly, and not from the same angle as proposed in this study. 'Political behavior and the power capacities of social groups are contingent, at least in part', one has claimed.[12] But there are instances, rare as they may be, when politics is more than just 'contingent'; therefore any approach to politics must take the possibility of randomness into account.

In short, the state-in-society approach needs certain refinements and modifications. There are a number of features to this paradigm that make it a particularly attractive framework for comparative analysis, but some clarifications of its core principles are definitely needed. Thus what follows is not so much a refutation of the approach's basic premises as it is an effort to make them as analytically sound as possible.

A SHARPER FOCUS

In understanding and conceptualising the political characteristics and dynamics of a polity, the focus must be on five distinct and yet highly entwined plains of analysis. These are, in order of importance, the state, society, political culture, political economy, and random occurrences. This call for a multidisciplinary paradigm is unlikely to be welcomed by purists. However, it is difficult to arrive at any comprehensive and accurate understanding of comparative politics in general, and of Third-World politics specifically, without examining the combined effects of all of these seemingly disparate fields. States do not operate in a vacuum. They operate in relation to other states, and their own and other societies. These interactions are facilitated by, and take place within the context of, existing national and political cultures. State and social actors each have their own social standing, political priorities, and cultural peculiarities. One of the elements that shapes and determines these characteristics is the economy. Thus the economic axis of state–society interactions cannot be ignored. Finally, there is a built-in element of uncertainty involved, a degree of chance based on such varied factors as historical accidents or the circumstances and opportunities that crop up and happen to be exploited by enterprising individuals. To accurately conceptualise the underpinning dynamics of a political system, therefore, attention must be focused on all four of the areas outlined above and on the ways in which they combine to give a political system its unique and individual characteristics.

The State

The state has not only long been a focus of scholarly attention; it has also been perceived as the ultimate institution responsible for bestowing on a system its essential political characteristics.[13] When, for a brief interlude in the 1960s and 1970s, the importance of the state was thought to have been eclipsed by those of society and of a larger 'system', 'neo-statists' immediately asked for the state to be brought 'back in'.[14]

There is clearly a danger in overstretching the importance of the state at the expense of other equally pivotal political forces. Nevertheless, the analyst cannot ignore that centre within the body politic that monopolises official sources of power.[15] The position of the neo-statists is straightforward: within any given political system, there are institutions and actors with officially-endowed powers, and there are those who are largely recipients of this power. These institutions and groups may or may not act in concert with the rest of the polity; they may foster a relationship with the society that is conflictual or consensual; and may rely on varying degrees of subjective legitimacy versus objective force in order to maintain their position *vis-à-vis* the rest of the system.[16] In one way or another, the role of the state cannot be overlooked or be seen as part of a larger systemic whole in the sense that the systems approach claims.[17] Exactly what roles states play within a given polity may differ considerably from one case to another. Some states may maximise their own powers in order to carry out far-reaching social and economic changes throughout their societies, as most communist and bureaucratic–authoritarian states tried to do in the Soviet bloc and Latin America respectively.[18] Others may facilitate the formation of a number of groups that seek to further their own corporate interests under a larger democratic rubric, as is common among the corporatist states found in northern Europe.[19] Still other states may relegate themselves to a largely regulative role, as most liberal democracies do, in order to ensure that the routinised flow of societal input into the political process is not interrupted.[20]

This discussion of the state is necessarily brief, but it is sufficient to reveal the crucial points that analysis of comparative and Third World politics must entail. First and foremost, the analyst must determine exactly what role the state intrinsically – rather than episodically – plays in relation to the rest of the body politic. Is the state simply performing a regulative function (as in democracies), or is it trying to implement societal and/or economic changes (as in bureaucratic–authoritarian cases)? Is it fostering co-operation among competing corporate groups (for example, in northern Europe), or is it ramming its own agendas through, irrespective of the priorities that society may have? Does the state simply exist in a predatory capacity (as in Zaire), or does it sustain itself through the inclusion of mobilised masses into its own institutions (as in Iran and Cuba)? Once this overall role is determined, attention must focus on the institutions through which the state seeks to carry out its functions and agendas. Exactly what each of these institutions is made of; how they operate; what are their capabilities; whether they tend to rely more on force or on a sense of legitimacy to operate; are they based a specific doctrinal blueprint socialism, for example, or have they evolved in response to prevailing past and present circumstances? And so on.

With these questions answered, the level of analysis must then be taken one step further by looking into the ramifications of the workings of each of the state's institutions. States operate at two levels. At one level, states operate amongst one another, as compellingly and convincingly argued by the dependency approach. At another level, states operate in relation to society. Naturally, this state–society interaction has several consequences, some of which may be political, some social and/or cultural, and still others that may be economic. The analyst must examine not only the ways in which states operate, but, equally importantly, the larger affects of this operation on such diverse facets of life as politics, economics, culture and society. Put differently, both the structures and the functions of the state need to be analysed.

Because of its special position in the world system and in relation to its own society, the role and importance of the state is all the greater. Whether older or newer, authoritarian or democratic, ideological or non-ideological, most of the states in the Third World have been crafted in relatively recent historical time periods: most contemporary states of the Middle East were founded between the 1920s (Turkey and Iran) and the 1940s/1950s (Iraq, Syria, Lebanon, Jordan, Israel and Egypt); in South and Southeast Asia from the 1940s to the 1960s (India, Pakistan, Indonesia, Malaysia and Sri Lanka); and almost all of Africa since the 1960s and 1970s (Zimbabwe, Djibouti, Eritrea and South Africa being among the latest).

Compared to most states in Europe and North America, these and many of the other states in the Third World are relatively young, having developed not so much through evolutionary, historical processes but often as a result of deliberate and rather sudden political crafting. As a result, these states have assumed a special posture toward their societies, often feeling less constrained by the forces of tradition and heritage, being more zealous in their promotion of various domestic and/or international agendas, and much more directly and purposefully involved in their national economies than their know-how or capabilities allow. Put differently, the Third-World state has occupied a special place in relation to other states and its own society by the very virtue of being 'Third World'.[21]

These are states for whom maintaining political power is often a crusade and a struggle, not a by-product of historical evolution and maturation.[22] These are also states that strive to effect purposeful and calculated change in their societies, often fighting the forces of history and tradition. That some are swept aside by the very forces they engender – as happened most dramatically in China, Ethiopia, and Iran, among others – only demonstrates the ineptitude of the state's stewards and the inherent dangers they face. And now that democracy is once again in vogue and when politicians are clamouring to be labelled as 'democrats', the task of the Third-World state is all the more difficult: how to survive if one is not democratic? And, if one is in fact a democrat, how to maintain the many delicate, fragile equilibria on which such a system relies?

In looking at the Third World, the state must be a more important focal point of analysis than might otherwise be the case.

Society

The above discussion inadvertently implies that society is always on the receiving end of state power. Though this is not always valid, there are instances, as in communist and bureaucratic–authoritarian cases, in which society's powers have been emasculated to the point of making social actors and institutions merely passive recipients of the state's powers and agendas. In these cases, the political powers of the state are often based either entirely on brute force or on a combination of force and psychological manipulation. Society is either forced into institutional submission, or, as the circumstances and capabilities of the state may dictate, is fooled into it (in which case, an 'inclusionary' polity often results). Frequently, a combination of state coercion and societal apathy result in the maintenance in power of an otherwise institutionally weak and unpopular regime. Military dictatorships rarely rely on much more than brute force to stay in power.[23] But there are those politicians who seek to enhance their repressive rule through personality cults or other populist mechanisms.

In any case, the penalties for non-conformity are likely to be severe. But while in exclusionary cases the state simply excludes society from the political process through repression, in inclusionary polities it represses but at the same time includes and co-opts large blocs of society within itself. In either case, society is something for the state to reckon with. Which one dominates the other, and at what particular historical moment this domination takes place, is a factor that varies from case to case. In fact, there are as many strong societies and weak states as there are strong states and weak societies, and there may even be cases in which neither the state nor society can interact effectively with one another over a reasonable period of time (witness the demise of political regimes in Somalia, Ethiopia, Liberia, the Sudan, Rwanda and Angola).[24]

The above discussion is not to imply that society's political significance can only be summed up in the context of its overt, direct relations with the state. What happens within society itself can also have considerable political significance. Various groups or institutions in society may jockey for position among themselves for greater societal power and privilege, as, for example, religionist and secularist activists are currently doing in many countries of the Middle East.[25] There are also complex webs of social interaction that give society its overall character and sense of individuality. In some political systems, there may be a large gap between the cultural dispositions of society and the institutional configurations of the state. Again, examples from the Middle East come to mind.[26] In these cases, society may have non-political priorities and agendas of its own that greatly determine the state's behaviour towards it in both the long and the short term. These characteristics, not all of which may at first seem to be politically relevant, in turn combine to influence the manner in which state and society interact with one another.

Of course, there is a point in social analysis at which the examiner must draw the line; not everything that happens in society has intrinsic political relevance. It is exactly this deciphering of the political relevance of various social phenomena that is the political scientist's main challenge. Nevertheless, while not everything that happens in society is politically important or relevant, a lot of it is. The task is to decide which social phenomena, institutions and forces are politically relevant and which are not.

In comparative political analysis, society must be examined not in only relation to the state but also as an entity in itself, one whose constituent institutions are politically relevant, both on their own and when they come into contact with state institutions. Society needs to be viewed neither as a passive recipient of state power, although in some cases it may be, nor as its holistic extension, which some of the proponents of the systems approach claim it to be. Analysing society is not, therefore, radically different from analysing the state. The central features to consider are simple enough: what are the institutions that make up society and what is the political relevance of each of them? What is the exact nature of the interaction, at both an institutional as well as a functional level, that takes place between society and the state? Societies are by nature changeable; which ones and how many of these changes are state-initiated, or indigenously initiated, and what are their overall political consequences? In what instances and under what circumstances are societies politically passive in respect to the state; are co-operative; or become rebellious? When and how does a society mould its state, or state mould its society, or the two remain oblivious of each other, or develop a routinised, consensual and equal pattern of interaction?

These questions are not meant to be definitive points around which analysis must revolve. Rather, they are intended to present general guidelines to consider in looking at social institutions; the routinised patterns in which they interact within themselves and with the institutions of the state; the underlying reasons for, and ramifications of, processes of social change; the causes and effects of society-wide dislocations; and the less pronounced, more subtle changes that take place in society's relations with the state over time. Again, societies that exist in the Third World by nature require special attention; Third-World societies change rapidly. Moreover, sometimes they may be subdued by an authoritarian state, while at other times they may become highly volatile and rebellious. At times they are so fragmented as to paralyse any power attempting to govern (for example, Lebanon in the 1970s and Rwanda in the 1990s), and on other occasions they may act as cohesive units. At times they may be taken in by the rhetoric and propaganda of the regime in power (for example, Juan Perón's Argentina), and at other times they may develop into civil society and vehicles for democratisation. Because of the changeability of their relations with the state over relatively short time periods, the potential political significance of Third-World societies is all the more pronounced when compared to those in Western Europe and North Africa.

However, there is more to society than a mechanical collection of institutions, individual actors, and groups who interact among themselves and between themselves and the state. There is an additional normative context, the political culture, that also influences the ways in which state and society relate to one another. In short, political analysis must go beyond the simple, objective circumstances of society and must take into account its subjective, cultural dispositions and priorities as well.

Political Culture

One of the important areas that the state-in-society approach has not taken into account *explicitly* is political culture.[27] This lack of attention is part of a long tradition in political science in which culture/political culture were not taken seriously. Culture was often seen as a slippery phenomenon, more a by-product of larger political developments than a determining force by itself. Depending on their field of expertise, area specialists are likely to ascribe different

degrees of significance to culture; it has long been an inseparable
feature of Middle Eastern politics, especially since the 1960s, whereas
it played little or no part in the bureaucratic–authoritarian regimes
of Latin America.[28] Clearly, an expert on the Middle East will have
a much harder time ignoring the region's cultural influences on
politics than would a Latin American expert.[29]

In my advocacy of the importance of culture, I propose a middle
line. In so far as politics is concerned, culture is not always a stand-
alone phenomenon: it can neither make or break politics by itself.
In fact, politics being the art of the possible, culture is often moulded
and shaped by the powers of the state. Nevertheless, culture does
form an overall framework within which communities and societies
formulate their thoughts and actions, interact with one another,
and form opinions towards those in power. Therefore, all macro
level political analyses that concern state–society relations must
necessarily consider the overall valuative context within which societies operate. In particular, attention must be paid to a polity's
political culture, which is comprised of cultural norms and values
that specifically govern state–society interactions.

In non-democracies, there are often sharp differences between
the public manifestations of political culture ('regime orientations')
and the real, private feelings that people have about politics ('political orientations').[30] Making such a distinction is not always easily
possible in non-democracies, as the absence of open political forums
and such mechanisms as elections make it all but impossible to
quantify or analyse empirically popular political perceptions. It is
no accident that *Civic Culture* was based on largely empirical observations in a number of democracies.[31] None the less, the analyst must see whether there is indeed a distinction between regime
and political orientations, and, if so, where the centres of gravity
of each of the poles lie. This entails investigation of the various
other phenomena that give rise to political culture, some of which
may be unique to a particular country (a traumatic historical experience such as a revolution, for example), and some of which are
found more universally (childhood socialisation, political experience and so on). Once the overall features of the political culture
have been identified, the task is to find out which complement and
which contradict the normative premises on which a political system is based. From here, one can examine the possible causal relationships that may exist between facets of the political culture on
the one hand and the overall nexus between state and society on

the other. Is the current governing regime in tune with the prevailing political culture of the masses? If not, is it being undermined as a result? Is the regime attempting to carve out a political culture of its own, or is it slave to the normative dispositions of the people who will settle for nothing less than the full gratification of their political ideals and beliefs?

But culture does not always have to be overtly political for it to be politically relevant. There are many subtle and pronounced aspects of culture that can have great political significance without being in any way political. The neo-Confucian element in Southeast Asian cultures, for example, has long resulted in a remarkable degree of political stability and cohesion in such countries as Singapore, Hong Kong, South Korea and Taiwan.[32] In the Middle East, cults of personality have similarly benefited from Islam's tendency to glorify the individual.[33] Moreover, a pervasive spirit of social and cultural inequality, running rampant despite Islam's pretensions to egalitarianism, is largely responsible for the maintenance of highly corrupt monarchical institutions throughout the Arabian peninsula.[34] Reverence for elders in Africa goes a long way in accounting for the political longevity of such figures as Jomo Kenyatta and Julius Nyerere.[35] In Latin America, the political importance of the *caudillo* mentality is especially important.[36] Cultures everywhere provide the norms and values, customs and habits, according to which people think, behave and live their lives. Some of these norms and values are consciously picked up and manipulated by politicians who seek to enhance their popular appeal and legitimacy, while others provide more subtle emotional and psychological links between political actors and the ordinary masses. Therefore, it is not always easy to determine where popular culture ends and political culture begins, but both can have significant, and sometimes subtle, political ramifications.

Political Economy

Political economy is another area that the state-in-society approach overlooks but needs to consider. Specifically, analysis needs to focus on the economic ramifications of state–society interactions, as well as the larger economic context within which these interactions take place. This is not a theme that the comparative literature has overlooked entirely; Dietrich Rueschemeyer and Peter Evans argued persuasively in the early 1980s that in order to 'undertake

effective interventions' in the economic realm, 'the state must constitute a bureaucratic apparatus with sufficient corporate coherence'
while 'retaining a certain degree of autonomy from the dominant
interests in a capitalist society' to be able to pursue a consistent
policy. Later, Rueschemeyer, Evelyne Stephens, and John Stephens
argued that state power is only one of 'three clusters of power' –
along with class power and transnational structures of power – that
may result in the emergence or demise of democracy in the process of capitalist development.[37] Ultimately, the question that comparative analysis must answer is how much economic power and/or
autonomy do the state and society have in relation to one another,
and whether their economic power capabilities affect their respective agendas and interactions.

State and social actors compete, sometimes violently, for access
to/control over economic resources. These contests may occur at a
variety of levels, from the national, where the state tries to regu-
late the overall economic picture, to local levels, where state agencies or officials interact economically with individuals and other
social actors. The nature and outcome of such contests largely
determine the degree to which state and society can act auton-
omously from one another and, in turn, influence each other. The
number of possible scenarios is rather limited and are often better
known by their corresponding labels: advanced capitalist economies;
socialist economies; and mixed economies.

In the first of these scenarios, social actors have acquired considerable control over economic resources. This degree of societal
affluence, itself the result of a historical progression of market forces,
is made possible and maintained through economic competition
among the social actors, and the best the state can do is to play a
largely regulative role in the economic agendas of the various social actors. In his insightful treatment of the subject, Barrington
Moore has shown how in eighteenth- and nineteenth-century Europe the bourgeoisie, through its increasing economic might and
autonomy, was able to press demands upon states that at the time
were only just becoming aware of the importance of market forces.[38]
What evolved, most purely in the young USA, was raw and savage
capitalism, fuelled by its two quintessential elements: the incentive
and the opportunity to compete. But as the hard lessons of the
1930s were to demonstrate, capitalism can run into serious problems, and successive capitalist-run societies saw the intervention of
the state into various economic fields. Some states in Europe went

overboard, to the point of becoming fascist and corporatist (Germany, Italy and Spain), only to be altered dramatically later.[39] Others (Britain, the USA, Switzerland and Scandinavian countries) gave themselves extensive regulative powers within the economy and sought to fill the economic voids that capitalism would not attend to on its own (social security or unemployment benefits, for example).[40] In essence, capitalism in these countries has surpassed and overcome its brutish phase and has reached a certain level of maturity in comparison with elsewhere. The economic interactions between state and society take place within the context of advanced capitalism, though they still revolve around the basic question of economic autonomy: social actors want as much autonomy as possible in order to let market forces yield the highest results, while the state seeks to ensure that the proper areas of the economy remain regulated.

This is not a scenario that is applicable to the advanced capitalist nations of Europe and North America alone. The same thing has occurred in East Asia and Latin America, although under decidedly different historical auspices. Here the state initially assumed an overarching, bureaucratic–authoritarian format, excluding the popular classes from both the political and economic processes but instead promoting 'patterns of capital accumulation strongly biased in favour of large, oligopolistic units of private capital and some state institutions'.[41] The state embarked on ambitious processes of economic and infrastructural development, a task at which it was initially somewhat successful.[42] But these experiments in state-sponsored capitalism often had peculiar results. The authoritarian state was always careful not to give too much autonomy to social actors, seeking to ensure that economic liberalism did not necessarily translate into political liberalism. At the same time, it revelled in laying the economic and infrastructural foundations for further capitalist development. In itself, there is nothing particularly damning in the pursuit of authoritarian capitalism. What often dooms authoritarian capitalism is the way in which it goes about its business. In East Asia (Singapore, Taiwan and Hong Kong, for example) and in Augusto Pinochet's Chile, the armed forces as a corporate unit largely stayed out of economic affairs, allowing considerable policy-making discretion to civilian economists. But elsewhere in Latin America – especially in Argentina, Brazil, and Uruguay – colonels and generals suddenly became economic policy-makers, and in the span of a decade or so ran their countries' economies into the ground.[43] By the time authoritarianism collapsed in Latin America in the 1980s, it had already left behind a capitalist legacy and an infrastructure (though very poorly managed under the military) that was second only to that of the newly industrialised economies of East Asia. At present, therefore, the economic interactions of state and society in East Asia and Latin America (especially in South America) revolve largely around the same set of premises as those in other advanced capitalist cases: the degree of economic autonomy of social actors versus the regulative reaches of the state.

The same is true of the formerly socialist economies of Eastern and Central Europe, although in their case it is much more difficult to disentangle the many intrusive control mechanisms that the state once imposed on social actors. In the socialist scheme of things, a 'dictatorship of the proletariat' sought to 'guide' society through historical stages by owning directly, in theory at least, all sources of economic production. It thus devised a comprehensive ideological blueprint and penetrative bureaucratic apparatus in its self-proclaimed march toward eventual liberation. The whole point of the venture, or at least its inadvertent outcome if not its purposeful goal, was to minimise any potential areas of autonomy that society might develop *vis-à-vis* the state, especially in the economic sphere, to which particular ideological significance was attached. In such a scenario, the economics of state–society interactions, as in other areas, were singularly one-sided, controlled, dominated, and overwhelmed by the state.[44] The lingering economic legacy of the socialist experiment is as pervasive in East and Central Europe in the late 1990s as the foundations of capitalism were in South America after the demise of authoritarianism there a few years earlier. Reconstituting the economic aspects of the state–society relationship, by transforming the state's economic role into a largely regulative one, giving autonomy to market forces and so on, is no easy task.

The final scenario involves mixed economies where, theoretically at least, control over economic resources is divided between public and private sectors. In these economies, found in most Third-World countries, especially in the Middle East and Africa, the state seeks to foster market economies while still retaining control over most major sources of production.[45] In Latin America in the 1970s and 1980s, when most of the region's countries also had mixed economies, the state often sponsored joint industrial ventures with foreign and domestic investors (called parastatals) in an attempt to ease some of its own burden for economic growth and develop-

ment.[46] Nevertheless, by their very nature, states with mixed economies are highly constrained in their economic and political manoeuvrability. On the one hand, the state must cater to and placate
the consumerist yearnings of the middle classes who, if left economically unhappy, are quick to blame the state for their deteriorating
circumstances. On the other hand, the state is often beholden to
special interest elite groups whose investments help to support the
backbone of the domestic economy. There is also the stigma attached
to too close an identification with foreign investors, few of whom,
even in the neo-liberal environment of the 1980s and 1990s, would
find favour with Third-World intellectuals and other members of
the educated classes.

There are further structural limitations that such states face. Unlike
socialist states, mixed economy states do not have a coherent and
comprehensive ideological blueprint for the economy. Instead, their
overall economic programmes often derive from a mixture of planning, catering to this or that elite group, and, at times, joint ventures with various multinational corporations. The state also lacks
the necessary resources to fully carry out its economic commit-
ments. This hybrid form of economics, which may best be described
as one of state socialism and societal capitalism, is rampant in the
Middle East and, to a somewhat lesser extent, in Africa.

All mixed economies invariably give rise to an expansive and highly
active informal sector. But, in the Middle East especially, there is
a sizeable portion of the *formal* economy that continues to operate
outside of the government's purview. In fact, much of the formal
economy in the Middle East, especially that involving the exchange
of goods and services among non-governmental actors, retains an
astounding level of informality, and therefore autonomy from state
regulations and other forms of government interference. This widespread informality of the formal economy has much to do with the
phenomenon of the 'bazaar economy'. The bazaaris, many of whose
economic activities fall outside the formal sphere and are rarely
ever regulated by the state, engage in capitalism *par excellence*, subject
at most to unofficial rules and conventions formulated by their own
guilds and associations.[47] Despite the seemingly small scale of their
operations, most bazaari merchants are often inordinately wealthy,
so much so that some can at times corner the entire market on a
particular product (say, onions or tyres), and by so doing significantly influence a commodity's supply and price throughout their
city or even the entire country. In turn, the raw and unregulated

capitalism in which the bazaaris engage has a multitude of facets and dimensions, spilling over into other informal, and at times even formal, economic spheres. The state, meanwhile, is often largely powerless in dealing with the bazaaris as it has neither the resources nor the political will to break their considerable economic might. What results, therefore, is a savage capitalism operating at the societal level side-by-side with a timid socialism at the national level espoused by the state.

The situation in Sub-Saharan African countries is somewhat different. With some exceptions, an independent, politically autonomous merchant class has not developed in black Africa. Some classes do exercise a measure of autonomy from the state: the merchant communities (*Bamilke*) in Cameroon, the ubiquitous 'contractors' in Nigeria, and the *magendo* (people in the upper end of the economic scale who are a 'mirror image of the informal sector at the lower end') in Uganda, Ghana and Zaire.[48] But there is nothing similar to the Middle Eastern bazaar economy in Sub-Saharan Africa, and the many bustling open-air markets that are a consistent feature of Africa's urban landscape do not afford opportunities for an economically and politically affluent merchant class as such to grow.

In many African and non-African examples, nevertheless, society does exercise some autonomy from the state, at times, in fact, to the point of making the country as a national unit dysfunctional. But this autonomy is caused by factors that are largely non-economic. In Western Europe, societal autonomy grew out of persistent demands for political space by various social actors. In South America and Eastern Europe, society gained autonomy (although in places the process continues to face obstacles) after the rolling back of states that had previously sought to overwhelm and subdue it. In the Middle East, in cases where autonomy from the state does exist, it is the prerogative of a distinct social class (the bazaaris) and its successive layers of clients, in relation to which the state is often ineffective and almost a non-factor. In post-colonial Sub-Saharan Africa, however, class factors have been less important than other systemic economic and sociocultural dynamics. Often, they tend to be products of inherent institutional weaknesses by the state on the one hand and society's multiple fractures (along ethnic, linguistic and cultural lines) on the other.

In short, a major obstacle faced by African states is incapacity (or timidity) in relation to society. Moreover, the prevalence of a stagnant 'semicapitalism' in much of the continent has greatly hampered the ability of either the state or society on its own to meet the challenges of development successfully.[49] As a result, the economic nexus between state and society remains small and relatively insignificant. In most of today's Sub-Saharan Africa,[50] political economy is not playing as influential a role in state–society relations as have such non-economic factors as ethnic and cultural heterogeneity. In Migdal's terms, most African societies may be considered 'strong' compared to the states that rule over them. However, this strength is not based on the social actors' greater access to economic resources. Rather, it has more to do with the state's inability to tackle the challenges it faces from a deeply divided society.

THE UNCERTAINTY PRINCIPLE

The final area that the state-in-society approach could greatly benefit from is closer attention to what a number of theorists have called 'contingency', or what may also be called randomness. Long a part of some historically-grounded political analyses, contingency points to the existence of those elements whose genesis and causes are not always empirically explicable; they are not quantifiable; and they are almost impossible to predict. As a factor of analysis, contingency (randomness) is elusive and evasive, a shadowy area where the best we can do is to offer educated guesses and recognise our limitations in precise, tangible, 'scientific' measurement and reasoning. This is more than the 'contingence' factor which some proponents of the state-in-society approach have mentioned (though not elaborated on).[51] Instead, this is an area in social analysis where a measure of randomness is both possible and probable, where something akin to 'the uncertainty principle' of quantum mechanics prevails. In the life of every country, whether in its politics or its history, its society or its economy, there is a certain amount of unpredictability, a number of accidental or unintended occurrences that have little or nothing to do with the national, political, or historical 'norm' of that country. Sometimes things can happen that have no causal relationship to political, economic, or sociocultural forces that exist in a particular society. All political systems and societies operate according to sets of rules and guidelines that can pretty much be accurately grasped and analysed. But, by nature, they also contain an element of uncertainty, when developments arise based on no rules or conventions, when society or politics assume directions that no one expected, when culture develops norms few thought possible, when history takes turns few ever imagined.

We must, of course, be careful not to stretch the boundaries of this accidentalism beyond reasonable limits. There are very broad and general limits beyond which random occurrences are not possible. Nevertheless, there is a general framework within which not every occurrence or development is predictable. To assume, for example, that China might tomorrow suddenly become democratic is unreasonable; but no one could account scientifically for Chairman Mao's political antics after the success of Chinese communists in 1949 (not the least of which were the Great Leap Forward and the Cultural Revolution). In *A Brief History of Time*, Stephen Hawking offers a layman's definition of quantum mechanics that seems to fit this model perfectly:

> In general, quantum mechanics does not predict a single definite result from an observation. Instead, it predicts a number of different possible outcomes and tells us how likely each of these is. That is to say, if one made the same measurement on a large number of similar systems, each of which started off in the same way, one would find that the result of the measurement would be A in a certain number of cases, B in a different number, and so on. One would predict the approximate number of times that the result would be A or B, but one could not predict the specific result of an individual measurement. Quantum mechanics therefore introduces an unavoidable element of unpredictability or randomness into science.[52]

The uncertainty principle can be caused by any one of four interrelated and complementary factors: circumstances and opportunities; historical accidents; unintended consequences; and personal initiatives. Unforeseen circumstances and random occurrences – the element of chance – can potentially play a crucial role in the uncertainty principle. Circumstances and opportunities often arise that, if properly situated or exploited, may significantly change the political life or social direction of a given country. The circumstances in which a country finds itself can potentially (and often, in fact, do) have an important bearing on its politics and society. These circumstances may result from accidental factors that initially have nothing to do with the country itself. The tragic example of the

link between the Holocaust and Palestinian politics may better illustrate the point. Who could explain rationally Adolf Hitler's crusade to annihilate the Jews? There is no single social, political or
historical explanation for the Holocaust; the man was simply a
pathological murderer. One can rationalise about the causes of the
Holocaust, but the reason as to why it was carried out, and why it
was carried out the way that it was, ultimately rests with Hitler
himself. Some other political leader might have carried out the
same murderous crusade, but probably he would have avoided it
altogether, or at least done it differently.[53] That some six million
Jews perished and countless others were displaced throughout the
globe was simply a matter of unfortunate chance, but still chance
none the less. But this poor luck on the part of the European Jewry
has dramatically altered the life, politics, and society of not only
Jews but also Palestinians in a way they could not have possibly
imagined before 1947. The irrational actions of a man in distant
Europe, resulting in the misfortunes of millions of people, influenced life in Palestine in a way that indigenous Palestinian factors
had little to do with. The unpredictable element of chance, or in
this case horrendous misfortune, has played a determining role in
the nature of Palestinian (and, of course, Israeli) politics, society
and economics. Hitler's madness alone is not responsible for every
aspect of Palestinian life or politics since 1947, but the coinciden-
tal connection between the two is more formidable than may at
first appear to be the case. Closely related to the randomness of
circumstances and opportunities that are thrust upon a country are
the role of historical accidents. Especially in the contemporary era,
rarely has an accidental historical act or a random discovery changed
or fundamentally altered the political life of an entire country. Yet
a credible argument could be made that the appearance of the
Age of Revolution in Europe, and particularly of industrialisation
in England, was quite accidental, and that such Asian countries as
China or Japan were initially better situated to be the birthplaces
of technological innovation and advancement.[54]

Similarly unpredictable are the important roles played by personal initiative and human agency. At whatever level one looks
there are the undeniable, constant men and women who, either
individually or collectively, are the benefactors, or initiators, or
recipients of political power. Even when political ideology, or cus-
tom and convention, heavily constrain the range of options open
to human free will, there is still a degree if not of independence

but of variance that one person's thoughts and actions have from another's. How that initiative has an impact on politics and how the fluidity of human individuality results in a certain political outcome that would have been different had someone else been involved is where the uncertainty of politics lies. Politics thus becomes especially problematical when a person decides to 'make history'; when a Napoleon Bonaparte attains power, an Ayatollah Khomeini tries to cling on to it, an Idi Amin enters the scene, or a Mikhail Gorbachev worries about how future Russians will remember him. In such instances, politics becomes erratic, highly personalised and unpredictable. It has few or no set patterns, and no overarching guiding principles other than what the political leader thinks is prudent for the moment and at the time.

CONCLUSIONS: ANALYTICAL APPLICATIONS

The analytical utility of the approach laid out above becomes apparent when it is applied to the totality that constitutes politics. Politics is a multifaceted realm in which a number of forces, disparate and often initially unrelated, combine to determine the nature and behaviour of state and social actors themselves and in relation to one another. In one way or another, previous approaches to comparative politics have failed to provide proper and sufficient analytical guidelines that would take all such diverse components into account. Although it is far more thorough than those preceding it, the state-in-society perspective fails to leave room for accidental occurrences or to take into account factors related to political economy and political culture. Here, I have cast an analytical net that, for now at least, appears wide enough to take into account the many forces and phenomena that make up politics. It also retains an internal logical consistency that enables the analyst to point to the causal connections that may exist in seemingly unconnected political domains.

This is a holistic view of comparative politics in which five areas of analysis have been highlighted: state; society; political culture; political economy; and random occurrences. The inner- and inter-workings of each one of these five areas form the blueprint that comparative analysis can follow. This larger model can then be applied to look at a specific political phenomenon or event from a comparative perspective. The comparativist must determine which one of the five areas best explains the characteristics and underlying causes of their particular subject of investigation; which other areas were directly or indirectly involved or affected; and how that specific phenomenon, which might have occurred in only one area, has an impact on the larger picture.

Building on the state-in-society approach to comparative politics, this chapter has sought to take the level of analysis one step further by proposing a more holistic perspective. To examine politics in general and Third-World politics in particular, it argues, analysis must focus not only on the state and society but also on the additional areas of political culture, political economy, and 'the uncertainty principle'. As the general umbrella under which popular norms and values toward political objects are formulated, political culture plays a decisive role in influencing a society's interactions with the state and, in turn, the degree of success or failure a state may have in carrying out its social agendas. Similarly important is political economy, in particular the economic contexts and ramifications of the interactions that take place between the state and society.

Finally, attention has been drawn to a certain amount of built-in unpredictability in politics, a degree of deliberate uncertainty based more on the laws of probabilities and accidental occurrences than on any tangibly predictable phenomena based on the laws of politics, society or economics. Politics is not in any sense mysterious or magical; it is not a discipline whose study and examination is a matter of pure speculation or abstract philosophising. Rather, it is not always wholly quantifiable or reducible to immutable mechanical laws and regulations. We must acknowledge that because of the involvement of humans in it politics can potentially result in outcomes that are not always precisely predictable. The best we can do in such instances of political analysis, as with physics, is to present ourselves with a range of possible options and speculate about their potential outcomes. Conceptualising politics in the Third World is a more complicated venture than was previously assumed. I do not suggest a definitive end to the ongoing debate, but present this modified methodology for the various areas of analysis where attempts at political conceptualisation must focus.

The assertions made here enjoy neither the elegant simplicity of the modernisation perspective nor the compelling convictions of the dependency approach. Politics is presented here as a messy, complicated, and at times accidental and unpredictable, web into which may enter a number of non-political forces and considerations. But that, as unfortunate as it may be, is precisely what politics is. As our understanding of comparative global politics becomes more thorough and sophisticated, so we must modify our perceptions and presuppositions of what *politics* is and how we must go about understanding it. Progressively greater levels of analytical and conceptual sophistication are to be expected in the future.

Notes and References

1. See S. Huntington, 'The Goals of Development', in M. Weiner and S. Huntington (eds), *Understanding Political Development* (New York: HarperCollins, 1987), pp. 3–32.
2. J. Migdal, A. Kohli and V. Shue (eds), *State Power and Social Forces: Domination and Transformation in the Third World* (Cambridge: Cambridge University Press, 1994), p. 1.
3. See, for example, J. Manor (ed.), *Rethinking Third World Politics* (London: Longman, 1991).
4. Although the approach informs the underlying premise of a number of case studies dealing with comparative politics, its theoretical parameters have been outlined explicitly in only a few publications. See, for example, M. Kamrava, *Understanding Comparative Politics: A Framework for Analysis*, (London: Routledge, 1996).
5. J. Migdal, *Strong Societies and Weak States: State–Society Relations and State Capabilities in the Third World* (Princeton, NJ: Princeton University Press, 1988), pp. 28–9.
6. See J. Migdal *et al.*, (eds), *State Power and Social Forces*.
7. M. Kamrava, *Understanding Comparative Politics*, pp. 2–3.
8. The dependency-modernisation debate has been treated extensively in a number of publications. See, for example, K. Clements, *From Left to Right in Development Theory: An Analysis of the Political Implications of Different Models of Development* (Singapore: The Institute of Southeast Asian Studies, 1980).
9. See J. Migdal *et al.* (eds), *State Power and Social Forces*.
10. M. Kamrava, *Understanding Comparative Politics*, pp. 2–3.
11. J. Migdal, *Strong Societies and Weak State*, p. 40.
12. See J. Migdal *et al.* (eds), *State Power and Social Forces*, p. 3.
13. J. Dearlove, 'Bringing the Constitution Back In: Political Science and the State', *Political Science*, vol. 37 (1989), p. 251.
14. T. Skocpol, 'Bringing the State Back In: Strategies of Analysis in Current Analysis', in P. Evans, D. Rueschemeyer and T. Skocpol (eds), *Bringing the State Back In* (Cambridge University Press, 1985), pp. 3–37.
15. A. Giddens, *Capitalism and Modern Social Theory: An Analysis of the Writings of Marx, Durkheim and Max Weber* (Cambridge: Cambridge University Press, 1991), p. 156.
16. M. Kamrava, *Understanding Comparative Politics*, pp. 43–4.
17. See, for example, G. Almond and G. Bingham Powell, 'The Study of Comparative Politics', in G. Almond and G. Bingham Powell (eds),

Comparative Politics Today: A World View, 5th edn (New York: HarperCollins, 1992), pp. 4–6.

18. S. White, J. Gardner and G. Schopflin, *Communist Political Systems*, 2nd edn (New York: St Martin's Press, 1987), p. 20.
19. B. Guy Peters, *European Politics Reconsidered* (New York: Holmes & Meier, 1991), pp. 171–2.
20. G. Loewenberg and S. Patterson, 'Legislatures and Political Systems', in L. Cantori and A. Ziegler (eds), *Comparative Politics in the Post-Behavioral Era* (Boulder, Col.: Lynne Rienner, 1988), p. 280.
21. S. Huntington, *Political Order in Changing Societies* (New Haven, Conn.: Yale University Press, 1968), p. 196.
22. Ibid.
23. For example, in Argentina's 'dirty war'.
24. These instances arise when there are multiple and competing centres of authority in both the state and society which can establish effectively their dominance over one another. Consequently, a broken state tries to govern a deeply fractured society, with a multi-authority polity being the outcome.
25. In Egypt, for example, there is a not-too-subtle competition among religious and secular professors over which group becomes more dominant on university campuses and in particular departments (personal interview, Professor Kamal El-Menouphi, Associate Dean of the College of Politics and Economics, Cairo University, Cairo, 2 June 1996).
26. I. Harik, 'The Origins of the Arab State System', in G. Salame (ed.), *The Foundations of the Arab State System* (London: Croom Helm, 1987), p. 24.
27. However, Migdal does allude to political culture when discussing civil society, which he claims to assume 'the existence of a normative consensus or hegemony of fundamental ideas among social forces ... this consensus represents a prevailing moral or social order' (J. Migdal, *Strong Societies and Weak States*, p. 28).
28. This is not to say that examinations of Latin-American culture and its political significance do not exist. For example, see J. Booth and M. Seligson, 'Paths to Democracy and the Political Culture of Costa Rica, Mexico, and Peru', in L. Diamond (ed.), *Political Culture and Democracy in Developing Countries* (Boulder, Col.: Lynne Rienner, 1994).
29. M. Kamrava and F. Mora, 'Civil Society in Comparative Perspective: Lessons from Latin America and the Middle East', Paper delivered in Conference on Democratisation and Civil Society, University of Warwick, UK, 15–16 February 1996.
30. M. Kamrava, *Understanding Comparative Politics*, pp. 144–5.
31. G. Almond and S. Verba, *The Civic Culture* (Princeton, NJ: Princeton University Press, 1963).
32. E. Vogel, *The Four Little Dragons* (Cambridge, Mass.: Harvard University Press, 1991), pp. 92–3.
33. J. Bill and R. Springborg, *Politics in the Middle East*, 4th edn (New York: HarperCollins, 1994), pp. 160–2.
34. H. Sharabi, *Neopatriarchy: A Theory of Distorted Change in the Arab World* (Oxford: Oxford University Press, 1988), p. 9.

68   *Modifications to the State-in-Society Approach*

35. J.-F. Bayart, *The State in Africa: The Politics of the Belly* (London: Longman, 1993), pp. 174–5.
36. S. E. Finer, *The Man on Horseback: The Role of the Military in Politics* (Boulder, Col.: Westview, 1988), pp. 214–5.
37. See D. Rueschemeyer, E. H. Stephens and J. Stephens, *Capitalist Development and Democracy* (Chicago, Ill.: University of Chicago Press, 1992), p. 269.
38. B. Moore, *The Social Origins of Democracy and Dictatorship: Lord and Peasant in the Making of the Modern World* (New York: Penguin, 1966), p. 415.
39. For a discussion of the nature of and relationship between corporatism and Fascism in inter-war Europe, see H. R. Kedward, *Fascism in Western Europe 1900–45* (New York University Press, 1971), pp. 207–19.
40. K. Laybourn, *The Evolution of British Social Policy and the Welfare State* (Keele University Press, 1995), p. 222.
41. G. O'Donnell, *Bureaucratic Authoritarianism: Argentina, 1966–1973, in Comparative Perspective* (Berkeley, Calif.: University of California Press, 1988), p. 32.
42. M. Foley, 'Debt, Democracy, and Neoliberalism in Latin America: Losses and Gains of the "Lost Decade" in M. Dorraj (ed.), *The Changing Political Economy of the Third World*, (Boulder, Col.: Lynne Rienner, 1995), p. 20.
43. Ibid., p. 21.
44. L. C. Bresser Pereira, J.-M. Maravall and A. Przewoski, *Economic Reform in New Democracies: A Social-Democratic Approach* (Cambridge: Cambridge University Press, 1993), pp. 132–3.
45. M. Todaro, *Economic Development in the Third World*, 4th edn (New York: Longman, 1989), pp. 20–1.
46. H. Wiarda, *Latin American Politics*, (Belmont, Calif.: Wadsworth, 1995), pp. 112–16.
47. C. Geertz, H. Geertz and L. Rosen, *Meaning and Order in Moroccan Society: Three Essays in Cultural Analysis* (Cambridge: Cambridge University Press, 1979), pp. 123–264.
48. C. Young, 'Patterns of Social Conflict: State, Class, and Ethnicity', *Daedlus*, vol. 111, no. 2, Spring (1982), p. 86.
49. See A. Gadzey, 'The Political Economy of Centralization and Delayed Capitalism in Sub-Saharan Africa', in M. Dorraj (ed.), *The Changing Political Economy of the Third World*, p. 89.
50. With the exception of South Africa. See S. Lewis, *The Economics of Apartheid* (New York: Council on Foreign Relations Press, 1990), pp. 17–18.
51. See J. Migdal *et al.* (eds) *State Power and Social Forces*, p. 3.
52. S. Hawking, *A Brief History of Time: From the Big Bang to Black Holes* (London: Bantam, 1988), pp. 55–6.
53. The argument that the responsibility for the Holocaust rests primarily with Hitler is not universally accepted. For more on this debate see, M. Marrus, *The Holocaust in History* (Hanover, Mass.: University Press of New England, 1987), especially pp. 1–30.
54. See the arguments made in J. Needham, *Science and Civilisation in China, Volume 5* (Cambridge: Cambridge University Press, 1976), pp. xxv–xxvi.

5 Globalism, Regionalism and the New Third World

Björn Hettne

Is the Third World, as commonly understood, at all a relevant concept as the Christian world reaches its second millennium? Many do not think so, and for good reasons. The old Third World, meaning the post-colonial states in Africa, Latin America and Asia, was never a very homogeneous category in the first place, and usually the Middle East was left out of this category altogether. In the late 1990s, Asia-Pacific is competing with the old North for world hegemony, while some of the northern regions are gradually becoming marginalised and sinking into the periphery. Thus the world of tomorrow will be different from the world of yesterday. But the world of today is not easy to define either. Is it still the old inter-state system; has it become global; or is it becoming regional? Has the Third World disappeared? If this is the case, poverty and misery have definitely not disappeared, and are still in need of explanation. For that reason the question 'What happened to the Third World?' is still relevant.

The thrust of my argument here is that a new world order will be a regionalised one, and that the phenomenon of regionalism should be seen basically as some sort of response (offensive or defensive) to globalisation, a process that is undermining and eroding the traditional position of the nation-state in the international system. There are, however, many regionalisms, and a rough distinction can be made between core and peripheral regions, with an intermediate category in between. The primary criteria for these distinctions have to do with performance in terms of security and development. The peripheral regions of the world can thus be seen as the 'New Third World', inheriting the structural problems of underdevelopment and domestic conflict, but largely different from the old post-colonial Third World. This chapter tries, from a structuralist point of view, to explain why. It then turns to a more actor-orientated approach and asks the question; what can be done? Structure is not seen as historical rigidities but as regularised patterns

69

of action that are amenable to change. But let us start with the global processes and their local repercussions.

GLOBALISM AND REGIONALISM

Globalism as an ideology can be defined as programmatic globalisation, a vision of a borderless world. Globalisation as process was made possible by the political stability of the American hegemonic world order, which lasted from the end of the Second World War until the late 1960s or early 1970s. The origins of globalisation may be traced far back in history, but one could also argue that the process reached a new stage in the post-Second World War era, because globalisation implies a deepening of the internationalisation process, strengthening the functional, and weakening the territorial dimension of development. I therefore see globalisation as a qualitatively new phenomenon. Some speak of 'the end of history', implying by that a systemic convergence in various parts of the world, which are also becoming increasingly interdependent. The subjective sense of geographical distance has also changed dramatically; thus some speak not only of the end of history, but also of 'the end of geography'. So, not very much seems to be left of the territorially organised Westphalian Old World.

Globalisation basically implies the growth of a functional world market, increasingly penetrating and dominating the so-called 'national' economies, which in the process are bound to lose much of their 'nationness'. Global economies are being delinked from culture and politics, both of which are becoming intrinsically mixed in 'the politics of identity'. The states are becoming spokespersons of global economic forces, rather than protecting their own populations and their cultures against these demanding and inexplicable changes. This implies that the state is becoming alienated from civil society, defined as inclusive institutions that facilitate a societal dialogue over various social and cultural boundaries, and, furthermore, that identities and loyalties are transferred from civil society to primary groups, competing with each other for territorial control, resources and security. This is a morbid replay of nineteenth-century Westphalian logic. The contradictions involved may end up in a collapse of organised society.

For this reason, there will eventually emerge a political project to modify, halt or reverse the process of globalisation, in order to safeguard some degree of territoriality, civic norms, cultural diversity, and human security – principles that we associate with organised society. One rather radical way of achieving such a reversal of trends (de-globalisation) could be through regionalisation as a neo-mercantilist political project, that is the building of (suprastate) regional communities. The regionalist response can, as we shall see, take different forms depending on the interests of the dominant actors.

The two processes of globalisation and regionalisation are thus articulated within the same larger process of global structural transformation, the outcome of which depends on a dialectical rather than a linear development. It cannot therefore be readily extrapolated or easily foreseen. Rather, it expresses the relative strength of contending social forces involved in the two processes. They deeply affect the stability of the traditional Westphalian state system, and therefore contribute to both order and disorder and, possibly, a future post-Westphalian world order of some sort. By 'Westphalian system' is implied an interstate system constituted by sovereign states and the particular political logic that characterises each single state. Inside the state are the citizens with obligations and rights defined by citizenship and allegiance to the nation-state. The outside world is conceived as anarchy, with neither rights nor obligations. The identity of the security of the citizens and the security of the state is taken for granted. The turbulence and uncertainties many people experience today come with the unpleasant realisation that this guarantee, historically associated with the status as citizen of a state, can no longer be taken for granted. Increasing numbers of people are international refugees without citizen rights, or a floating domestic population, similarly without substantive rights and unwelcome everywhere.

REGIONALISM AND 'REGIONNESS'

The awkward situation sketched above raises the question of how essential security as a human need can be maintained in a world of eroding nation-state structures. Are there emerging structures to compensate for the, if not vanishing, at least transforming, nation- state? Post-Westphalian rationality, on the other hand, would assert that the nation-state has lost its usefulness, and that solutions to problems of security and welfare therefore must be found increasingly in different forms of transnational structures, multilateral or, as this chapter argues, regional. The 'world region' can, by maintaining the territorial focus and the stress on the role of 'the political', be said to constitute a compromise between Westphalian and post-Westphalian in the sense that the world regions combine economies of scale and large markets with some degree of territorial control. Since the mid-1980s the issue of regionalism has once again 'been brought back in', albeit in a different form compared to the debate on regional integration of the 1960s and 1970s. Thus, there is a 'new regionalism' or, more correctly, 'new regionalisms'. There are consequently many definitions of the new regionalism, and, just as is the case with globalism, some are enthusiastic, some more alarmist. For the critics, the regionalist trend constitutes a threat to the multilateral system as well as violating the ideal of UN multilateralism. For the enthusiasts, on the other hand, the new regionalism might form the basis for an improved multilateral system, including a better deal for the poor regions. I shall argue that we are dealing with a 'new' regionalism. I shall also argue that this regionalism is largely a political response to the market-driven process of globalisation and the social eruptions associated with this process. In particular I shall discuss what happens to the Third World in the overall process of globalisation and regionalisation.

The basic problem with globalisation is, in my view, its unevenness and selectiveness. Exclusion is inherent in the process, and the benefits are balanced by misery, conflict and violence. It is in this way that a new Third World may be said to be emerging. Poverty and violence are the crucial criteria in identifying this world. The negative effects are incompatible with the survival of civil society, and thus, in the longer run, a threat to all humanity.

The new regionalism, I suggest, would include economic, political, social and cultural aspects, and go far beyond free trade arrangements. Rather, the political ambition of establishing regional coherence and regional identity, apart from security and welfare, seems to be of primary importance. This I call 'the pursuit of regionness', which can be compared to 'the pursuit of stateness' in classic mercantilist nation-building. What shall we understand more exactly by 'regionness'? It means that a region can be a region 'more or less'. There are five generalised levels or stages of 'regionness', which may be said to define the structural position of a particular region in terms of regional coherence. Of course, the 'region' can only be identified *post factum* and it is therefore only potential in the first two stages. The actual regionalisation happens in stage three, where, as stages four and five show, the outcome in terms of actual regional formations, such as the EU (so far the only one). In the main, when 'regions' are spoken of, what is in fact meant is 'regions in the making'.

1. Region as a *geographical unit*, delimited by more or less natural physical barriers and marked by ecological characteristics: 'Europe from the Atlantic to the Urals', 'Africa South of Sahara', Central Asia, or 'the Indian subcontinent'. This first level can be referred to as a 'proto-region', or a 'pre-regional zone', since there is no organised international society. In order to further regionalise, this particular territory must necessarily be inhabited by human beings, maintaining some kind of translocal relationship. This brings us to the social dimension, which is the real starting point for the regionalisation process.

2. Region as *social system* implies ever widening translocal relations between human groups. Such relations of embryonic interdependence constitute a 'security complex', in which the constituent units, as far as their own security is concerned, are dependent on each other as well as on the overall stability of the regional system. Thus existing social relations may very well be hostile and completely lacking in co-operation. The region, just like the larger international system of which it forms part, can therefore on this level of regionness be described as anarchic. The classic case of such a regional order is nineteenth-century Europe. At this low level of regionness, a balance of power, or some kind of 'concert', is the sole security guarantee. This is a rather primitive security mechanism. Similarly, the exchange system tends to be based on symbolic kinship bonds rather than on trust. We could therefore talk of a 'primitive' region, exemplified, as far as security is concerned, by East Asia (in spite of a high degree of spontaneous economic integration) or the Balkans in the 1990s.

3. Region as transnational *co-operation*, organised or more spontaneous and informal, in any of the cultural, economic, political or military fields, or in several of them at the same time (multidimensional regionalisation). In the case of more organised co-operation, region is defined by the list of countries that are the formal members of the regional organisation in question. The

more organised region could be called the 'formal' region. In order to assess the relevance and future potential of a particular regional organisation, it should be possible to relate the 'formal region' (defined by organisational membership) to the 'real region', which has to be defined in terms of potentialities, convergencies and through less precise criteria. This is the stage where the crucial regionalisation process takes place. This process can be described as a convergence along several economic, political and cultural dimensions.

4. Region as *civil society* takes shape when an enduring organisational framework (formal or less formal) facilitates and promotes social communication and convergence of values and actions throughout the region. Of course, the pre-existence of a shared cultural tradition (an inherent regional civil society) in a particular region is of crucial importance, particularly for more informal forms of regional co-operation, but it must be remembered that culture is not only a given, but also being created and re-created continuously . However, the defining element here is the multidimensional and voluntary quality of regional co-operation, and the societal characteristics indicating an emerging 'regional anarchic society'; that is, something more than anarchy, but still less than society. In security terms the reference is to 'security community.'

5. Region as *acting subject* with a distinct identity, actor capability, legitimacy and structure of decision-making. Crucial areas for regional intervention are organised conflict resolution (between and particularly within former 'states') and creation of welfare (in terms of social security and regional balance). This process is similar to state-formation and nation-building, and the ultimate outcome could be a 'region-state', which in terms of scope and cultural heterogeneity can be compared to the classical empires, but in terms of political order constitutes a voluntary evolution of a group of formerly sovereign national, political units into a supranational security community, where sovereignty is pooled for the good of all. This is basically the idea of the EU as outlined in the Treaty of Maastricht. The gap between the ideal and reality is still great. Thus, 'region' in this sense is still something for the future, particularly outside Europe. It should be emphasised that conflict resolution in order to properly reflect this stage implies the existence of institutions and mechanisms, not *ad hoc* interventions of the type that are hap-

pening today. However, these attempts at crisis management underline the need for more institutional forms of conflict resolution at the regional level.

These five levels or stages may express a certain evolutionary logic, but the idea is not to suggest a progression but simply to provide a framework for comparative analysis of emerging regions. Since regionalism is a political project and therefore devised by human actors, it may, just like a nation-state project, fail. For example, the Amsterdam Summit in June 1997 was a failure for the European project; how big remains to be seen. This, similarly, means decreasing regionness and peripheralisation for the 'region' (or rather geographical area) concerned. Changes in terms of regionness thus imply changes of the structural position in the centre–periphery order. A region in decline means decreasing regionness and ultimately a dissolution of the region itself. The reference here is to the peripheral regions or the 'New Third World'. The struggle against peripheralisation is the struggle for increasing regionness, from a very low level of potential or 'primitive' region.

The new regionalism is, as I pointed out before, linked in different ways to globalisation, and can therefore not be understood merely from the point of view of the single region in question, whether South East Asia, South Asia, Southern Africa or the Southern Cone of Latin America. Rather, it should be defined as a world order concept, since any particular process of regionalisation in any part of the world has systemic repercussions on other regions, thus shaping the way in which 'the new world order' is being organised. The emerging global power structure will thus be defined by the world regions, but by very different types of region. To clarify this pattern, I shall fall back upon dependency theory and the familiar division of the world into Centre (or Core) and Periphery. However, this is a dependency analysis at a stage of higher integration and interdependence of the world, where the 'delinking' option is ruled out in any way other than involuntary marginalisation.

REGIONALISM AND GLOBAL STRUCTURE

In spite of current post-structuralist thinking in international relations theory, it still makes sense to conceive the world as a structural system; that is, a system defined by certain regularities and rigidities in the relationships among its constituent units. What is new with the system in the late 1990s is that various structural positions, as a consequence of transnationalisation processes, can be defined increasingly in terms of regions rather than nation-states. This makes it important to understand the nature of the emerging regionalisms around the globe. A rough distinction can be made between three structurally different types of region: core regions, peripheral regions and, between them, intermediate regions. How do they differ from each other? There are two basic character-istics. The regions are distinguished by their relative degree of econ-omic dynamics and by their political stability.

The core regions are thus politically stable and economically dynamic. They organise for the sake of being better able to con-trol the rest of the world – the world outside their own region. One important means of control is ideological hegemony. The pre-dominant economic philosophy in the core is neoliberalism, which, with varying convictions, is preached throughout the world. As has always been the case, the stronger economies demand access to the less developed in the name of free trade. We can thus speak of 'neoliberal regionalism', although it may sound like a contradic-tion in terms. This is the 'stepping stone' (rather than 'stumbling block') interpretation of regionalism with respect to its relationship to globalisation. There are, however, different emphases among the core regions, differences that may become more important depending on which form of capitalism turns out to be the more viable in the longer run.

The intermediate regions are closely linked to one or other of the core regions. They will be incorporated gradually as soon as they conform to the criteria of 'core-ness'; that is, sustained econ-omic development and political stability. This means that the 'poli-tics of distribution' has probably been thrown in the historical dustbin, but the praise for free trade is here somewhat more reserved. The expression used in both South East Asia and Latin America is 'open regionalism', which means open economies, albeit with some pref-erence for one's own region, as well as a rather precautionary atti-tude as far as the core regions and their assumed adherence to free trade is concerned.

The peripheral regions, in contrast, are politically turbulent and economically stagnant. War, domestic unrest and underdevelopment constitute a vicious circle which makes them sink to the bottom of the system (a zone of war and starvation). Consequently, they have to organise in order to arrest a threatening process of marginalisation. At the same time, their regional arrangements are fragile and ineffective, and they must first of all tackle acute poverty and domestic violence. Their overall situation thus makes 'security regionalism' and 'developmental regionalism' more important than the creation of free trade regimes, or even adhering to 'open regionalism'. They are necessarily more introverted and more interventionist, as we shall see. This is what lies behind the protectionist ('stumbling block') interpretation of the new regionalism.

Let us now look at these structural levels in more empirical terms. The core regions are politically capable, no matter whether such capability is expressed in the form of a formal political organisation or not. So far, only one of the three core regions, namely Europe, aspires to build such an organisation. Despite setbacks, Europe is the paradigm of regionalisation, serving both as a model, stimulating other regions to become more integrated, and as a threat, provoking other regions to be prepared for a protectionist turn in the world economy. As a model the EU looks less and less union. The single market is a fact, that is true. The monetary union is still on the cards, but a joint defence identity now appears to be a fairly distant dream. The third pillar (interior affairs) is slowly beginning to be erected. The enlargement towards Central Europe will most probably be delayed, which shows a general lack of concern for the overall stability and peace of Europe. The process of regional integration is slowing down and neo-nationalism is rising. However, so far there is no change in the general direction and, as before, co-operation will come because it is necessary.

The other two core regions – North America and East Asia – are both economically strong, but they so far lack a regional political order. This is particularly true for East Asia, where tensions between nation-states are just below the surface. The whole region is, in terms of security, an enormous vacuum, and from this point of view, it is marked by a rather low level of regionness. East Asian regionalism is often described as *de facto* regionalism, whereas regionalisation is supposed to take place *de jure* in Europe and to a lesser extent North America. This contrast may be because of differences in political culture, but an alternative explanation could lie in the fact that the interstate relations in East Asia are to some degree tense and unsettled (albeit not openly hostile). Thus a growing maturity of the regional security complex may lead to a more formal regionalism, just as the normalisation of the relationships among the countries in Southeast Asia has been accompanied by a more formal and predictable regional arrangement than seems to be possible in East Asia. This having been said, it is obvious that on levels other than the interstate one, there has been an impressive process of regionalisation. The future of the region is either very gloomy – in case the potential conflicts are translated into war – or very bright – if the degree of interdependence proves to be a point of convergence of interests where every state gets a stake in stable peace.

The North American region, on the other hand, is threatened by social upheaval as the neoliberal doctrine translates into growing cleavages, geographically, socially and ethnically. Mexico has seen guerrilla fighting in two states, Chiapas and Guerrero; in the USA there are internal low-intensity social wars going on in the big cities; and in Canada national identity is being reformulated and transferred from the federal to the provincial level, suggesting that the integrity of the Canadian nation is endangered. Thus, even in the core itself there are problems on the political front in spite of the fact that the economies are said to be in excellent shape.

Structurally close to the core are the intermediate regions, all of them in preparation for being incorporated in the core, the speed depending on their continuous good, 'core-like', behaviour. This implies maintaining economic growth in a context of openness and deregulation, as well as eliminating, and if necessary repressing, domestic conflicts. ASEAN provides a good example of the successful handling of these imperatives. The intermediate regions are as listed below.

Central Europe, obediently waiting in line for membership of the EU. At the front of the queue are the Czech Republic, Poland and Hungary, but with a big question mark over Slovakia. On the other hand, this group is joined by Slovenia, having escaped from the Balkan imbroglio and now behaving exceedingly well as a Central European candidate for EU membership. Croatia intends to follow a similar route, although held back because of its miserable human rights record. It will most probably remain in the Balkans.

Latin America and the Caribbean, now in the process of becoming 'North Americanised', but with an important southern bloc, MERCOSUR, which puts up some resistance to the neoliberal logic, and presumably will also become more defensive about Latin culture. The future relationship between NAFTA and MERCOSUR is crucial but hard to foresee.

South East Asia, the European Pacific (Australia, New Zealand) and the South Pacific are all now being drawn by Japanese capital into the East Asia economic space.

Coastal China, following in the footsteps of Southeast Asia and becoming part of a Greater China, together with Hong Kong and Taiwan.

Southern Africa (or at least parts thereof) has, after an impressive record of conflict resolution, the potential to become an intermediate region. This is, however, on condition that South Africa plays the role of benevolent regional hegemon and becomes the engine of economic development, as well as the guardian of regional peace. North Africa, also a potential candidate, is unfortunately about to sink into the periphery, because of the domestic unrest in Algeria (with spill-over risks) that has been on the increase during the mid-1990s. To end this destructive process is necessary in order to avoid sinking further into the periphery. The question is how this should be done without further violence.

Remaining in the periphery are the following seven regions or subregions.

The post Soviet area, the major parts of it (with the exception of the Baltic region) now in the process of being reintegrated in the form of Commonwealth of Independent States (CIS), perhaps laying the ground for a future core region. This large area is, of course, not a real region. Central Asia is more peripheral than the Western part of the former Soviet Union, and there is little likelihood of them sticking together, unless a new empire of the old type is formed. Major changes, as far as new alignments are concerned, can be expected in the Balkans, where the countries have lost whatever little tradition of co-operation they might once have been involved in. This is a region which can only be negatively defined as an explosive regional security complex.

The current degree of regionness in *the Balkans* is low indeed. One can, of course, speak of a geographical region, and of a regional security complex (with high security interdependence), but there is no formal regionalism, few spontaneous regional activities, certainly no regional civil society, and the Balkans are very far from being actors in their own right and with agendas of their own.

The Middle East, a region originally defined from outside and with a most unsettled and very explosive regional structure.

South Asia has, in spite of SAARC, so far shown a very low level of 'regionness', because of domestic violence and the 'cold war' (sometimes getting hot) between the two major powers, India and Pakistan. To the extent that this hostility can be overcome (and such attempts are now being made), the region may quickly reach intermediate status, but probably at the cost of new internal divisions.

The former *Indo-china subregion of South East Asia together with Burma*, all on their way to ASEAN membership in spite of their economic and political problems. As with the southern extension of the EU this may stabilise the whole region and even these additional states, foremost among them Vietnam, could reach intermediate status.

Inland China, which has not been part of the modernisation process and is lagging far behind the rest of China. This may endanger the coherence of the Chinese state/empire and destabilise the intermediate Chinese region as well.

Most of *Sub-Saharan Africa, particularly Central Africa and the Horn of Africa*, where in many countries the political structures called 'states' are falling apart. As noted above, South Africa, along with a substantial part of the Southern African region, may emerge as an intermediate region. In *West Africa*, where there exist similar potentials, Nigeria, for various mixed reasons, keeps the regional peace, but is itself politically divided and internationally isolated.

Thus the peripheral regions are 'peripheral' because they are stagnant, turbulent and war-prone. This is, of course, no explanation of their status, merely a structural analysis of their relative positions in the world system. Underdevelopment generates conflicts, and conflicts prevent necessary steps to get the economy in order. To the extent that the structural criteria change by purposive state action, the region 'moves' from one structural position to another. The exact borderlines delimiting this 'new' Third World are impossible to draw. The dividing line sometimes goes within large countries (China, India and Brazil for example). It seems likely that attempts to reach intermediate status by linking up to the world market will lead to deeper internal divisions, with destabilising consequences. There are also cases where individual countries are lingering between two structural positions (for example, Slovakia, Ukraine, Peru and Vietnam).

The only way for these poor and violent regions to become less peripheral in structural terms is to become more regionalised; to increase their levels of 'regionness'. Otherwise, their only power resource would rest in their capacity to create problems for the core regions ('chaos power'), thereby inviting or provoking some sort of external engagement. This mechanism can be seen in Southern Europe's concern for North Africa, *Mitteleuropa*'s concern for eastern and south-eastern Europe and Russia, Scandinavia's concern for the Baltic States, and in the growing emphasis put by the Chinese (PRC) authorities on spreading some of the economic dynamics from east and south to west and north, so as to avoid the prosperous areas being invaded and thereby undermined by desperate paupers, the so-called floating population of perhaps a hundred million, fleeing the nameless misery of interior China. Nothing can illustrate more drastically the delinking of 'peripherality' from territory in the new world order.

AN ACTOR APPROACH: SECURITY AND DEVELOPMENT REGIONALISM

So far this chapter has dealt with the structural pattern. The definition of this pattern in terms of established and repeated behaviour has been made deliberately to avoid the image of a structural trap, which characterised much early dependency theory. The structural problems are to a large extent internal and can be dealt with by changed policies in the various states, but a change that goes in the same direction among a group of neighbouring countries. Let me therefore turn to the problem of purposive change of structural positions, through the help of regional co-operation and integration. The issue I want to discuss here concerns the strategic value for various actors, this brief discussion being confined to state actors, of a conscious regionalisation policy in the interrelated fields of security and development in peripheral areas, or what may be said to constitute the 'new' Third World. *Violence* and *underdevelopment* are the two problems that define 'peripherality'.

What are the security problems to which regionalisation may provide a solution? They can be summarised by the metaphor of 'black holes', or what, in UN terminology, are referred to as 'failed states'. These constitute a problem for neighbouring states who rely on a stable regional environment for their international credibility. Therefore they are liable to intervene if something goes wrong in one particular state. Nigeria thus takes an interest in stabilising the West African region in spite of being itself rather shaky, and Brazil explains to the military in Paraguay that coups will not be

accepted in the new era of MERCOSUR. National disintegration
in fact seems to reinforce the process of regionalisation via threats
to regional security, provoking some kind of reaction at the regional level. National disintegration may even be said to form part
of the process of regionalisation, since the enlargement of political
space provides opportunities for different subnational and micro-
regional forces, previously locked into state structures, to reassert
themselves in peaceful (as in the case of micro-regionalism) or violent
(as in the case of ethno-nationalism) ways.

We discussed earlier the undermining effect of globalisation on
the Westphalian state system and on the internal legitimacy of weak
state formations. The collapse of political authority at one level of
society (the nation-state) tends to open up a previously latent power
struggle at lower (subnational) levels, and in a complex multiethnic
polity the process of disintegration may go on almost indefinitely.
But only 'almost'. The world does not appreciate a vacuum. Sooner
or later there must be some reorganisation of social power and
political authority on a higher (transnational) level of societal organisation, to my mind most probably the region. Why? Since most
wars today are civil wars, and a region facing in one of its states a
Hobbesian situation must provide some substitute for the vanishing state authority.

This regional arrangement is, however, likely to be preceded by
some form of external intervention, with the purpose of reversing
the disintegration process, threatening to become a regional security
crisis. Again, the region may play a role as an actor, but there are
also other far more important ones. In making an inventory of
possible actors, a distinction can be drawn between no less than
five different modes of external intervention in regional security
crises: unilateral, bilateral, plurilateral, regional and multilateral.

The *unilateral* can be carried out either by a concerned neigh-
bour trying to avoid a wave of refugees, or by a regional superpower also having strategic interests in the region. The many US
interventions in Central America are the most obvious case in point.
Regarding neighbourly interventions such as Tanzania's in Uganda
and Vietnam's in Cambodia, it is interesting to remember that they
were highly controversial in spite of the fact that there were rather
good reasons behind them.

In the *bilateral* case there is some kind of (more or less voluntary) agreement between the intervener and the country in which
the intervention is made. One such, rather unusual, case was the
intervention of India in Sri Lanka's civil war.

The *plurilateral* variety can be an *ad hoc* group of countries or some more permanent form of non-territorial alliance, such as NATO or the Islamic Conference. The intervention in Bosnia was at the same time multilateral (UN) and regional (EU), but the more effective interventions were plurilateral.

The *regional* intervention is carried out by a regional organisation and thus has a territorial orientation. One such, rather unexpected, intervention was the ECOMOG-force in Liberia, organised within the framework of ECOWAS.

The *multilateral* intervention normally means a UN-led or at least UN-sanctioned operation. The most spectacular such operation to date was the one in Cambodia. The operation gave an opportunity for Japan to participate in a large international operation, probably indicating a deeper security interest in the region. For Cambodia, several question marks remain, above all the question of how the Khmer Rouge may rejoin the national community and on what conditions. Only when a solution has been found to this problem can we talk about real conflict resolution. At present, this is rather a case of multilateral conflict management with a strong regional component, with Japanese involvement and a strong ASEAN interest in regional peace.

These distinctions are not very clear-cut, and in real world situations several actors at different levels may be involved, the number usually increasing with the complexity of the conflict itself. However, it is my understanding that future external interventions will prove to be a combination of regional and multilateral operations, but with an increasingly important role for the former. Unilateral action lacks legitimacy and raises suspicion in the international community. Bilateral action, such as the Indian intervention in Sri Lanka, could, were it not for India's persistent bilateralism, have been organised as a regional (SAARC) operation. This would presumably have made it more legitimate. In cases where there are sleeping regional organisations, such as the case of ECOWAS in West Africa, they may be revived and even find a new task for themselves by a regional crisis. Even when there are no regional organisations at all, regional initiatives (however feeble) are nevertheless taken, as in the crisis of Central Africa (Rwanda, Burundi and Zaire) and West Asia (Afghanistan). The legitimacy of such actions rests in the fact that no organised actor with sufficient legitimacy is prepared to get involved. This may, however, be a security imperative for neighbouring states, since inactivity may mean their own undoing. This also suggests a stronger regional interest in a durable solution. For a multilateral force the intervention is a task with a definite end (the soldiers move out), but for regional actors the problem remains unless it is solved. A regional solution must be embedded in the larger regional power structure. A cease-fire between the belligerents is not enough. A stable solution demands the building of a regional security community.

The record of regional intervention in domestic conflicts and regional conflict resolution is a recent one, and therefore the empirical basis for making an assessment is weak. However, in almost all world regions, there have been attempts at conflict resolution with a more or less significant element of regional intervention, often in combination with multilateralism (UN involvement). Perhaps the preferred future world order can be characterised as regional multilateralism? In contrast with the chilling 'clash of civilisations' scenario, this would be a world with largely introverted regions in symmetric balance and involved in a multicultural dialogue and constructive political relationships.

The new regionalism may also provide solutions to development problems. This can also be seen as a form of conflict prevention, since, as was noted above, many of the internal conflicts are rooted in development problems of different kinds. Under the old regionalism, free trade arrangements reproduced centre–periphery tensions within the regions, which made regional organisations either disintegrate or become dormant.

Let me now propose seven arguments in favour of a more comprehensive development regionalism:

1. Although the question of size of national territory might be of lesser importance in a highly interdependent world, regional cooperation is nevertheless imperative, particularly in the case of micro-states, who either have to co-operate to solve common problems or to become clients of the 'core' (the *sufficient size* argument).
2. Self-reliance was rarely viable at the national level and has now lost its meaning, but a strategy of development from within may yet be a feasible development strategy at the regional level, for example, in the form of co-ordination of production, improvement of infrastructure, and making use of various economic complementarities (the *viable economy* argument).
3. Economic policies may remain more stable and consistent if underpinned and 'locked in' by regional arrangements, which cannot be broken by a participant country without provoking

some kind of sanctions from the others (the *credibility* argument).
4. Collective bargaining on the level of the region could improve the economic position of marginalised countries in the world system, or protect the structural position and market access of emerging export countries (the *effective articulation* argument).
5. Regionalism can reinforce societal viability by including social security issues and an element of social or regional redistribution (by regional funds or specialised banks) in the regionalist project (the *social stability* argument).
6. Ecological and political borders rarely coincide. Therefore few serious environmental problems can be solved within the framework of the nation-state. Some problems are bilateral, some are global, quite a few are regional, the latter often related to water: coastal waters, rivers, and ground water. Like a regional security complex, we can speak of a regional ecology complex. The fact that regional resource management programmes exist and persist, in spite of nationalist rivalries, shows the imperative need for environmental co-operation or 'environmental regionalism' (the *resource management* argument).
7. Regional conflict resolution, if successful and durable, eliminates distorted investment patterns, since the 'security fund' (military expenditures) can be tapped for more productive use (the *peace dividend* argument).

In sum, development regionalism contains the traditional arguments for regional co-operation of various relevance for different actors, such as territorial size and economies of scale, but, more significantly, also add some that are expressing new concerns and uncertainties in the current transformation of the world order and world economy.

CONCLUSION: HOW TO ESCAPE THE PERIPHERAL TRAP?

The Third World, as it was known some decades ago, no longer exists, and, similarly, the North–South distinction that has become an alternative conceptualisation makes equally little sense. Yet poverty, underdevelopment and violent conflict remain, and these are characteristics usually associated with the 'Third World'. We may therefore see the peripheral or peripheralised regions that are

marked by economic stagnation and civil war, sometimes referred
to as the 'zone of war', as the 'new' Third World. This peripheral
situation was defined above as a low level of regionness, possible
to change by purposeful political and economic action at the
suprastate regional level. This structural problem is a vicious circle,
where conflict and underdevelopment feed on each other. But the
circle can also become positive. Regional co-operation for development would reduce the level of conflict and the peace dividend
could facilitate further development co-operation. Regional peace
thus becomes a comparative advantage in an integrating but turbulent world economy.

Security situations differ from region to region, with great vacuum
problems in East Asia, eruptions of older conflicts in South Asia
and the Middle East, and breakdowns of political order leading to
'tribalism' in parts of Africa and the Balkans. The ASEAN component of the Southeast Asian region is a good demonstration of the
economic value of regional stability. Another former Third World
region experiencing relative peace in the late 1990s is Latin America,
which therefore may be said to have gained a comparative advantage in peace and political stability. In Central America, formal
regional institutions have done nothing to facilitate a process of
regional integration, but during the mid-1990s conflict resolution,
in combination with more compatible and internationally acceptable economic policies, have not only moved the small and fragile
states closer together but also created a new dynamism in the region. Similarly, Southern Africa can, through the new political order
established in South Africa, begin to strive towards intermediate
status, whereas North Africa is about to sink into the periphery
because of persistent internal violence. The peace in East and Southeast Asia now seems to be relatively stable, but there are many
unsettled issues that must be resolved. In view of the high degree
of economic interdependence, the states in this region have a very
high stake in regional stability. There is a great risk that a conflict
(interstate or domestic) in East Asia or South-East Asia (where
former the Indo-China is still part of the periphery) may peri-
pheralise areas that now are described as 'intermediate' – for example,
Indonesia.

Europe, where the core is being organised into a political union,
is not immune to the forces of peripheralisation. Because of economic chaos and threatening civil wars, large parts of the post-Soviet
area must be described as peripheral, in spite of its great potential

in terms of resources and people. The Balkan region (including Romania and Bulgaria) also belongs to the new global periphery because of its many manifest and latent conflicts, and because of its poverty. The countries here must either increase their regionness or sink together. 'Balkanisation' is another word for disintegration, but the concept is typically applied to other regions as a negative example. Applied to the region itself, 'Balkanisation' should mean increased 'regionness'. The current degree of 'regionness' is here low indeed. However, as in the case of South Asia, there is an inherent civil society, in terms of an inherited shared culture (including language), but (also as in South Asia), this important potential for regionness is destroyed by the current policies of the nation-states (pathological Westphalianism).

Security and development form one integrated complex, at the same time as they constitute two fundamental imperatives for regional co-operation and increasing regionness. Thus, political will and political action will play their part in breaking the vicious circle of uneven globalisation, regional conflict, underdevelopment and human insecurity. This is particularly the case in the peripheral regions of the 'New Third World'.

6 Globalisation and Sovereignty: Implications for the Third-World State

Norman Lewis[1]

Since the end of the Cold War a dramatic shift in the presentation of the so-called 'Third World' has taken place in the West. Until the late 1980s, the 'South' commanded considerable moral authority and credibility in international affairs. The Non-Aligned Movement occupied the moral high ground; its concerns were debated in international institutions and both sides of the Cold War could not ignore its aspirations. It was during the post-war period, particularly in the 1950s and 1960s, that the moral authority of Third-World movements gained ground. This process coincided with the discrediting of Western imperialism to the extent that it was generally acknowledged in the West that the social, economic and political problems of the Third World were intimately connected with the colonial past. However, by the end of the 1980s the moral balance between the Third World and the West had been reversed. The end of the Cold War and the triumph of a new conservative orthodoxy provided the West with an unexpected opportunity to claw back the moral high ground by pointing to the failures of the various radical national experiments in the South. By highlighting the plight of Southern societies, the West quite self-consciously rehabilitated its imperial past; the moral condemnation of the South, especially of Africa, retrospectively vindicated colonialism.[2]

The remarkable expression of this transformation is clearly highlighted by the widespread acceptance within the West of its right to intervene in the internal affairs of Southern states. Underlying this sentiment is the hotly debated question of globalisation, particularly with regard to the future of sovereignty itself. While erosions of sovereignty and questions of legitimacy were raised in the past, these discussion were framed in terms of a world of states. Differences arose over the degree of centrality state sovereignty had in international affairs. Discussion in the 1990s has gone a lot further. According to its protagonists, we are witnessing a process in which long-standing conditions of time, space and territoriality have undergone transformation.[3] As a result, it is held, the nation-state itself has been compromised and superseded. In this view, these developments call into question (more acutely than ever before) pillars of the 'old world order' such as sovereignty and national self-determination, with particular perverse implications for Third-World states.

For the purposes of this chapter, the new moral rehabilitation of imperialism forms the context rather than the focus of discussion. Instead, the chapter is concerned primarily with the notion of globalisation and its implications for the Third World. More specifically, the chapter highlights how most theories of globalisation (particularly with regard to sovereignty) strengthen rather than undermine the new interventionist consensus against Third-World states.

GLOBALISATION AND SOVEREIGNTY

During almost every decade of the twentieth century, sovereignty has been declared to be under threat from international economic changes, and before the ink has dried on the death certificate, the 'corpse' of sovereignty has risen from the grave to haunt the world yet again. Before the First World War, it is worth recalling, many leading Europeans believed that integration of the world economy rendered interstate conflict and war 'the great illusion'. Hilferding speculated on the nature of nationally-based but internationally co-ordinated corporate capitalism, where capital appeared as a unitary power exercising 'sovereign sway over the life processes of society'. Cross-border tie-ups were rife. America's General Electric worked with Germany's AEG and, in a strategic alliance signed with Tokyo Electric in 1904, gave birth to Toshiba. Before 1914, Britain gained a tenth of its income from foreign assets; imported more than 80 per cent of its synthetic dyes from Germany; and a comparable amount of chemicals, optical glass and sophisticated electrical goods from the same source. Yet, interstate conflict, world war and the assertion of sovereignty in the most glaring manner occurred, not just in 1914 but again in 1939.

In the post-war period, the same debate re-emerged as early as the 1960s after the French Europeanist Jean-Jacques Servan-Schreiber complained of the *American Challenge* (1967). It seemed that multi-nationals in general, and those in the US in particular, could trample their way round national governments. By 1971, US scholar Raymond Vernon had declared multinationals the victors over nation-states. The recessions of 1973 and 1979 altered the discussion and introduced the new concept of 'globalisation' into the discourse. Theodore Levitt, then editor of the *Harvard Business Review*, first used the term as a sound bite when he told multinationals that they had to deny local subsidiary autonomy and turn, instead, into global concerns. Nationalism in product tastes, he explained, was 'obsolete'; economies of scale on a global basis now prevailed.[4] But Levitt's top-down, homogenising approach to corporate strategy was soon overturned. By the late 1980s, theorists agreed that product branding, market positioning, promotion and distribution should have different mixtures of internationally standard and nationally specific elements, depending on the product at issue.[5] By the end of the decade, the call was made for 'managing across borders' and for the creation of 'world' products with modular structures; for basic components and core designs to be internationally stan-dardised, but features and styling to be differentiated by national markets.[6]

By 1990, the world's 100 largest non-financial corporations had $1.2 of their $3.1 trillion assets 'abroad'. There were 35 000 multi-nationals in the world, complete with 170 000 subsidiaries. The tone of the discussion on globalisation at the end of the Cold War was optimistic; Kenichi Ohmae, head of management consultants McKinsey in Japan, argued that the world was now 'borderless, and that national trade statistics were meaningless.'[7] Robert Reich, the US Secretary of Labour, agreed. There would be no 'national products or technologies, no national corporations, no national industries', and there would 'no longer be national economies.'[8] While Francis Fukuyama declared 'the end of history', the talk in business was the end of geography, while the talk in International Relations (IR) was 'the end of sovereignty'.[9] Now globalisation spelt the end of the nation-state and the end of the national corporation.

For Philip Cerny, for example, the globalisation of financial markets has not only eroded the state but has also fundamentally trans-formed it within a wider structural context; 'the international sys-tem is no longer a states system; rather, it is becoming increasingly characterised by a plural and composite ... "plurilateral" structure'. According to Cerny, the globalisation of finance has increasingly divorced finance capital from the state, a process that has been 'virtually synonymous with the rapid development of electronic computer and communications technology.'[10] Mary Kaldor argues that the changed structural context; the 'post-industrialisation or at least . . . entirely new phase of industrialisation comparable with the original industrial revolution's does speed up global integration as well as greater de-centralisation of both production and consumption. The net effect being that the 'ability of nation-states to influence national economies continues to be eroded'.[11] Jan Aarte Scholte captures this erosion of sovereignty well when developing his concept of 'post-sovereignty'. He argues that 'in a globalised condition, power relates largely to the control of *flows*, whereas state sovereignty is premised on the control of *places* . . . whereas in the past a state could by strengthening its apparatus graduate from the mere legal sovereignty to positive sovereignty, in a globalised world no amount of institution building will allow a state to achieve absolute control of its realm. At most, unilateral state action can shift the content, intensity or direction of global flows.'[12] A world in which 'global flows', free from constraint and outside the structures of the sovereign-states system, now seems to dominate.

The couplet of the autonomy of globalisation fuelled by new technologies are the key assumptions underlying this emerging consensus of the 'post-sovereign' condition. The development of information technology (IT) since the late 1960s has been seen to have defined a new 'techno-economic paradigm' with 'such pervasive effects on the economy as a whole that they change the style of production and management throughout the system'.[13]

There is another dimension to this technological deterministic paradigm; namely, the question of uncertainty this has brought to international relations. David Held (writing in the same book as Kaldor above) endorses globalisation as a distinct new phase of industrialisation. But he adds that the absence of control by the nation-state, together with the nature of 'modern communications', which virtually annihilate territorial boundaries, can also create 'political uncertainties'.[14] John MacMillan and Andrew Linklater spell out further to what these uncertainties refer:

> environmental degradation, nuclear safety, refugees, global warming, drugs, disease, population, international trade and investment, the issues of the new agenda . . . invoke images of a global lifeboat rather than the billiard-ball model of old.[15]

The metaphor of the 'global lifeboat' aptly portrays the fears and uncertainties these changes have brought to the world (and to IR itself). In the post-Cold War era, it seems that threats have multiplied, or 'diffused', as John Lewis Gaddis puts it.[16] The erosion of sovereignty, what Molly Cochran calls the 'artificial anchor of international relations' has lost its hold and now the world is anchorless and rudderless; a 'global lifeboat' in a sea of turbulence and threats with a seeming incapacity to control the forces beneath the waves.[17]

This uncertainty lies behind much of the loss of faith in the agency of the nation-state. The real cumulative experience of the failure of national economic policies to curtail the recessions in the USA and Europe has expressed itself in the scapegoating of global forces and of global competition. At the end of the 1990s, the local, the regional and the international are counterposed to the failed national entity. Even the critics of globalisation (a growing band) go along with the assumption that the nation-state is less effective or not in control, and draw fairly negative conclusions about what this means for intervention in general.[18] But for many of the upholders of globalisation, the uncertainty underlying the theory itself has turned many of these theories into a kind of chaos theory for the social sciences.

While it is the case that many upholders of the globalisation thesis recognise that the process they describe is not entirely a new one (some date it from the dawn of history or the Middle Ages; others from the Renaissance, or from 1972) the sense of chaos and uncertainty that informs the discussion in the 1990s is new.[19] For Anthony Giddens and the German environmentalist Ulrich Beck, globalisation has transformed long-distance causation. This is no longer a one-way exercise in which Western nations unilaterally affect other, less fortunate ones and remain immune from the results of their handiwork. Now, it is argued, no country can avoid the global; 'what goes around, comes around', as the Americans have it. Beck refers to a 'boomerang effect'; when Western companies invest in polluting industries in the Third World, they can now expect the waste they have created to come back and haunt the West. Similarly, the Mexican peso, though 'Made in America', came to exert the effects of its 1994 decline not just in Guadalajara, but in Washington and Wall Street too.

Causality is rarely unidirectional, then, given the multiplied interconnections and compressions of the 1990s. Instead, phenomena are the creation of multiple causes, with influences from various localities. Indeed, the roots of some events are so complex that their causes are unlikely to be known. So, while causation exists, it may consist of so many elements, conscious and unconscious, that the outcomes of our actions are likely to be unintentional. Conversely, it becomes impossible to establish the real determinants of particular outcomes. When Giddens turns to use the example of the High Street shopper he implicitly recalls the famous butterfly whose flapping wings can effect colossal meteorological changes:

> Our day-to-day activities are increasingly influenced by events happening on the other side of the world. Conversely, local life-style habits have become globally consequential. Thus my decision to buy a certain item of clothing has implications not only for the international division of labour but for the earth's ecosystem.[20]

Giddens suggests that a dynamic independent of human beings (impersonal autonomous) has brought us to a new era. In this new era, most day-to-day activity has all sorts of unintended repercussions. There is nothing particularly new or mysterious about this. What are being described are the phenomenal forms thrown up by the anarchy of the market. The problem, however, is that these forms are never explained, nor is there any attempt to root any of these forms, through a series of mediating links, to what are merely, in the final analysis, the unfolding structures of the world market. The market is now held to be eternal, immutable and invisible, with its anarchic character held to be a fact of nature and therefore not subject to human modification. Roland Robertson, for example, insists upon this method in his approach to globalisation:

> We are still left with a common problem or question which unites the old and the new ... the crucial question remains as to the basic form or structure in terms of which the shift [in order] has occurred. That form has been imposed upon certain areas of the world is, of course, a crucial issue but until the matter of form (more elaborately structuration) is adequately thematised our ability to comprehend the dynamics of the world-as-a-whole will be severely limited.[21]

Robertson accepts the market's existence and its centrality to the global is taken for granted. The privileging of 'form' as logically prior in the analysis cannot begin to deal with the critical question

Robertson himself poses of the unity between 'the old and the new'. In other words, without rooting this analysis in the market relations that gave rise to the sovereign state in the first place, it is difficult to see how changes to sovereignty have come about. At best, such an approach can 'comprehend the dynamics of the world-as-a-whole' but cannot begin to explain why any changes have taken place. This is quite remarkable because it expresses how many of the theories of globalisation, while seeking to account for change at an international level, have no theory of change itself. Change happens – just feel the quality of the depth.

In fact, and ironically, the methodology underlying many of the theories of globalisation in fact betrays an excessively state-centric view of international relations. The counter position of the erosion of sovereignty today to the sovereign state of yesterday betrays an uncritical acceptance of the claims that states (and their IR theoreticians) made for themselves in the past. This positivist methodology underlying the globalisation discourse accounts for the excessively exaggerated claims made regarding the erosions of sovereignty today. The questions that need to be posed at this point are: What has really been eroded, sovereignty or the perception of sovereignty? Are the claims made about IT and globalised financial markets justified or exaggerated? What significance should we attach to these phenomena, and how would we explain them in the first place?

While it is the case that nation-states' ability to control international operations and transactions of the market have certainly been altered, the question remains: Why? Is it the case, for example, that telecommunications networks are simply and effortlessly built and then just as magically, traffic on them multiplies? Or are such networks more a response to a prior internationalisation of business?

Many technological breakthroughs sit in the laboratory or the patent office until there is a demand for them. Yet the American George Gilder is not alone in arguing that telecommunications advances as a 'kinetic force of change in the "information economy"'.[22] In fact, however, investment in IT requires enormous sums of money. As a result, networks will only be built if there is business to be had from them; IT cannot be regarded as a kind of autonomous dynamo behind globalisation. On the contrary, the development of communications and transport networks has long been an absolute necessity for the development of the world market. And precisely because market relations are intrinsically *inter-*

national, modern society is forced to develop the means of gaining knowledge of far-away economic events. In this sense, the 'information superhighway' is an entirely predictable, rather than autonomous mystical development. Information, and gaining access to it, becomes a *sine qua non* for survival on the world market. Because globalisation assumes the fantastic form of an objective relation which appears to be independent of human agency and intervention, it obscures the human-made social relations underlying the phenomenon itself, and, as a result, elevates indeterminacy to almost an organising principle.

No doubt IT substitutes for labour, reduced turnover time, speeds time to market and lowers transaction costs between organisations. But the export of commodities, capital and new product development drives the extension of IT networks much more than IT drives globalisation. To ascribe an independent, autonomous dynamic to global IT networks is an error of technological determinism. At best an 'enabler', IT is rarely a 'driver'. The technological determinism underlying much of the globalisation discussion highlights how many of these theories enumerate phenomena they seek to explain, rather than offer a logical understanding of them. In the international capitalist system, speculations and transactions follow not from new networks, but from the motive force of capitalist production: the quest to make profits. Falling rates of return and a broader stagnation in the industrialised world are the factors that accelerated commodity and capital exports to the USA and Europe before the Cold War was over, and to Asia afterwards. These same factors explain other new phenomena – for example, the vogue for cross-border tie-ups, and a relentless search for partners with whom to share costs.

The case of research and development (R&D) is particularly illuminating. On the one hand, the cost of skilled Asian labour in this field is low. That is one reason why British Telecom and Fujitsu pay Indian programmers $200 a month to write software. On the other hand, differentiation of products according to local tastes must be researched locally, if Asian markets are to be developed successfully. Studies now reveal how Japanese multinationals, for example, see global R&D as central to survival in the future. Nor is it surprising that the West learns much to its own benefit from products designed to chase local Asian demand. Especially in IT, it is the vibrant Asian market, not the West, that often generates world-beating innovations. In the early 1990s, the struggle to survive in these markets forced many IT companies to tailor their global survival along these lines. The development of IT and *transborder* data flows to accommodate national and cultural differences to facilitate competitiveness was driven by the struggle for survival in the fiercely competitive world market, rather than by the technology itself.

These examples suggest something entirely missing from the theories of globalisation discussed above; the trends they describe and the phenomena they elevate, particularly the growing dominance of the global over the national, are the consequence of survival strategies that have discernible causes. Today, in the last years of the 1990s, the internationalisation of its operations is the only way the capitalist corporation can deal with stagnatory conditions at a national level. The need to escape the limitations of the national, to cross borders, is not a question of choice, but of survival. The rise of global money markets and that of the notorious global market for financial 'derivatives', for example, owes much to the decline of the USA relative to Germany and Japan, and the consequent descent of the dollar. The relative decline of the USA also, paradoxically, explains the unprecedented and global impact of 'American culture' today. Relatively weak in sectors such as cars, superconductivity, advanced microelectronics and integrated optics, the USA is forced to play to its strengths (IT, media, fast-moving consumer goods and defence) on the world stage, and as never before. Overcoming stagnation, therefore, accounts for the global flows that have become so central to economic activity.

However, there is a dimension to the claims of these globalisation theories which suggests that the explanation offered above may be incorrect. This relates to the idea of 'national capitals' – the assumption that capital remains tied to a national base rather than existing as global, internationalised, and free from the constraints of the nation-state. This is a critical question which needs thorough investigation, because it challenges the analysis presented in this chapter on sovereignty as the necessary form of capitalist social relations.

Cerny begins to raise this point in his discussion of 'plurilateral structures', mentioned above. His argument is that 'the logic of collective action is becoming a heterogeneous multilayered logic, derived not from one core structure, such as the state, but from the structural complexity embedded in the global arena'. What follows from this is what is important:

Globalization does not mean that the international system is any less structurally anarchic, it merely changes the structural composition of that anarchy from one made up of relations between sovereign states to one made up of relations between functionally differentiated spheres of economic activity, on the one hand, and the institutional structures proliferating in an *ad hoc* fashion to fill the power void, on the other.[23]

Cerny is wrong to counterpose sovereignty to spheres of economic activity, because the separation and unity of the two is the distinctive feature of international market relations. However, Cerny does uphold the separation of politics and economics when he posits the 'institutional structures proliferating in an *ad hoc* fashion' as the new arena of 'politics'. He thus draws out the logic of those making these claims – namely, that market relations can exist without the state, although what form the new political relations will take remain open. Stephen Gill, on the other hand, argues that economic globalisation has not been matched by political globalisation.[24] The question this poses is whether those arguing that sovereignty no longer exists are right, and capitalism has changed and thus globalisation holds out the possibilities of a new, just and equitable 'governance'; or these phenomena express the mechanisms through which capitalist social relations are being reformed and re-legitimised at the end of the twentieth century. The latter case suggests that while this reorganisation is taking a new form, their essential content (a global order in which the North dominates the South) remains unchanged.

GLOBALISATION AND INEQUALITY

If there is another aspect of the globalisation process that requires investigation it is the process through which global economic integration has reproduced – indeed, *increased* – the structural inequalities of the world order. While changes have shifted the centre of world interest from the Atlantic to the Pacific, and the old Cold War category of the 'Third World' has become less relevant than it once was, it cannot be deduced that the nations of the world are now converging. For each of the four Asian 'tiger' economies (South Korea, Hong Kong, Taiwan and Singapore) there is more than one nation in Sub-Saharan Africa being bled dry by World

Bank structural adjustment programmes. It is worth remembering that the half billion people who live in Sub-Saharan countries (excluding South Africa) have a combined gross domestic product (GDP) on a par with Belgium, whose population is only 11 million. The North–South gap has not only widened throughout the lost decade of the 1980s, it has also increased during the 1990s. Between 1985 and 1992, Southern nations paid $280 billion more in debt service to Northern creditors than they received in new private loans and government aid.

Today, the advanced industrialised countries, with one-sixth of the world's population, produce at least two-thirds of its total output. These countries also account for three-quarters of world exports and almost all foreign direct investment (FDI). In Asia, as elsewhere, the competition among Western powers for the international sphere has begun to unleash diplomatic manoeuvres of a remarkable character. Both Chancellor Helmut Kohl of Germany and President Bill Clinton of the USA have gone out of their way to woo Beijing. The more they and other rivals jockey for position, the more it is clear that there will be both winners and losers in the race to 'civilise' the 'Middle Kingdom'.

At the same time, the contrast between Africa and Asia confirms that there will be winners and losers among the recipients of FDI too. In 1994, a record $80 billion of FDI went to the developing countries. A third was committed to China alone; another third was split between just four countries (Malaysia, Thailand, Argentina and Mexico), and a further quarter was split among another fifteen countries.[25] In other words, some twenty countries in Asia and Latin America took 90 per cent of FDI flows. The other 130 states were left to scramble for the residual 9 per cent. Africa, it seems, will remain completely marginalised for the foreseeable future. When one considers that output and income per head fell absolutely in the 1980s, and that most Africans are poorer today than they were in the 1970s, it becomes clear how the process of globalisation has intensified the structural inequalities in the world. Indeed, the UN Summit for social development, held in Copenhagen in March 1995, accepted that impoverishment and social polarisation have reached dramatic and threatening proportions.[26]

The question of FDI also reveals another structural inequality which is masked by appearances. Besides the points made above concerning the destination of global FDI flows, when one examines the types of FDI behind many of these heady figures, the picture is less upbeat than claimed. According to World Bank figures, roughly half of the new foreign direct investment by global corporations in the South in 1992 quickly left those countries as profits. Several of the ten so-called emerging markets (Brazil, India, Mexico, South Korea and Taiwan) have attracted substantial short-term flows by opening their stock markets to foreigners and by issuing billions of dollars in bonds. Between 1991 and 1993 alone, FDI as a share of all private capital flows into poor countries fell from 65 to 44 per cent as these more speculative flows increased. The fickleness of these speculations are revealed by the example of Mexico; during the last week of 1994, an estimated $10 billion in short-term funds left the country.[27] When one takes into account the decline in the terms of trade between the North and the South (between 1985 and 1993 when real prices of primary commodities fell 30 per cent, which for Africa, for example, cost the continent some $3 billion). Ramond Broad and John Cavanagh have a point when they characterise the world of the twenty-first century as one of economic apartheid: 'there will be two dozen rich nations, a dozen or so poorer nations that have begun to close the gap with the rich, and approximately 140 poor nations slipping further behind'.[28]

One of the more important, but rarely commented upon, new realities of the globalised world is the growth of the 'other' North–South gap; the increasing stratification and division of the world, wherein about one-third of humanity is being integrated into a complex chain of production, consumption, culture and finance, while the remaining two-thirds of humanity (from the slums of New York to the *favelas* of Rio) who are not hooked into the new global network are losing out. The gap between rich and poor *within and across* nations has widened dramatically. In the 1960s, the income of the richest fifth of the world's population combined was thirty times greater than that of the poorest fifth. Today, in the late 1990s, the income gap is more than sixty times greater. Over this period the income of the richest 20 per cent grew from 70 to 85 per cent of the total world income, while the global share of the poorest 20 per cent fell from 2.3 to 1.4 per cent. To spell this out further: approximately 45 per cent of the world's population eke out an existence using just under 4 per cent of the world's GNP. At the top, 358 individuals own the same percentage.

The impact of the adoption of free-market policies imposed by Western institutions and banks in these concentrations has been particularly noticeable in those countries marked for special attention.

Mexico is a case in point as the model of the so-called success of these policies. In 1987 there was just one billionaire in Mexico. By 1994, there were twenty-four, who accounted for $44.1 billion in collective wealth. This exceeded the total income of the poorest 40 per cent of Mexican households. As a result, the twenty-four wealthiest people are richer than the poorest 33 million people in Mexico. This is not to mention the effect these same policies had upon the coffers of Western bankers and institutions.

This example suggests something quite critical for our discussion of globalisation: the erosion of sovereignty in the South is intimately linked to the ability of the free market to function on a world scale. The 'winners and losers' scenario described above is not an accidental outcome. The fact that the gap between the North and South is not merely a geographical distinction expresses the fact that this is how the global market system operates.

However, in the relations between the North and the South it is the case that erosion of sovereignty has proceeded at an alarming pace. Institutions such as the World Bank have embraced globalisation as the new stick with which to beat the old Third World. While recognising the plight of Africa, the World Bank admonishes it to liberalise its economies and to open them up to the ruthless sway of international market forces still further than they have already. Obscuring the fact that Africa's plight has everything to do with the continent's relationship to the world economy, the World Bank now presents the relatively impotent Third World and ineffective Third World state policies as one of the biggest potential sources of global risk.[29] Conditionality has rendered many of these states even more impotent in terms of control over their own national economic policies. Of course, it is never pointed out what a double standard is at work here; technologically determined global flows, beyond the control of the state, are a source of fear and the claims about the ineffectiveness of the nation state in the West. Yet, when it comes to the Third World, these states are told to embrace their lack of control as the only way in which to advance themselves.

Ironically, in Eastern Europe an opposite tendency, with similar results, appears to be taking place. Here the West is forcing these states to exercise their 'sovereignty' in the form of passing legislation giving Western conglomerates monopolistic control over local markets. Thus Volkswagen (VW) required monopoly-protecting tariffs on Czech car imports before investing in Skoda; Hunslet, the British rolling-stock maker demanded similar monopoly rights when it bought Ganz in Budapest; and General Motors required the right to import its cars duty-free into Poland as a condition for investing in FSO in Warsaw, while requiring high tariffs on non-GM cars.[30] In Hungary, Suzuki has obtained trade protection for its cars and Samsung has done the same for its televisions. Here we see an apparent strengthening of sovereignty to open these economies to monopolistic, and not free-market relations.

The example of Eastern Europe is apposite. It shows how, even in the strengthening of sovereignty, one can have its erosion at the same time. These outcomes are neither fortuitous nor unexpected. The growth and reproduction of international inequality reflects the overwhelming content of globalisation – the process through which the structural problems in the market at both domestic and international levels are being negotiated. What should be clear from the above as well, is that this is not some altruistic dynamic taking place in a vacuum. On the contrary, it is driven by interests backed by power. Moreover, far from these phenomena representing something distinct, a fundamental change from the past, these developments suggest that a fundamental continuity is at work.

In fact it is precisely this continuity that needs discussion and analysis which is obscured in many of the theories of globalisation. Concepts such as 'reflexive modernity', or 'global risk' or 'globalisation', while stressing contradictory tendencies, eradicate some of the critical continuities that exist in the world in the 1990s. The evocative and powerful metaphor of the 'global lifeboat' mentioned above illustrates this profoundly.

At first glance, the metaphor appears to evoke accurately the condition of the world in the post-Cold War era. After all, there is greater uncertainty in the world in the closing decade of the twentieth century than in previous decades. The problem is, however, that it obscures more about the world than it illuminates, and exaggerates this uncertainty. In presenting culpability for this state of affairs as being the responsibility of us all, the authors mystify the processes at work, as well as who is really responsible. According to MacMillan and Linklater, we are all in the 'global lifeboat' together. True, but as we have seen above, in reality, we are not all equally at risk nor equally responsible for the state of the world as it stands. The 445 billionaires who together command over half of the world's resources and wealth are certainly not in the same position as most people in the 'global lifeboat'. The idea that peasants from Bangladesh, unemployed workers roaming China or Eastern Europe, and billionaires such as Bill Gates of Microsoft and George Sorros, are all in the same position within the boat is patently absurd. The latter not only have the power to do something about the condition they are in, their position is very much based upon the monopoly of power they hold. No doubt alongside these travellers in our boat we would find a host of their policemen, security experts and armed services personnel.

This fundamental difference in, and reality of, power relations is obliterated altogether. And that is not all. The responsibility for this state of affairs is also obscured because it presents the threats to society as being extraneous to any interests within society; indeed, as extraneous to the way society is organised. The threats facing mankind have become as natural as the sea and the tides. Man-made relations of power are thus transformed, naturalised and placed above human intervention. In the face of humanity's apparent helplessness in the face of the power of nature, an inherently conservative moral message is suggested – we are all in the same boat and if we are to survive we should alter our behaviour in order not to rock this boat. The solution implicit in the global lifeboat is the moderation of individuals' behaviour – the limiting of demands upon society and each other.

Thus, the metaphor of the 'global lifeboat' does more than efface the relationship between interests, power and responsibility. It naturalises the very social processes that need to be investigated and places them above human intervention. The market and its unfolding structures across the globe at the end of the twentieth century – the source of all the phenomena these theorists enumerate but fail to explain – is now taken for granted. Since the market is now believed to be eternal, immutable and invisible, its anarchic character is held to be a fact of nature and thus beyond human modification.

GLOBALISATION AND THE EROSION OF SOUTHERN SOVEREIGNTY

From everything that has been said above it is clear that the erosion of sovereignty in the late 1990s represents a complex process by which international economics and politics are being reorganised. Giddens and others may speculate about prospects for 'dialogic democracy'; a global politics of 'world governance', interpersonal relations and identity construction, but for every speculation there is a World Bank to warn that while globalisation offers real openings, these are matched by risks 'for those who ignore the rules of the game'. For developing countries, privatisations, open markets and cuts in state expenditure, hold out, the World Bank believes, new-found prospects for economic advancement. In short, what is being said is that the South cannot buck the market: the same market that has produced the process of globalisation and its reproduction of the structural inequalities in the international system.

The example of the World Bank expresses the need for a cautious approach to the central question addressed in this chapter; namely, the claims of the effect of globalisation upon the concept of sovereignty. In the context of the new moral climate of Western condemnation of the South, these claims, and the uncritical content of many globalisation theories, merely serve to legitimise further intrusions into the affairs of Southern societies. The couplet of the South as the source of global risk together with the reported moral and political collapse in these societies has produced a new consensus that now the West has to save not just the West from the South, but these societies from themselves. Today, moral lessons orientated towards cultural practices and intimate individual behaviour have been propagated through Western non-governmental organisations (NGOs) and international institutions. High profile international conferences are routinely held (in Rio, Cairo and Beijing, for example) which lecture representatives from the South about their responsibilities for maintaining the environment, how to reduce their rate of population growth, and how to treat their women and children.

In this new climate of Western moral intrusion, all aspects of the domestic affairs of Southern societies have become subject to scrutiny. And precisely because these interventions focus upon issues of women and children, human rights and the environment, and are presented in the vocabulary of rights, they are endorsed by Western liberals, and left-wing and feminist activists. Yet such intrusions represent a form of cultural warfare against the societies of the South. In this instance, the 'globalisation' of culture represents the internationalisation of Western values; a case of endorsing uncritically the notion that 'the West knows best'. The globalisation discourse merely adds another uncritical voice to the consensus about North–South relations which embraces virtually the entire political spectrum in the West. In the globalised world, there are two kinds of societies: problem ones and those that provide solutions. The qualifications of sovereignty through this new moral agenda (from human rights to gender rights) serves to legitimise the fact that the democratic right to self-determination (the right to national sovereignty) is now a thing of the past.

This consensus is most clearly illustrated by the democratisation debate.[31] In the past, Western intervention in the internal affairs of former colonies would have been regarded with outrage. In the 1990s, however, whether or not an election in Asia or Africa is democratic is determined not by the indigenous electorate, but by a commission of Western election monitors under the auspices of the United Nations. It seems that only Western officials have the capacity to recognise a fair election when they see one. Yet if it were the case that globalisation was leading to 'one world', as Giddens and many others have suggested, then how long is it before we have some Rwandan or Angolan monitors pronouncing on the outcome of the next British general election? No doubt this will never happen. Indeed, the very suggestion would be considered ludicrous. But when it comes to Western interference in the domestic affairs of Southern states, this is regarded as legitimate and morally defensible. But in the South, national sovereignty has ceased to be an issue. This is not intervention into the internal affairs of a sovereign state, but merely 'world society' upholding universal moral standards.

Thus, before we rush to declare the sovereign state redundant in the 'globalised' landscape we should recognise how its erosion has so far been an uneven process. While it is the case that 'global flows' have intensified a sense of a loss of control in the West, in the South these same dynamics have been devastating. The exacerbation of inequality in the world has everything to do with the adoption by the G7 powers of an increasingly differential approach to focusing their international energies. The erosion of sovereignty in these conditions does not represent anything positive. On the contrary, from everything that has been discussed above, the questioning of sovereignty that globalisation has given rise to, represents the reorganisation of the international relations of domination. Indeed, the implication is that, in the face of globalised risks and eroded sovereignties, more rather than less intervention on the part of the powerful states will be increasingly called for and legitimised. This is why it is important to insist upon a more thorough investigation of what precisely the new process of globalisation represents.

Notes and References

1. Thanks are due to Dr Jan Aarte Scholte, Zdenek Kavan, Dr Frank Furedi, Phil Murphy and Gemma Forest for their critical input into the preparation of this chapter. What follows is my responsibility.
2. See F. Furedi, *The New Ideology of Imperialism* (London: Pluto, 1994).
3. See J. A. Scholte, 'Governance and Democracy in a Globalised World', Paper for the ACUNS/ASIL Summer Workshop on International Organisation Studies (1995). Also J. Saurin, 'The End of International Relations? The State and International Theory in the Age of Globalisation', in J. MacMillan and A. Linklater (eds), *Boundaries in Question: New Directions in International Relations* (London: Pinter, 1995); and D. Held, 'Democracy, the Nation-State and the Global System', *Economy and Society*, vol. 20, no. 2, May (1981).
4. T. Levitt, 'The Globalisation of Markets', *Harvard Business Review*, May–June (1983).
5. M. Porter (ed.), *Competition in Global Industries* (Cambridge, Mass.: Harvard University Press, 1986).
6. C. Bartlett and S. Ghoshal, *Managing Across Borders: The Transnational Solution* (New York: Hutchinson, 1989).
7. K. Ohmae, *The Borderless World* (London: Fontana, 1990).
8. R. Reich, *The Work of Nations: Preparing Ourselves for 21st Century Capitalism* (New York: Vintage, 1992).
9. J. Camilleri and J. Falk, *The End of Sovereignty? The Politics of a Shrinking and Fragmented World* (Aldershot: Edward Elgar, 1992).
10. P. G. Cerny, 'Globalisation and the Changing Logic of Collective Action', *International Organization*, vol. 49, no. 4, Autumn (1995), p. 617.
11. M. Kaldor, 'Europe: Nation-Sates and Nationalism' in D. Archibugi and D. Held (eds), *Cosmopolitan Democracy: Agenda for a New World Order* (Oxford: Oxford University Press, 1995), p. 79.
12. J. A. Scholte, 'Governance and Democracy in a Globalised Word', p. 8.
13. C. Freeman, 'Information Technology and Change in the Techno-economic Paradigm', in C. Freeman and L. Soete (eds), *Technical Change and Full Employment* (Oxford: Basil Blackwell, 1987), p. 130.
14. D. Held, 'Democracy, the Nation-State and the Global System', p. 101.
15. J. MacMillan and A. Linklater, *Boundaries in Question*.
16. J. L. Gaddis, 'The Post-Cold War World', *Foreign Affairs*, Spring (1991), p. 113.
17. M. Cochran, 'Cosmopolitanism and Communitarianism in a Post-Cold War World', in J. MacMillan and A. Linklater, *Boundaries in Question*, p. 41.
18. See P. Krugman, 'Dutch Tulips and Emerging Markets', *Foreign Affairs*, July/August (1995).
19. A. G. McGrew and P. G. Lewis, *Global Politics: Globalization and the Nation State* (Cambridge: Polity Press, 1992).
20. A. Giddens, *Modernity and Self-Identity: Self and Society in the Late Modern Age* (Cambridge: Polity Press, 1991).
21. R. Robertson, *Globalization: Social Theory and Global Culture* (London: Sage, 1992), p. 25.

22. G. Gilder, 'The Network as Computer', *Northern Telecom Annual Report* (1995), p. 16.
23. P. G. Cerny, 'Globalisation and the Changing Logic of Collective Action'.
24. S. Gill, 'Economic Globalisation and the Internationalisation of Authority: Limits and Contradictions', *Geoforum*, 1992.
25. World Bank, *Global Economic Prospects 1995* (Washington, DC: World Bank, 1995).
26. UN Summit for Social Development, *Declaration and Programme of Action: Outcome of the World Summit for Social Development* (New York: United Nations, 1995); and R. Vernon, *Sovereignty at Bay: The Multinational Spread of US Enterprise* (London: Basic Books, 1971).
27. R. Broad and J. Cavanagh, 'Don't Neglect the Impoverished South', *Foreign Policy*, Winter (1995–6).
28. Ibid.
29. World Bank, *Global Economic Prospects 1995*.
30. R. Parker, 'Clintonomics for the East', *Foreign Policy*, Spring (1994).
31. See G. Hyden and M. Bratten (eds), *Governance and Politics in Africa* (Boulder, Col.: Lynne Rienner, 1992); and T. Ranger and O. Vaughan, *Legitimacy and the State in Twentieth-Century Africa* (London: Macmillan, 1993).

7 World Cities, Capital and Communication
Peter Wilkin

The aim of this chapter is to illustrate and examine the ways in which the modern capitalist world order (CWO) is developing in its current phase of political, economic and social restructuring. The implications of these quantitative and qualitative transformations in the CWO are profound, and are of particular significance for any redefinition of the Third World in international relations (IR). My argument will be that while the categories of core and periphery are central to any political geography of the current CWO, the ways in which they have been developed in both Dependency Theory and World-Systems Theory are not sufficiently sensitive to the fluid and uneven nature of global development, broadly construed.

My intention in focusing upon the rise of 'world cities' is to illustrate what I see as the increasing complexity of the way in which core–periphery relations manifest themselves in the CWO. The crucial factor to be borne in mind here is that we are concerned with a CWO that is composed of complex and integrated levels of action, structure and change – in essence, a social totality.[1] I will turn to the importance of this for IR shortly. While the CWO is an integrated system connecting the economic, political and cultural-ideological levels, this chapter is expressly concerned with the global movement towards urbanisation, and in particular the rise of what are generally called 'world cities'. These developments reflect the central role that revolutionary innovations in new information technology (NIT) have played, and continue to play, in the current wave of capitalist development.[2] In practice these trends have tended to lead to the increased spatial dispersal of production processes in the world economy and at the same time the centralisation of management and control, invariably from these world cities.[3] As I will set out in this chapter, these transformations in the CWO have important implications for social and political change, continuity and conflict.

Underpinning these objectives is a concern with the relationship between the restructuring of the CWO and the spread of democracy in international politics. The rise of world cities and the movement towards a social world that for the first time in human history will be largely urban rather than rural brings with it many sites of social and political conflict. Already there are numerous developments in world cities that indicate the varying forms of conflict that are likely to ensue as a result of this restructuring.[4] Familiar themes from 'the end of the Cold War' have been both the triumph of capitalism and the alleged intrinsic link between capitalism and democracy.[5] However, the uneven nature of the restructuring of the CWO illustrates that the link between capitalism and democracy is far more complex than this. Robert Dahl has illustrated that historically it is societies that are split by deep forms of social, economic and political inequality that are likely to lead towards conflict and increasingly authoritarian political practices.[6] The balance between democracy and freedom is a fragile one, according to Dahl, and wide inequalities of private power will render, in practice, formal political freedoms increasingly empty.

When seen in the context of the deepening forms of global inequality and exploitation that are accompanying the current phase of global social, economic and political restructuring we are left with a sombre portrait of the possibilities of democracy becoming substantively embedded in the CWO. In fact, as I will argue, the movement towards forms of procedural over substantive democracy is part and parcel of this process of restructuring at the level of the state in the CWO. World cities serve to illustrate this point as they become sites of increased social regulation on the part of public and private institutions. *This is occurring as these world cities come to mirror the inequalities of social, economic and political power that are the defining features of the transformations in the current CWO.* Indeed, it is the ensuing naturalisation of poverty and the denial of human needs that are primary sites of conflict in international relations. If substantive forms of democracy involving participation and the empowerment of ordinary citizens are to become embedded in the current restructuring of the CWO, then the world cities will become primary locations for such practices. As I shall illustrate in the course of this chapter, it is my contention that the current tendencies in the CWO are leading away from the likelihood of embedded substantive democracy. Before turning to the role of world cities in the CWO, I want to deal briefly with what I take to be most significant about globalisation for the current restructuring of world order.

UNDERSTANDING GLOBALISATION

One of the most contentious issues surrounding the idea of globalisation is the very meaning of the term. Some writers have taken this conceptual struggle to mean that it is little more than an academic discussion that serves to obscure more than it reveals.[7] Conversely, others have noted that the problem is not with the processes that the concept aims to describe and explain, but with the way in which it is presented as either a neutral process of progressive change in the world order or else as an almost inescapable form of technological determinism.[8] Equally problematical is the assumption that globalisation is so all-embracing a concept that it offers to explain both everything and nothing. By this is meant that it exists as an almost metaphysical explanation of all events: when in doubt, blame it on globalisation. There is no doubt that these and other problematical issues can be located in writings on globalisation but I do not see this as a reason to dispense with the concept totally. Rather, my intention here is to outline what I take to be the four main strands of globalisation that are central to an understanding of economic, social and political change in the world order and which are important to the emergence of world cities.

GLOBAL CAPITAL ACCUMULATION

The main mechanism driving globalisation is the continuing integration of capitalism as a world economic system in which capital accumulation is increasingly taking place on a global rather than a national scale.[9] As has long been argued, it is transnational corporations and international financial institutions (IFIs) that are the primary agents for this restructuring of the global economy, as private institutions increasingly take control of investment and trade.[10] In effect, this transformation of the world economy has been developing rapidly since the decline of the Bretton Woods system in the early 1970s, and has been amplified by the liberalising economic reforms of the period. The collective power of these transnational capitalist institutions to set the global political, economic and social agendas represents the most important tendency in globalisation since the 1970s. While various writers have correctly noted that globalisation, when understood as the movement towards an integrated capitalist world order, has been an inherent feature of modernity, I would argue that it is only with recent developments in communications technology and transportation that the full complexity of this process has begun to gather speed. In addition to the power that accrues from the control of capital and existing in complex relationship to it comes an accumulation of other forms of power that are part of the hierarchical structure of power in the world order; in particular, power over knowledge and information, power over regulation of trade and investment, and, finally, the accumulation of military power.

GLOBAL AND LOCAL PATTERNS OF INEQUALITY AND POVERTY

Directly related to the movement from forms of national capital accumulation to those that are increasingly taking place on a global scale are the widening forms of social and economic inequality and exploitation that are a defining feature of the world order. As TNCs utilise the access that a 'liberalised'[11] world economy brings to their capacity to seek out the most profitable forms of investment and locations for production, so we are witnessing a substantive global social restructuring.[12] This sees the movement of manufacturing industries from traditional locations to a number of key Third-World regions. At the same time, there has been a steady transformation in the older industrial areas to new forms of production and accumulation. The social consequences of these changes have led to starkly uneven forms of development. In the traditionally rich states, forms of social deprivation, poverty and ill-health have re-emerged with a vengeance alongside areas of comparative wealth and general affluence.[13] While the Third World is still the overwhelming site of absolute poverty in the world order, there has been a significant redistribution of resources, not only from 'South to 'North in geographic terms, but from 'poor' to 'rich' in global terms.[14] This presents a far more complex picture of inequality in the world system and these transformations are perhaps best captured in the idea of global cities that has taken root in a wide range of social-science literature. As cities throughout the world expand to incorporate historically unprecedented waves of migration from rural areas to urban in search of work opportunities, so there is a build-up of urban poverty alongside the astonishing ar-

chitectural and financial riches that are the ultimate symbols of
the nodes of political, economic and cultural power that are global
cities.[15] The combined impact of mass unemployment, migration
and economic retrenchment portends, as many are noting, social
disasters of unparalleled proportions.[16] Thus the patterns of inequality
that are developing in the world order are best understood as features of local, regional *and* global patterns of inequality as opposed
to patterns that are seen as features of the relations between and
within nation-states.

NEO-LIBERAL IDEOLOGY AND HEGEMONY

The third and related strand of globalisation that I emphasise is
the hegemony of neo-liberal ideology. The ideas and values associated with contemporary liberal capitalism have gained international
ascendancy since the 1970s through the increasing confidence of
major economic actors to assert the authority of private institutions to control the direction that economic policy takes, from the
national level through to the workings of various IFIs.[17] When coupled
with the impact of world-wide movements towards liberalised trade,
privatised economies and deregulation of state controls, these neo-
liberal values and ideas have taken on the form of a new common
sense, at an elite level at least.[18] In effect, there is a dominant
ideology that has served to unite the interests of a range of powerful political and economic actors under the guise of providing a
universal blueprint for development. While there are functional
aspects to this ideology (for example, it reinforces the power of
private capitalist interests over those of both the workforce and
those excluded from work), it is not all-embracing and, as I will
illustrate later, it is part of an ongoing struggle for control over
the direction that social, political and economic organisation will
take in the early party of the twenty-first century.

THE CHANGING ROLES, POWER AND AUTONOMY OF STATES

A common theme in globalisation literature, and one already mentioned here, is that both the sovereignty and autonomy of nation-
states have been diminished seriously by the movement towards a

globalised economy.[19] No single nation-state is said to be able to resist the power of continually transforming patterns of global investment and the relocation of capital as private investors seek out the most efficient and profitable locations. Indeed, this belief is an important strand of the current hegemony of neo-liberal capitalism and has found widespread acceptance among political parties of all persuasions. *While I do not seek to deny the power of the increased mobility and volatility of capitalist transactions, equally I do not subscribe to the view that there has been a general levelling down of the power of nation-states. Rather, what needs to be emphasised is that changes in the sovereignty and autonomy of nation-states is differentially distributed in the world order.* For example, while even major economies such as those of Eastern Europe or Mexico are either directly or indirectly organised under the auspices of representatives of the IFIs, it is still the case that the powerful Northern states remain dominating actors in the world order.[20] There are strong reasons to suppose that, contrary to neo-liberal orthodoxy, TNCs in fact need nation-states to remain strong and powerful actors in certain areas.[21] For example, strong nation-states are needed to maintain social order and to help discipline populations in both employed and unemployed sectors. While nation-states may have retreated increasingly from certain forms of economic activity (for example, public welfare), they have expanded their powers in other areas, most generally concerning domestic surveillance, policing and control.[22] Nor should we overlook the fact that it is nation-states that have brought about and helped to legitimise the changes to the global economy that have taken place. A consequence of this has been that the economic role of nation-states has been redrawn substantively towards providing incentives for private investors to utilise the resources that a nation-state has to offer. This takes the form of a familiar litany of requirements, from tax-free trade zones, general reductions in direct corporate and personal taxation, and increases in regressive taxation, to reductions in public welfare, and the selling-off of public assets to private investors and corporations. All this amounts to the *embedding of the principle of public investment for private profit and power on the assumption that it will lead to the maximum utilisation of resources.*[23]

I conclude, then, that while many nation-states can certainly be said to have seen their autonomy and sovereignty significantly diminished, it is also the case that other states have more power than ever in terms of military and political authority in the world order. These states are, unsurprisingly, familiar and reflect well-entrenched patterns of power in the world order. The G7 states, Russia, China and a few of the emerging nations represent this group. The point here is to stress that there is an absence of the kind of anarchy in the international system posited by realists. In fact, this is a hierarchical and well-ordered system in which the multiple forms of power (economic, political, military, cultural and ideological) help to maintain and stretch the structure of power over time. The relations of domination that persist and develop in the world order are complex, combining local, regional and global relations around a range of issues such as class, gender and ethnicity.

GLOBALISATION IN CONTEXT: STATES, SOCIETIES AND GEOPOLITICS

Alan Jarvis, utilising insights from historical sociology, has suggested a useful way of understanding the complex and stratified ontology of world order, tracing the historical emergence, continuity and change of what he calls the 'fit' between states, societies and geo politics. Such an account recognises the fact that there is both movement and change as well as continuity through embedded structures and practices in the CWO, and it is the 'fit' between them that we need to trace over time. Thus it is a concern with understanding the broad tendencies of historical change and continuity as well as the concrete practices, divergences and ruptures to these processes. It is a rejection of social science as science that looks into the future and promises certainty, calculation and prediction. The rise and emergence of world cities is a crucial site of the 'fit' between states, societies and geopolitics that Jarvis is concerned with, and this is what I will illustrate in the rest of the chapter.

UNDERSTANDING WORLD CITIES, CAPITALISM AND MODERNITY

The movement towards an urbanised CWO in which mega-cities of 8 million or more inhabitants come increasingly to dominate social, economic and political life is best understood within the context of two distinct but interwoven processes. First, the rise of urbanism in its modern context can be seen as part of the historical process of integrating a CWO within which such factors as the private appropriation of land and the rationalisation of production processes have been central factors determining the direction of subsequent uneven development. Second, the city is an embodiment of aspects of the much contested idea of modernity, which I would argue is a concept that must be kept distinct from the rise of a CWO. Notions of modernity have their roots in Enlightenment ideals of progress and the empowering role that knowledge about the world and society might play in transforming how we live. The classical ideals of the Enlightenment and modernity are in part about the (self) emancipation of people from the drudgery of life lived under conditions of deprivation, ignorance and poverty.[24] Urbanism is one trend within modernity, which in its progressive intent is about the construction of more cosmopolitan forms of social order. In the current CWO, world cities are quintessential features of the modern nation-state, representing sites of economic, cultural and geopolitical power. I will turn to the implications of this shortly, but in concluding this section it is important to emphasise that the relationship of a CWO to what I take to be the classic Enlightenment ideals of progress, freedom and equality has, in practice, been to subvert and undermine these aspirations. The mistake that the more brutal forms of post-modern and post-structuralist thought tend to make is to confuse these two trends of modernity, and a CWO as being in essence part of an integrated process of so-called oppressive 'grand narratives'.[25]

WORLD CITIES IN A CWO: HISTORICAL STRUCTURES

If it is true to say that cities have always played an important part in the progress of human history, it is equally important to stress that they have not always played similar roles and symbolised similar forms of social, economic and political power. In the modern context we are concerned with two related processes when interpreting the development of modern world cities. First, these developments must be understood within the historical context of the expansion of Europe into the rest of the world, with the conquest of the Americas from 1492 representing an appropriate starting place for such a history. The ensuing history of colonialism and imperialism have been the most significant determining factors in the shaping of the CWO, as they helped to establish the rise of nation-states and centralised political and military power, the structures of trade, transport, communication and cultural exchange that continue to define the current world order. It is the past and ongoing history of colonialism and imperialism that must always be considered when attempting to understand the current structures of power, hierarchy and order in international relations. In many respects the construction of a CWO and the modern nation-state can be seen as part of a European process of conquest and domination whose legacy continues to plague the majority of the world's population.

As well as the expansion of European power and the construction of a CWO through colonialism and imperialism, a defining feature of the historical context underpinning the rise of world cities has been the establishment of capitalism as a mode of production within which social power is determined significantly by ownership of the means of production. This twin axis of relations of production and exchange has helped to structure the forms of social power in modernity, dividing a stratified world order along such geo-political lines as First World–Third World, core–periphery and also in terms of class relations within states. The development of the world's major cities has reflected the geopolitical and economic aspirations of states, the economic ambitions of corporate actors as well as the wider social and cultural expressions of contrasting social forces. In this sense the movement towards an urban social order in modernity is a global trend that reflects the interests of a range of social, corporate and statial actors regarding questions of political power, cultural activity, social control and the centralisation of economic decision-making. Fundamentally these are developments taking place within the tracks of a CWO in which sites of social, economic and political power have long been established through colonialism and imperialism.

The current tendency towards world cities is driven by a similar panoply of factors, but importantly has also to be understood within the context of the current phase of the restructuring of capitalism that I mentioned earlier.[26] This restructuring is concerned with four processes:

1. The spatial dispersal of production processes throughout a global system where deregulation, liberalisation and privatisation as *de facto* global economic norms have enhanced the speed and power of capitalist institutions.[27]
2. The concentration and centralisation of managerial control of the production process through the utilisation of what I would refer to as the NIT revolution of the past two decades, with telecommunications and computers as the crucial developments here.[28]
3. The flexibility of labour as a global tendency representing a mechanism for increasing both productivity and profits in order to take maximum advantage of these technological developments.
4. The broader agenda is the need on the part of capital to overturn the post-war gains made in the core states by labour that led to increased wages, welfare and so on.[29]

These developments provide us with the historical–structural context within which the current rise of world cities can be understood, connecting as they do the ongoing balance of social forces, state institutions and geopolitical concerns. I shall return to these four features elsewhere, but before doing so it is important to explain why the emergence of world cities is an uneven phenomenon in the CWO.

CITIES AND UNEVEN DEVELOPMENT IN A CWO

There is a tendency in even the best of works on the rise of world cities to present these developments within a structural framework that would appear to leave little room for the role of politics and culture in the movement towards an urbanised CWO. Such analyses have the common weakness of analysing the city solely in terms of the expansion and integration of global capitalism without paying due regard to the part that both geopolitical and cultural factors play in these developments. As a consequence, a common accusation that is labelled against important writers such as Immanuel Wallerstein and Saskia Sassen is that they are either reductive in their analyses or over-determining in the relationship between capital and urbanisation. I would concede immediately that these writers have been crucial in providing us with the background for an understanding of world order as a complex and stratified totality, and of an understanding of the relationship between urbanisation and political economy. All that I would hope to offer here is the suggestion that an account of urbanisation in the CWO has to be sensitive to the following criteria:

1. *Historical structures.* The main structural forces driving the development of the modern CWO are historical structures. As such they have to be understood as structures that are differentially embedded in the CWO over time and space. They are not the ahistoric and detached structures of neo-realism, but are both shaped by, and shaping of, movement and change within the CWO. In this sense, such structures connect the different levels of a stratified CWO and provide the framework within which the various causal mechanisms act.[30]

2. *Contingent factors.* The development of cities into world cities is in part to do with the structural context within which political, economic and cultural agents act – the necessary structures and relations of the CWO. Crucially, however, it is also to do with the impact of contingent factors upon the concrete development of particular cities in particular times and places. For example, both Kuala Lumpur and Beirut had the possibility of transforming into important regional economic cities in the current CWO, but only Kuala Lumpur has achieved this. This cannot be understood simply in terms of its spatial relationship to the flow of capital in a CWO, but has to be understood in the context of the concrete cultural, political and economic circumstances affecting the cities, the states in which they are situated and the balance of social forces surrounding the transformation of those cities and regions. In addition, such contingent factors as geographical location, environment, and natural resources might all play a part in the success or failure of cities in a CWO to transform into world cities. It is only through empirical study that we can answer such questions. Thus the uneven nature of the emergence of world cities in a CWO will reflect the dynamic of the historical structures that have emerged through colonialism and imperialism and that have been embedded over time and place, with the contingent factors of culture, politics, geography, environment and so on.

Having set out an abstract schematic for understanding the uneven development of the emergence of regional and global cities,
we need to turn briefly to the problem of defining these urban
forms.

DEFINING CITIES IN A CWO: WORLD CITIES AND SOCIAL POWER

There is no consensus as to the way in which cities are defined,
incorporating as they do polarised areas of extreme wealth and poverty,
innovative architectural designs alongside slum dwellings and shanty
towns. What I do want to set out here is the way in which a more
elaborate model of the idea of world cities could be constructed
which pays due regard to the complexities of a CWO shaped by
uneven development. It is worth noting that Sassen classifies global
cities in terms of their economic location in global capitalism, the
extent to which they are the HQs of major capitalist firms. While
she concedes that there are a growing number of major cities around
the world, she is left with only London, Tokyo and New York as
genuine examples of what she calls global cities. My contention is
that such a categorisation does not pay due regard to the stratified
levels of power and significance in international relations, in particular
to issues of cultural and geopolitical concern.

A more complex framework for understanding the network of
world cities would seek to categorise them according to a broader
range of criteria than simply the location of the HQs of major
capitalist corporations. By building upon Alan Jarvis's framework
of the 'fit' between societies or social forces, states and geopolitics
in a CWO, we can categorise cities in a more elaborate manner.[31]
Thus a classification of world cities might see them located within
a grid that assesses in the manner of Table 7.1.

In this table, the horizontal axis indicates the form of social power
by which the city is assessed, while the vertical axis defines the
type of the city in a CWO. Thus the term 'world cities' is a generic
category under which different types of cities and social power can
be assessed as follows:

1. *National*. A city that has national significance within the boundaries
   of a specific nation-state in at least one area of social power.

Table 7.1   The classification of cities

	Economic	*Geopolitical*	*Cultural–ideological*
National	Cities that are sites of national economic importance	Cities that are sites of national military importance	Cities that are sites of national cultural importance
Regional	Cities that are of regional economic importance	Cities that are of regional geopolitical importance	Cities that are of regional cultural–ideological importance
International	Cities that are of international economic importance	Cities that are of international geopolitical importance	Cities that are of international cultural–ideological importance
Global	Cities that are of global economic importance	Cities that are of global geopolitical importance	Cities that are of global cultural–ideological importance

Horizontal Axis = Form of Social Power
Vertical Axis = Type of World City

2. *Regional.* A city that has significance in at least one area of social power which stretches across the boundaries of the state within which it is located.
3. *International.* A city that has significance in at least one area of social power and which stretches across at least two continents in geographical terms.
4. *Global.* A city that has a global reach in at least one area of social power.

In using such a matrix to examine the emergence of world cities in a CWO it enables us to draw out the complex and stratified nature of social power in international relations. Previous models that have utilised core–periphery frameworks have tended to be overly rigid and structural in their map of the world order and social power. The rise of world cities as centres of social power in a CWO is a process that establishes a network of social power operating on three related levels:

1. Social forces at national, regional, international and global levels.
2. The geopolitical interests of state actors.
3. The increasingly transnational interests of corporate actors.

Such a model of world cities cannot be seen simply in terms of established ideas of First World–Third World, as such approaches tend to simplify social power rather than allow for the stratified and complex account that is put forward here. While the CWO is hierarchical, in line with the forms of social power I have outlined here, there is also a danger in core–periphery analyses of oversimplifying this hierarchy so that it takes on an almost monolithic structure that seems to deny both the possibility and reality of social change. As I have said, structures are historical and differentially enduring over time and space; they do not simply determine the actions of agents but are both constraining and enabling of events. For example, cities the periphery can emerge as world cities, for reasons that may be both structural (their location and development in the history of colonialism and imperialism) and contingent (the geopolitical and economic policies of state and corporate actors and the interests of conflicting social forces). There is movement in this account of the rise and fall of world cities in a CWO that any model has to take account of, always bearing in mind that this movement always *begins* within the context of established structures of power and hierarchy.

The consequence of such categories of world city for how we understand idea about the Third World is of considerable substance. For example, a city such as Vienna would undoubtedly fall into the category of a global city in terms of culture, but not in any other category. Equally, Washington DC, the *de facto* world capital in geopolitical terms, must surely be included in any account of world cities that is attuned to the role that political factors play in the development of the CWO. In the Third World, cities such as Baghdad and Jerusalem are undoubtedly global cities in cultural terms, but in geopolitical terms are only regional. What I hope to show is that a matrix of world cities presents us with a more dynamic picture of the stratified nature of the CWO and one that is explicitly conscious of the fact that there are other levels of power than economic in the shaping of that order. Having set out the grounds for a matrix by which world cities might be assessed (recognising that this is both a quantitative and qualitative judgement and not simply reducible to numbers), I can now turn to the sig-

nificance of these developments for our understanding of the Third
World in a CWO and for ideas of core–periphery.

CITIES AND THE THIRD WORLD: STATE, SOCIETY AND GEOPOLITICS

The matrix of world cities and social power set out in this chapter
present us with an understanding of core–periphery relations in a
CWO that recognises the uneven nature of the distribution of social power in a global system. While a 'North–South' model is pertinent in terms of the way in which the spread of capitalism through
colonialism and imperialism constructed a hierarchical CWO, it is
insensitive to the stratified nature of social power that I have set
out in this chapter. For this reason, a form of core–periphery model
is needed that seeks to explain the diverse forms of social power
and hierarchy in a CWO that are in themselves not simply reflections of interstate relations. Thus hierarchies of class, gender on
ethnicity, for example, are all important tendencies within the modern
CWO that are phenomenan connecting local, regional and global
social forces. The absolute majority of the poor and exploited undoubtedly reside in the Third World, but so too do a significant
stratum of the world's wealthiest citizens. Equally, there are various objective tendencies in the North regarding matters of health,
unemployment, poverty and ownership of wealth that are part of a
general trend towards what we might call the 'Third-Worldisation
of the North'.[32] World cities are sites within which this meeting of
the powerful and the powerless increasingly occur.

As we have seen, the model of world cities and social power
presented here allows for significant degrees of movement and change
in the CWO. Hence so-called Third-World states have some opportunity to develop key cities within their territory so that they
might fit within the framework of social power that I have described.
As I have said, the development of world cities will depend on a
range of necessary and contingent factors that reflect the co-deter-
mination of structure and agency in a CWO:

1. *National policies.* Governments do have the ability to make policy
   choices that will make a difference in attracting capital to their
   cities. As I mentioned earlier, the application and promotion of
   the global economic norms of liberalisation, deregulation and

privatisation, when coupled with economic incentives to attract core investors, might all be significant in the growth of world cities in general. Thus in the current phase of the CWO it is of geopolitical interest for governments and state institutions that they pursue such policies in order to promote and defend their own world cities.

2. *Systemic factors*. Within a CWO there are structural or necessary factors that will be crucial in the development of potential world cities. The needs of capital may change over time in many respects, but the central dynamics of the pursuit of profit and the reduction of costs are systemic factors that are central to the calculations of corporations. In the wake of an increasingly deregulated, liberalised and privatised world economy they are also central to the geopolitical calculations of state institutions. The ramifications of this can be seen in terms of the continued attempt on the part of powerful social forces in the CWO to accumulate capital at the expense of the vast majority of people in the periphery and a significant sector of the population in the core.[33]

3. *Contingent factors*. Finally, a range of contingent factors will be crucial in the potential emergence of world cities in different areas of social power. The cultural and historical importance of cities for religion, politics, trade and communication will play a part in this process, as will the range of social forces generating them.

The rise of world cities in a CWO is of great importance because it presents us with an account of power that is located increasingly in urban areas and which is complex and stratified. World cities can be seen as sites within which processes of globalisation from above and below are meeting in diverse ways. If globalisation from above is the result of the actions of powerful institutions and processes in a CWO such as the actions of state institutions, corporations and national governments, globalisation from below is the fragmented and diffuse response to such developments from those social forces on the receiving end of this. A key question that remains is to what extent these tendencies represent a movement towards transnationalism in the CWO between core and periphery? Before answering this question, it is important to set out the way in which the relationship between capital and NIT has helped to fuel the rise of world cities.

CAPITAL, COMMUNICATION AND TECHNOLOGY

The development of world cities must be seen within the context of the restructuring of capitalism. In particular, the development and application of NIT (essentially telecommunications and computers, now converging into what is often called 'telematics') has been central to these related processes. As David Harvey has noted, the history of capitalism is in substantial part the history of systems of communication, and in conjunction with the aforementioned contemporary global economic norms the current innovations in NIT have been fundamental in allowing for the dispersal of sites of production around the world.[34] This, in itself, has helped to facilitate the expansion of urban areas in the CWO while at the same time enabling the possibility of increasingly sophisticated forms of centralised managerial control and decision-making. The impact of this on the CWO has been to integrate in unprecedented, though uneven, ways a global system within which world cities as contrasting sites of social power are transformed into a qualitatively new kind of infrastructure. This is an important theme I shall turn to shortly, but before doing so it is important to establish how these developments in capital and communication with their importance for the rise of world cities have come about.

THE NIT REVOLUTION

NIT has largely been developed by two main actors since the Second World War: states (military) and TNCs, both situated in core states. Manuel Castells, for example, notes that this military–industrial relationship was central to the USA's economy as it sought to utilise a form of 'military Keynesianism' to generate growth in its domestic economy.[35] Equally, telecommunications has become, and continues to be, an area of huge economic importance for the world economy in its own right and for the range of largely core state corporations that dominate this strand of production. The principle established within this sector was the idea of large-scale public funding for private companies to carry out research into areas that would benefit both military power and the economic power of core states. In recent years, the so-called 'Star Wars' project inaugurated by the Ronald Reagan's Presidency in the USA has been the latest and grandest manifestation of this tendency towards public subsidy for private corporations carrying out research primarily for the military.

The priority in the development and application of these innovations in NIT has been towards both private profit and state power, with questions of the satisfaction of general needs largely of limited importance. Indeed, one of the effects of the introduction of NIT into the world economy has been to worsen the satisfaction of human needs by encouraging a general tendency towards increased and unprecedented levels of unemployment, of which the world cities are prime sites. In practice, the development and application of NIT is a clear example of the relationship between knowledge and interests that critical theorists have rightly focused so much attention upon.[36]

Thus with these developments in the restructuring of capitalism world cities become sites of geopolitical importance for states; of economic importance for TNCs; and of social and cultural importance for the vast numbers of people drawn to these urban environments. But in what sense do these transformations represent the transition towards a global economy within which world cities are the key nodes of social and economic relations?

WORLD CITIES AND A GLOBAL ECONOMY?

The idea of a global economy has slipped into popular political discourse since the mid-1980s as governments and analysts alike highlight the constraining effects that the transformation in the movement and organisation of capital and production are said to have brought to the autonomy of states. While the notion of the global economy appears to reflect a range of developments in the CWO it is important to locate the real pressures and meaning of these changes in the CWO. However, it is necessary first to highlight exactly what is implied by the idea of a global economy before turning to the problematic nature of the concept. The movement towards a global economy is usually seen to rest upon two related processes that have their roots in the two decades since the 1970s. First is the expanded role that TNCs have come to play in world trade and production, a common point noted by many commentators. This expanded role has been fuelled by the global economic norms of deregulation, liberalisation and privatisation, all policies introduced by governments that have worked to increase the mobility and importance of TNCs in the world economy. Second, when coupled with the speed and mobility of investment, decision-making and general capitalist transactions (largely underpinned by the NIT infrastructure), then it is reasonable to argue that this represents a qualitative transformation in the nature of the organisation of production and social relations in the CWO. World cities can be seen as the key sites of control and communication in this integrated system.

The practical impact of these developments has been to free capital of its dependence upon labour, as investors and producers can continually seek out the most profitable sites under the rubric of 'efficiency' and the necessity of competition in a market economy.[37] As a consequence, it is increasingly the case that it is the demands of working people that are seen as being either out of date or conservative, standing in the face of the progress and modernisation of a continually innovative capital. Despite huge shifts in social power away from working people generally and towards capital in a global economy we need to qualify the analysis, for a number of reasons. For example, there is undoubtedly a major polarisation in the global economy, with a sizeable portion of the world's population not even a part of any market relations. As various writers have noticed, the great majority of trade and investment is still tied to the core states, even if there are important and powerful developments in the world cities of the periphery.[38] More significant, perhaps, is the fact that for all the much-vaunted mobility of capital it is still rooted in particular areas of the world, and particular urban locations. Investors and corporations may be able to relocate from one region to another with comparative ease in a global economy, but there are only a limited number of locations that will be attractive and these are invariably situated around the most important of the world cities.[39] Thus it is important not to lose sight of the fact that, as Karl Polanyi observed, markets and capital are also vulnerable to the activities of social forces that might try to shape investment and production for the satisfaction of human needs rather than the interests of private profit. Of course, these tendencies in the history of capitalism to which Polanyi refers require active resistance on the part of social forces and it is for this reason that the emergence of world cities would seem to be of such importance as centres of possible social change in the CWO.

CONCLUSIONS

The picture of the CWO that has emerged in this chapter suggests that world cities are becoming increasingly important centres of social power in a complex and stratified system. I want to finish by drawing out the some of the key ways in which these forms of social power are manifested in existing social relations in the world cities of the CWO and what, in turn, this means for the problems of democracy raised by Robert Dahl that I mentioned at the beginning.

World Cities and Economic Power

The most prominent feature in the structure of world cities has been the emergence of what is often referred to as a dual economy. Major corporate institutions are central to the establishment of this dual economy as they help to redevelop and expand these world cities. In addition, there is the construction of something like a transnational network of elite corporate actors whose working lives see them located within the world cities. The other side of this dual economy is the creation of a service economy of unskilled and semi-skilled workers, invariably low-paid and largely subordinate and responsive to the needs of the elite groups that dominate world cities. This dual economy is more complex than a simple division of class as it is increasingly pitching different social groups into conflict with each other. For example, young people are common targets for the violent punishment of state and private institutions in a range of world cities. Also, the patriarchal nature of work in this dual economy is a central dynamic as women are increasingly drawn into manufacturing and service economies, where they suffer even greater levels of exploitation. This gender conflict is a central part of the restructuring of the CWO. In addition to this it is also the case that the elderly in many parts of the world are particularly vulnerable to the vagaries of life in world cities, where there has been for some time a global attack on welfare, pensions and service provision for the elderly. Finally, impoverished migrants to world cities in both the core and the periphery have tended to fill the most poorly paid and insecure jobs as well as being the subject of racism from state institutions and the wider population. Thus the idea of a dual economy has to be severely qualified to take into account the deeper features of oppression in the restructuring of social relations in the CWO.[40]

World Cities and Cultural–Ideological Power

The question of cultural-ideological power in the CWO is important on a number of levels, and world cities are central to this. As
Julian Saurin has noted, there is in practice a dual culture–ideology
in the CWO that is concerned with what we might call official or
public history, as opposed to lived history.[41] What is meant here is
that an important form of power is the power to impose a meaning and interpretation upon events in the CWO, their significance,
and their relationship to ideas of progress, freedom, justice and so
on. As Saurin has noted: internationally, official history and lived
history present us with a stark dichotomy in the sense that official
history is concerned not only with a narrow range of states but
also with around just 15 per cent of the world's population. Invariably, the producers of official history are located in world cities of
great cultural–ideological importance, working within what we might
broadly refer to as the culture industries. None of this is a question of the effects of culture–ideology in the CWO but it is an
attempt to understand why the official accounts of the history of
international relations have been so narrow in their range of assumptions. In essence, the mode of thought and understanding
developed over time in the official history has been shaped and
developed in the context of prevailing forms of dominant social
power, something that both feminist and critical theory approaches
have emphasised. These pressures tend to reflect the prevailing
structure of social power in a CWO, where elite institutions and
actors attempt to promote ideological accounts of international
relations that reflect, as far as possible, their own interests.

World cities are increasingly becoming locations within which the
official culture–ideology and the lived cultural experience of the
world's excluded 85 per cent clash. If world cities are polarised in
terms of the range of cultural ideas and practices they provide for
their populations there is little doubt that the movement towards
an increasingly urbanised world will have profound implications for
the direction that future social change will take, given that it is
bringing together, into comparatively small areas, a vast sector of
the world's population.

World Cities and Political Power

I have already highlighted the way in which the emergence of world
cities in part reflects the ongoing geopolitical concerns of national

governments and state institutions, but it is also important to draw out the political developments internal to the structure of world cities that are emerging. There are, in practice, many features that are transforming the organisation of the world cities we are concerned with, but there is one in particular that concerns me here. The application of NIT by state and corporate institutions intensifies the surveillance power of states and corporations over ordinary citizens. As Giddens has often noted, surveillance power is a central tool in the armoury of modern states as they seek to control and organise populations. It is also of increasing importance to private corporations as they seek to organise production, workers and investment as well as targeting potential markets for their products. Thus surveillance is a crucial disciplinary feature for social control in world cities and as population density increases it seems likely to remain so, particularly in the core state, where regular and overt state repression of general populations is largely illegitimate. In the peripheral world cities (São Paulo, for example), violence remains a regular tool for social control.[42]

World Cities, Democracy and Globalisation

The overall picture that emerges here is one in which the rise of world cities both mirrors and represents the deepening nature of poverty, inequality of social power and exploitation in the CWO. While Dahl's argument is that property rights and economic inequality within a state will ultimately raise major problems for the possibility of democracy, it would seem to be equally applicable to the possibility of embedded democratic practices being established globally. World cities are sites of manifest and deep inequalities of wealth and social power, the very conditions that Dahl notes have led historically to social conflict and the erosion of substantive democracy. The difference now is that such conflicts connect social forces in an ever more integrated CWO. In practice, the impact of these inequalities leads to the transcendence of procedural over substantive forms of democratic practice, with a nexus of party–state–corporate institutions tending to dominate the process of democratic representation in most of the core states in the CWO. In part it is world cities that are the centres of these political processes and the areas within which these party–state–corporate institutions tend to reside. As Dahl says, the root of the obstacle to the possibility of embedded democratic practice in which people have meaningful control over their own lives is that the economic institutions that underpin capitalism are fundamentally anti-democratic. TNCs are manifestly not democratic organisations, and the tendency towards the increasingly private control of wealth and resources only exacerbates the way in which inequalities of social power undermines the possibility of substantive democratic social orders emerging.[43] World cities remain as the key locations within a CWO where these conflicts of social power will be played out as we move towards an increasingly urbanised system. As such they are of central concern in understanding a redefined Third World, precisely because they illustrate the difficulties and complexities of the idea of core–periphery in the CWO.

Notes and References

1. D. Harvey, *Social Justice and the City* (London: Edward Arnold, 1973), pp. 290–2.
2. J. S. Nye and W. A. Owens, 'America's Information Edge', *Foreign Affairs*, vol. 75, no. 2, March–April (1996), pp. 20–36.
3. D. Sudjic, *The 100 Mile City* (London: Andre Deutsch, 1992), p. 239.
4. See N. Megalli, 'Hunger Vs the Environment', in C. Kegley and E. Wittkopf (eds), *The Global Agenda* (New York: McGraw Hill, 1995).
5. On the end of the Cold War and capitalism and democracy see, for example, F. Fukuyama, *The End of History and the Last Man* (Harmondsworth: Penguin, 1992); and F. Halliday, 'The End of the Cold War and IR', in K. Booth and S. Smith (eds), *IR Theory Today* (Cambridge: Polity Press, 1995).
6. R. Dahl, *A Preface to Economic Democracy* (Los Angeles: University of California Press, 1985), pp. 4–5.
7. W. Hutton, 'Myth That Set the World to Rights', *Guardian*, 12 June (1995).
8. M. Ferguson, 'The Mythology About Globalisation', *The European Journal of Communication*, vol. 7 (1992), pp. 69–93.
9. D. Drache, 'From Keynes to K-Mart: Competitiveness in a Corporate Age', in R. Boyer and D. Drache (eds), *States Against Markets* (London: Routledge, 1996), pp. 31–61.
10. S. Burchill, 'Liberal Internationalism', in S. Burchill and A. Linklater (eds), *Theories of International Relations* (London, Macmillan, 1996), pp. 50–63, illustrates the level of intrafirm trade in the global economy.
11. The liberalisation of the world economy needs to be understood in the context of the skewed nature of these processes of liberalisation that have evolved in recent decades, primarily through the GATT framework. See C. Raghavan, *Recolonisation: GATT, The Uruguay Round and the Third World* (Penang: Third World Network, 1990).

12. R. Cox, 'Production, the State and Change in World Order', in E-O. Czempial and J. N. Rosenau (eds), *Global Changes and Theoretical Challenges* (Lexington, Mass.: Lexington Books, 1989), p. 46.
13. N. Chomsky, 'The Third World at Home', in N. Chomsky, *Year 501: The Conquest Continues* (London: Verso, 1993).
14. L. Brown and H. Kane, *Full House: Reassessing the Earth's Population Carrying Capacity* (London: Earthscan, 1995), p. 46 for information on the widening levels of global income distribution.
15. S. Castles and M. J. Miller, *The Age of Migration* (London: Macmillan, 1993).
16. Various authors, 'A World in Social Crisis', *Third World Resurgence*, Special Issue, December (1994).
17. M. Bienefeld, 'Is a Strong National Economy a Utopian Goal at the End of the Twentieth Century?', in R. Boyer and D. Drache (eds), *States against Markets*.
18. S. Gill, *American Hegemony and the Trilateral Commission* (Cambridge: Cambridge University Press, 1990).
19. R. Reich, *The Work of Nations* (New York: Vintage Books, 1992).
20. P. Gowan, 'Neo-Liberal Theory and Practice for Eastern Europe', *New Left Review*, vol. 213, September–October (1995).
21. R. Jenkins, *Transnational Corporations and Uneven Development* (London: Methuen, 1987), p. 177.
22. M. Shaw, *Global Society and International Relations* (Cambridge: Polity Press, 1994), pp. 72–9.
23. See P. Krugman, 'The Case for Stabilising Exchange Rates', *The Oxford Review of Economic Policy*, vol. 15, no. 3, Autumn (1989).
24. E. M. Wood, *Democracy Against Capitalism* (Cambridge: Cambridge University Press, 1995).
25. F. Lyotard makes this point in his *The Postmodern Explained* (Minneapolis: University of Minnesota Press, 1992), pp. 77–8.
26. E. Linden, 'The Exploding Cities of the South', *Foreign Affairs*, vol. 75, no. 1, January–February (1996), pp. 567–93.
27. E. B. Kapstein, *Governing the Global Economy* (London: Harvard University Press, 1994).
28. M. D. Alleyne, *International Politics and International Communication* (London: Macmillan, 1995), p. 21.
29. S. Sassen, 'Economic Globalisation', in J. Brecher *et al.*, *Global Visions* (Boston, Mass.: South End Press, 1993).
30. On the idea of structures and historical change, the social ontology of critical realism offers perhaps the most substantive insights into this. See R. Bhaskar's seminal *The Possibility of Naturalism* (Brighton: Harvester Wheatsheaf, 1979).
31. A. Jarvis, 'Societies, States and Geopolitics', *Review of International Studies*, vol. 15, no. 3 (1989), pp. 281–93.
32. N. Chomsky, 'The Third World at Home'.
33. S. Sassen, 'Economic Globalisation'.
34. D. Harvey, *Social Justice and the City*.
35. M. Castells, *The Informational City* (Oxford: Basil Blackwell, 1989), pp. 238–69.

36. D. Harvey, *Social Justice and the City*, p. 147.
37. See T. Lang and C. Hines, *The New Protectionism* (London: Earthscan, 1993).
38. R. Jenkins, *Transnational Corporations*, and S. Chan (ed.), *FDI in a Changing Global Economy* (London: Macmillan, 1995).
39. D. Sudjic, *The 100 Mile City*, p. 5, notes that culturally global cities have more in common with each other than they do with the rest of their respective countries.
40. D. Sudjic, *The 100 Mile City*, p. 49, notes how the development of global cities depends very much upon public subsidies or handouts for the rich corporations that are subsequently regenerating them. This is an irony made all the more stark by the fact that this form of public investment is taking place around the world at exactly the same time as there are general cutbacks on the principle of public welfare for the poor.
41. J. Saurin, 'Globalisation, Poverty and the Promises of Modernity', *Millennium: Journal of International Studies*, vol. 25, no. 3, Winter (1996).
42. P. Virilio, *Open Skies* (London: Verso, 1997).
43. R. Dahl, *A Preface to Economic Democracy*, pp. 54–5; and N. Chomsky, *The Prosperous Few and the Restless Many* (Berkeley, Calif.: Odanian Press, 1993), p. 20.

8 Urbanisation and the Third-World City: The Need for a Reconsideration
Giok-Ling Ooi

This chapter contends that efforts to reconsider the meaningfulness and current-day relevance of the concept of the Third World should include a reconsideration of the Third-World city. The focus is on the review and reconceptualisation of the role of the Third-World city in national development. The discussion considers cities and development in the period following the end of colonial rule, and then the more recent contribution and role of cities in the economic development of Third-World countries. In a broader context, this chapter also questions whether using the term 'Third World' in referring to cities in Asia, Africa and Latin America needs reassessment in the light of increasing similarities between cities everywhere: 'In every First World city, there is a Third World city of malnutrition, infant mortality, unemployment and homelessness and in every Third World city there is First World city of high tech, high finance and high fashion.'[1]

A BRIEF HISTORY OF URBANISATION STUDIES IN THIRD-WORLD CONTEXT

Third-World urbanisation has become a major focus of academic attention in recent times. The reason, however, appears to be diametrically opposed to those that shaped urban studies in developing countries in the 1960s and 1970s.[2] While studies in the earlier post-colonial period concentrated on urban problems and issues, the more recent studies have centred on issues related to rapid industrialisation and economic growth and their relationship to large cities.

Indigenous urban centres that developed in the Third World were eventually superseded by colonial centres in many countries. Due in large part to colonial influence, urbanisation in Third-World countries was propelled less by industrialisation, as had been the case in advanced industrialised countries of the West, and more by mercantilist imperatives. Studies of Third-World urbanisation in the wake of independence from colonial rule have therefore highlighted many of the problems related to the process and rapid rate of urbanisation without industrialisation in many large Third-World cities.

In their review of post-war developments in urban studies in developing countries, Victoria Savage *et al.*[3] have noted how the post-colonial era generated great interest in the Third-World city. In particular, questions were raised regarding the state of primacy[4] and the problems of rural–urban migration, such as the existence of slum and squatter settlements.[5] Views that the process in developing countries was pseudo-urbanisation because colonial cities had not contributed to economic development have been countered by scholars who have argued that the city is a beach-head and centre of modernisation.[6] Arguments concerning planning for urban growth centred on the relationship between urbanisation and modernisation/development. In the post-independence period through to the 1970s, literature on urbanisation and urban policy tended to have a marked anti-urban bias. There were arguments against large cities in particular, which were considered to be anti-social evils and probably also anti-developmental.

During the 1960s and 1970s, Third-World cities shared a wider range of common problems than they have the 1980s and 1990s. Economic growth in many Asian countries now makes it difficult to justify reference to cities in Asian, African and Latin-American contexts as Third-World cities without any differentiation among them. Yet just as studies of the Third World and its development and urbanisation were shaped by the problems besetting these countries, so current research on urban growth/urbanisation is similar. If formerly the discussion focused on primary cities and the negative impact these had on their countries' economic development, studies now tend to be concentrated on mega-cities and extended metropolitan areas.

Before moving on, it should also be pointed out that urban theorists have tended to view cities as if they were isolated in space and time such that urban system boundaries are usually drawn at the edge of the city, region or nation.[7] Such delineation of cities is inaccurate, particularly in the context of an interlocking capitalist world economy. Urbanisation in Third-World countries has not simply reflected an internal, spatial division of labour, but rather global patterns of labour and resource exploitation.[8]

ORIGINS AND NATURE OF THE THIRD-WORLD CITY

Many cities in Southeast Asia were founded following Indian and Chinese influences.[9] Indian influence was concentrated around the coastal fringes of Southeast Asia while the impact of the Chinese tended to be in mainland Southeast Asia with the migration of people away from an expanding Chinese empire. Some countries had no cities until Western colonialisation. There are thus few cities in the Philippines and much of mainland Southeast Asia, including Myanmar. Writers on colonialism such as Keith Buchanan[10] have argued that 'while the metropole developed industry, the rest of the world developed underdevelopment. Before capitalist development there may have been non-developed regions; but there were no underdeveloped regions, much less under-developed peoples'.[11] Accordingly, urban centres that developed in the colonies were the outposts of metropolitan powers. Cities such as Kuala Lumpur have been built on the trade in commodities, in this case tin, that have helped to develop colonial economies.

Throughout the colonial period and even after the early years of independence from colonial rule, Singapore served as the entry port for the region's trade in raw products that were exported to the industrialising countries of the West, as well as the import and then re-export of industrial or manufactured goods from the West to the colonies. Like Manila, Singapore is thus viewed as lacking a concern for regional culture and is focused on its interest in world trade.[12]

Third-World cities thus have many different histories, and in some the impact of world trade and the search for new markets and sources of labour supplies and raw materials has been highly significant. Their importance in the late 1990s is sometimes disputed in an age of interlocking urban economies, instant global communications, transnational corporations and world trade areas. However, apart from the colonial origins of many cities in the developing world, rural–urban disparities have reinforced the view that the Third-World city has less in common with the rest of the developing country in which it is located than with other Third-World cities, or even cities in the rest of the world.

The demographic underpinnings of the urbanisation process in the Third World during the 1960s and early 1970s have generated two sets of polarised assumptions about the role of cities in Third-World countries.[13] At one pole is the view that growth, and particularly occupational formation, in Third-World cities is basically because of the combination of very high rates of natural increase in both countryside and city, and a large volume of actual and potential rural–urban migration involved in urban transformation. This, in turn, has placed grave demographic constraints on the possibility of labour absorption in high-productivity and capital-intensive sectors so that an increasing proportion of the urban population has been forced into low-productivity activities.

At the second pole is the view that cities can generate evolutionary growth. So, while in transition, occupation formation creates lags that lead to sectoral imbalances in employment absorption and opportunities, but both occupational mobility and economic growth will eventually correct such imbalances so that occupational structures will become more similar to those in the developed world.

POPULATION, PRIMACY AND PROBLEMS

The pattern of urbanisation in much of the Third World, where the process was often started off by colonial rule rather than industrialisation, led to one view that Third-World countries were undergoing 'pseudo-urbanisation'. However, the consequences have been very real. The urban population in the Third World increased threefold between 1950 and 1975,[14] has showed no signs of stopping, and now comfortably exceeds that of the more developed countries. Such rapid urbanisation has been attributed to the natural increase of the population, net migration, and the reclassification of rural to urban areas.

Urbanisation has been characterised more often than not by the 'primary city'. The most often cited example is the Bangkok Metropolitan Area in Thailand, where two-thirds of the country's urban population live and which is approximately fifty times that of the second largest city, Chiengmai.[15] Such primacy has been viewed negatively, with much of the growth unplanned.[16] The growth of primary cities has also been considered to be at the expense of a more 'natural' development or evolution of the urban system, including smaller cities where services and facilities are located and needed by their respective population catchment areas. Primacy, however, is not an exclusive trait of the Third World, even though its most extreme forms are to be found there.[17] Among the world's twenty largest agglomerations, twelve are in the developing world.[18]

While there was an expectation that modernisation and development would bring about a more balanced urban system in developing countries,[19] many factors (including the disintegration of rural economies because of the expansion of large-scale commercial agriculture at the expense of smallholder and small-scale rural enterprises, together with traditional spatial inequalities between rural and urban) have contributed to an increasing tendency towards primacy. Although a deceleration in primacy was in fact documented in some Latin-American countries in the 1980s[20] (development planning and shifts in growth strategies which emphasised smaller cities helped provide more alternatives to primary cities for migration), even here there are cities such as Guatemala City which has an extremely high level of urban primacy, with hardly any city in Guatemala functioning as an alternative growth pole.[21]

In the rapidly growing mega-cities of the Third World, the number of migrants and the population growth rate in the cities have increased ahead of the cities' ability to absorb them into new jobs or offer employment opportunities.[22] At the same time, the provision of affordable housing and infrastructure has also lagged behind demand, so there has been a sprouting of squatter settlements in many cities, housing as much as 25 to 35 per cent of the population.

Squatter settlements (for residential, industrial and commercial purposes) pose many problems. The settlements complicate the effort to plan for the provision of basic urban services such as sewerage and water supply, with need already outstripping resources. By squatting on land that usually belongs to public-sector agencies, squatter settlements are taking up space that would have been allocated to needed public services and infrastructure. Urban authorities are often concerned that the extension of urban services to squatter settlements would be construed as a *de facto* recognition of the unauthorised and illegal occupancy of the land, especially since such settlements often breed anti-government resentment, or even operate as semi-autonomous kingdoms.[23]

CITIES AND DEVELOPMENT PLANNING

Much urban planning effort in the 1960s and 1970s was focused on decentralising the urban population, with an anti-urban bias in development planning reflected in massive regional development schemes such as those in Venezuela and Malaysia.[24] However, the focus of regional development schemes was on new *towns* and growth poles which were effectively medium-sized and small urban centres. In socialist developing countries, such as Vietnam, the emphasis in development planning has been on correcting rural–urban disparities (a deliberate de-urbanisation programme) but even here reality has seen priority given to urban centres, albeit smaller ones such as district towns. Accordingly, planning priorities in the 1960s and 1970s encouraged growth poles in rural areas; the development of medium-sized and smaller towns; and the facilitation of 'counter-urbanisation'. Development policies were focused on rural areas in order to encourage more people to remain on the farms and not seek economic opportunities in the cities. The effects of such policies were somewhat of a contradiction in that while essentially anti-urban, the strategy in fact promoted urban growth around new growth poles.

Growth poles were planned on the premise that cities played a catalytic role in economic development,[25] since cities are places of prestige, status, modern symbols of educational importance, and civilised elites.[26] In Malaysia, growth poles were located in less developed and less urbanised areas and states in order to stimulate development of the surrounding areas, and were linked to a policy of industrial dispersal throughout the country. Generally these policies have 'failed to expand fast enough to provide employment opportunities for the rural population ... provid[ing] little scope for the rural population to enjoy the full range of urban facilities and services'. Consequently 'it is doubtful as to whether rural new towns have the vitality to bring about an equitable distribution of development benefits within Malaysia'.[27]

Similarly, in socialist Vietnam, districts or small towns in rural areas which were planned to eliminate the differences between rural and urban areas and promote a controlled form of urbanisation to facilitate the industrialisation of agriculture, have floundered because of major problems, such as the failure to link agriculture and industry. Instead, the liberalisation of the economy in recent years, and its opening up to foreign investment capital, have tended to reinforce the growth of Ho Chi Minh City and Hanoi.

In some Latin-American countries, the deceleration in primacy, though it has not eliminated the growth of mega-cities, has been attributed to the impacts of economic globalisation, and the subsequent restructuring demands of global financial institutions, rather than set priorities.[28] The overall shift in growth strategies towards export-orientation has created growth poles that have emerged as alternatives to primary cities for capital as well as migrant labour.[29]

GLOBALISATION AND THE CITY IN THE THIRD WORLD

The foregoing and extended introduction to the Third World city has sought to sketch its origins, highlight the reasons for, and problems associated with, primacy, and finally to suggest that planning has not always proved an effective way to deal with the situation. Indeed, the case of Latin America suggests that, in this context at least, external pressures generated by global processes have had at least as much success in creating alternative growth poles. It is now time to move on to a reconsideration of urbanisation and the Third-World city in the context of globalisation.

With the decline in the world economy of the role of material resources in production, there has been a concomitant rise in the internationalisation of capital as a major driving force.[30] Global restructuring, resulting in capital migration from old centres of the world economy, now in decline, to the major cities in selected developing countries, is reflected in the growing number of export processing zones (EPZs). Many of these zones are in Asia (Hong Kong, South Korea, Singapore, Indonesia, the Philippines, Taiwan, Malaysia) and South America/Caribbean Basin (Colombia, El Salvador, Mexico, Haiti), although a new series of zones are being located in the Middle East (Syria, Egypt, Jordan) and South Asia (Sri Lanka and India).[31] This shift in industrial location has eroded the economic base of First-World cities[32] and there has been a historical switch to production/reassembly of manufactured products in Third-World cities for export/re-export to home markets in First-World cities.[33] Furthermore, newly industrialising economies have developed their own transnational corporations to exploit undeveloped markets, especially in the region in which they are located. As a result, new economic relationships now link cities in Third-World countries with other cities across national borders largely because of the development of multinational networks of affiliates and subsidiaries typical of major firms in manufacturing and specialised services such as banking and finance.

Accordingly, cities play pivotal roles in an increasingly interconnected network of multinational firms;[34] modern capitalism is both a world-wide net of corporations and a global network of cities in which capital mobility facilitates a new international division of labour.[35] In Latin America and the Caribbean, the above process has led to new growth poles (EPZs) which have emerged outside the existing major urban agglomerations.[36] However, elsewhere, the growth of primary urban agglomerations has been reinforced with growth poles located close by. Most major cities in the Asia-Pacific region have followed a similar pattern of reinforcing primary urban agglomerations.

Throughout the Third World, therefore, the rate of urbanisation has been rapid. In a majority of the developing countries, the growth of the population living in cities has either paralleled or, more usually, exceeded the countries' population growth rates (see Table 8.1).

Yet it is a Third World that is becoming increasingly differentiated because of uneven growth. The problems facing Asia, Africa and Latin America are quite different. Latin America, however, in the context of population increase has already attained somewhat stable urban population levels similar to those of developed countries.[37] Meanwhile, Africa and Asia-Pacific still appear to be in a transitional phase, with further proportions of the population to absorb (see Table 8.2).

THE DOUBLE-EDGED SWORD OF MEGA-CITIES

The area covered by Bangkok in 1974 was already double that of 1960, and by 1984 its boundaries had reached the fringes of surrounding provinces. Areas within 40 kilometres of the city had become built up with housing estates, commercial establishments and recreational places such as amusement parks and golf courses, largely because of the economic boom of the 1980s.[38] Similarly, in the period between 1960 and 1980, Jakarta expanded and practically doubled its size, and between 1980 and 1990 the population grew again, from 6.5 million to 8.2 million.[39] The result has been incorporation into the metropolitan boundaries of the neighbouring regencies of Bogor, Tangerang and Bekasi.

Table 8.1   Urban population growth patterns in selected developing countries

Country	Average Rate of Growth Urban Population (%)		Rural Population (%)	
	1980–85	1995–2000	1980–85	1995–2000
Argentina	1.88	1.39	—	—
			0.87	0.88
Mexico	3.36	2.39	0.34	–0.07
Colombia	3.11	2.29	0.28	–0.07
Brazil	3.71	2.28	–1.27	–1.00
Algeria	3.71	3.85	2.51	1.25
Morocco	4.28	3.42	1.40	0.50
Ivory Coast	6.63	5.24	2.54	2.26
Nigeria	6.07	5.33	2.22	2.02
Kenya	8.06	6.72	3.17	2.78
Zaire	4.41	4.73	2.29	1.80
India	3.91	3.96	1.65	0.93
China	1.44	2.95	1.18	0.58
Indonesia	4.6	3.62	1.13	0.14
Malaysia	4.51	3.32	1.06	0.15

Source: World Bank, *Urban Policy and Economic Development: An Agenda for the 1990s* (Washington, DC: World Bank, 1991).

Table 8.2   Urban population in urban areas by major regions, 1950–90

Region	1950	1960	1970	1980	1990
World total	29.2	34.2	36.6	39.5	45.2
Developed regions	53.8	60.5	66.6	70.3	72.6
Developing regions	17.0	22.1	24.7	28.9	37.1
Africa	14.5	18.3	22.9	27.8	33.9
Asia	16.4	21.5	22.9	26.3	34.4
Latin America	41.5	49.3	57.3	65.0	71.5

Source: United Nations, *World Urbanisation Prospects* (New York: UN/Department of International Economic Affairs, 1991).

Mega-cities have generated increasing academic interest not only because of the concentration of economic growth and industrialisation but also the deteriorating urban conditions to be found in them.[40] Pressures from high rates of population growth plus demands from burgeoning urban economies have meant that infrastructural development has not been able to keep up in a majority of the cities. If problems in the 1960s and 1970s were caused in large part by the problem of insufficient jobs for a rapidly growing urban population, current ones would appear to be related to infrastructural requirements. Land has to be found and urban sites developed for industry, commerce, mass transport services, housing, modern sanitation and sewerage works, energy and water supplies, as well as a whole range of other urban services, from schools to parks.

Despite such problems, in many developing Asian countries, urban centres and urbanisation have been the major factors in the economic boom often referred to as an economic miracle. The idea of an extended metropolitan area[41] explains the tendency for cities effectively to grow outwards into their hinterlands through networks involving either subcontracting of work or flows of money sent from cities to families in the rural areas.

In explaining the transformation of urban growth processes and urban areas, three factors appear particularly important: foreign trade, foreign investment, and international tourism. Scholars who have focused on the development of extended metropolitan areas have identified Hong Kong and Singapore's mega-urbanisation process as essentially an internationally-driven one.[42] In the case of Hong Kong, the EPZ developed in Shenzhen has provided the opportunity for urbanisation and industrialisation to spread from the city-state to this southern part of the Guangdung province in China. For Singapore, the extension of its urban space-economy has been through the growth triangle agreement forged with neighbouring Malaysia and Indonesia. This triangle, driven by growth generated from capital and infrastructural developments financed by Singapore, is a complex arrangement predicated on international comparative advantage, geopolitics and the mixing of national political economies.[43]

IMPACT AND IMPLICATIONS

Rapid urbanisation has stretched the demand on resources of cities well beyond the ability of Third-World governments to cope.[44] Continually high rates of urban growth mean that national development efforts will have to focus on providing jobs, housing and services for urban dwellers as well as resources such as water and energy for the population, commerce and industry. In many senses a losing battle, the management of urban development, and particularly its environmental risks, in terms of degradation of re-sources such as water, will continue to be of major policy concern in the coming decades.[45] Bangkok's legendary traffic problems are increasingly matched in other major Third-World cities. Similarly, the pollution of the groundwater upon which 40 per cent of Jakarta's population relies, presents a serious problem that is far from unique to this city.[46]

Scarcity in provision translates to persistent urban poverty. Squat-ters frequently have no legal tenure for their land and homes, nor government licences for their petty trades. Facing such uncertainty discourages the investment which might lead to higher productiv-ity and income.[47] According to scholars such as Sassen, accompany-ing the problem of poverty itself, Third-World countries have to cope with increasing interurban inequality: a vast terrain of cities, towns and villages increasingly detached from the new international growth dynamic. Sassen argues that 'this dissociation is not simply a question of city size, since there are long subcontracting chains connecting workers in small villages to the world markets. It is rather a question of how . . . emergent transnational economic sys-tems are articulated, how they connect specific localities in less developed countries with markets and localities in highly devel-oped countries'.[48] In other words, inequality arises because there are some cities and sectors within cities that are linked to the glo-bal economy and others which are not. The new inequality is therefore different from the inequalities that have existed in the past and the challenges for government correspondingly new.

SUMMARY

Urbanisation has been discussed here with a view to illustrating the major changes that have been seen since the 1960s/1970s, and the increasing differences that have emerged among the regions that together comprise the Third World. Unevenness of develop-ment has seen major differences in the levels of urbanisation. At the same time, however, there are common features, including the emergence of mega-cities and mega-urban regions. More strikingly, much of the recent economic growth and industrialisation in de-veloping countries has been concentrated in such cities and urban regions. There is also a great deal of evidence that an evolving system of urban linkages between the mega-urban regions in Third World has developed or is emerging rapidly.[49]

Differentiation in the urbanisation process and the level of urbanisation are presenting a variety of issues and problems that will have to be addressed by urban governments and the state in the Third World. Though regions of Africa and Asia are experiencing an accelerated phase of the urban transition, which Latin America has largely already gone through, population growth itself will imply problems for the latter. However, in addition to problems with managing the growth of the urban population (Latin America's chief concern), African and Asian developing countries will have to continue the effort to absorb the population moving from rural to urban areas.

CONCLUSION

Studies of Third World urbanisation have changed substantially since an initial concern with primary cities. Cities which often share common origins in colonial rule have created academic interest in their subsequent growth, which has largely been driven by different external forces, and which has reshaped societies radically. As a consequence of the restructuring of the world economy and the internationalisation of capital, many of the largest cities and their urban regions are contributing the majority share of Third-World economic growth. As the rate of urbanisation and the growth of the largest cities continues unabated, interest will surely be maintained. While earlier attempts to understand the nature of the urbanisation process and the role of the Third-World city were informed more by the experiences of developed Western countries, more recent attempts have found it necessary to rationalise the different urbanisation experiences of developing regions through theoretical explanations drawn from neo-classical theory, world system theory and convergence theory.[50] However, whichever way we look at the phenomenon, any attempts to redefine the Third World in the sense of its boundaries will need to take account of the important transformations taking place from within, and the problems associated with these, which have been the subject of this chapter's discussion.

144   *Urbanisation and the Third-World City*

Notes and References

1. See J. Perlman, *Concordare*, no. 2, Summer (1992), p. 1.
2. T. G. McGee, 'The Persistence of the Proto-proletariat: Occupational Structures and Planning of the Future of Third World Cities', Paper presented to the Comparative Urban Studies and Planning Program, School of Architecture and Urban Planning, University of California, Los Angeles (1974). Also T. G. McGee, 'On the Utility of Dualism: The Informal Sector and Mega-urbanisation in Developing Countries', *Regional Development Dialogue*, vol. 17, no. 1 (1996), pp. 1–15.
3. V. Savage, L. Kong and B. S. A. Yeoh, 'The Human Geography of Southeast Asia: An Analysis of Post-War Developments, *Singapore Journal of Tropical Geography*, vol. 14, no. 2 (1993), pp. 229–51.
4. D. W. Fryer, 'The Million City in Southeast Asia', *Geographical Review*, vol. 43 (1953), pp. 474–94. Also N. Ginsburg, 'The Great City of Southeast Asia', *American Journal of Sociology*, vol. 60 (1955), pp. 171–209.
5. See, for example, S. R. Aiken, 'Squatters and Squatter Settlements in Kuala Lumpur', *The Geographical Review*, vol. 71 (1981), pp. 158–75.
6. R. A. O'Connor, *A Theory of Indigenous Southeast Asian Urbanism* (Singapore: ISEAS, 1983).
7. M. Timberlake (ed.), *Urbanisation in the World Economy* (Orlando, Fla.: Academic Press, 1985).
8. S. E. Findley, 'The Third World City – Development Policy and Issues', in J. D. Kasarda and A. M. Parnell (eds), *Third World Cities – Problems, Policies and Prospects* (London: Sage, 1993), pp. 1–31.
9. W. L. Thomas and J. E. Spencer, *Asia, East by South – A Cultural Geography* (New York: John Wiley, 1971).
10. K. Buchanan, *The Southeast Asian World: An Introductory Essay* (London: Bell, 1967).
11. Ibid., p. 79.
12. W. L. Thomas and J. E. Spencer, *Asia, East by South*.
13. T. G. McGee, 'The Persistence of the Proto-proletariat'.
14. United Nations Economic and Social Commission for Asia and the Pacific (UNESCAP), *Human Settlements Atlas for Asia and the Pacific, Part III* (New York: United Nations, 1980).
15. Ibid.
16. G. Breese, *Urbanisation in Newly Developing Countries* (Englewood Cliffs, NJ: Prentice-Hall, 1966).
17. S. Sassen, *Cities in a World Economy* (Thousand Oaks, Calif.: Pine Forge Press, 1994).
18. United Nations, *The Prospects of World Urbanisation* (New York: UN Reports, 1987).
19. See, for example, M. Edel, 'Capitalism, Accumulation and the Explanation of Urban Phenomena', in M. Dear and A. Scott (eds), *Urbanisation and Urban Planning in Capitalist Society* (New York: Methuen, 1986).
20. S. Sassen, *Cities in a World Economy*, p. 34.
21. S. Sassen, *Cities in a World Economy*, p. 37.

22. In Bolivia, for instance, El Alto, an outgrowth of La Paz, grows un-planned at 10 per cent per year. Here, at least Santa Cruz, on the country's eastern lowlands, is providing an alternative growth pole.
23. Certain *favelas* of Rio offer the most obvious example of this phenomenon.
24. N. Ginsburg, 'Planning the Future of the Asian City – a Twenty-five Year Retrospectives', *Occasional Paper, Institute of Asia-Pacific Studies, Chinese University of Hong Kong*, No. 36 (1994).
25. J. Friedmann, *Regional Development Policy: A Case Study of Venezuela* (Cambridge, Mass.: MIT Press, 1966).
26. R. A. O'Connor, *A Theory of Indigenous Southeast Asian Urbanism*.
27. M. Sulong, 'New Towns in Malaysia's Regional Development Planning', in R. B. Potter and A. T. Salau (eds), *Cities and Development in the Third World* (London: Mansell, 1990), p. 136.
28. S. Sassen, *Cities in a World Economy*, p. 4.
29. P. Landell-Mills, R. Agarwala and S. Please, *Sub-Saharan Africa: From Crisis to Sustainable Growth* (Washington DC: World Bank, 1989).
30. I. Wallace, *The Global Economic System* (London: Unwin Hyman, 1990).
31. S. Sassen-Koob, 'Issues of Core and Periphery: Labour Migration and Global Restructuring', in J. Henderson and M. Castells (eds), *Global Restructuring and Territorial Development* (London: Sage, 1987), pp. 60–87.
32. E. Soja, 'Economic Restructuring and the Internationalisation of the Los Angeles Region', in M. P. Smith and J. R. Feagin (eds), *The Capitalist City: Global Restructuring and Territorial Development* (London: Sage, 1987), pp. 178–98.
33. Ibid.
34. See, for example, A. D. King, *Global Cities: Post Imperialism and the Internationalisation of London* (London: Routledge, 1990).
35. M. P. Smith and J. R. Feagin (eds), *The Capitalist City*.
36. S. Sassen, *Cities in a World Economy*, p. 37.
37. T. G. McGee *On the Utility of Dualism*, p. 7.
38. M. Krongkaew, 'The Changing Urban System in a Fast-growing City and Economy: The Case of Bangkok and Thailand in F.-C. Lo and Y.-M. Yeung (eds), *Emerging World Cities in Pacific Asia* (New York: United Nations University Press, 1996).
39. B. T. Soegijoko, 'Jabotabek and Globalisation', in F-C. Lo and Y-M. Yeung (eds), *Emerging World Cities in Pacific Asia*.
40. M. Timberlake, *Urbanisation in the World Economy*.
41. Identified and conceptualised by N. Ginsburg, B. Koppel and T. G. McGee (eds), *The Extended Metropolis: The Settlement Transition in Asia* (Honolulu: University of Hawaii Press, 1985).
42. S. Macleod and T. G. McGee, 'The Singapore–Johore–Riau Growth Triangle: An Emerging Extended Metropolitan Region', in F.-C. Lo and Y.-M. Yeung (eds), *Emerging World Cities in Pacific Asia*, pp. 417–64.
43. See G.-L. Ooi, 'The Indonesia–Malaysia–Singapore Growth Triangle: Sub-regional Economic Cooperation and Integration, *GeoJournal*, vol. 36, no. 4 (1995), pp. 337–44.

44. H. W. Richardson, 'Efficiency and Welfare in LDC Mega-Cities', in J. D. Kasarda and A. M. Parnell (eds), *Third World Cities*, pp. 32–57.
45. M. Douglass, 'The Future of Cities on the Pacific Rim', *Discussion Paper, Department of Urban and Regional Planning, University of Hawaii*, no. 3 (1987).
46. W. M. Donovan, 'Managing the Urban Environment: Problem-solving Approaches in Five Mega-cities, *The Journal of Environment and Development*, vol. 1, no. 1 (1992), pp. 187–90.
47. B. Sanyul, 'Intention and Outcome: Formalisation and its Consequences', *Regional Development Dialogue*, vol. 17, no. 1 (1994), pp. 161–78.
48. S. Sassen, *Cities in a World Economy*.
49. T. G. McGee, 'On the Utility of Dualism: The Informal Sector and Mega-Urbanisation in Developing Countries', *Regional Development Dialogue*, vol. 17, no. 1, pp. 1–15 (11).
50. W. Armstrong and T. G. McGee, *Theatres of Accumulation: Studies in Latin American and Asian Urbanisation* (London: Methuen, 1985).

9 Neo-Liberalism in Latin America: 'Triumph' and Institutional Deficiencies

Frank O. Mora and Karl Kaltenthaler

Nothing short of a sea change has occurred in the political economies of Latin-America since the 1980s. Almost every Latin-American state has engaged in a profound process of political-economic liberalisation and reform. Some have compared this dual transition process to the transformation that occurred in the 1930s, when most states replaced the oligarchic and self-regulating political economy of the late nineteenth and early twentieth centuries with an authoritarian-populist model.[1] By and large, Latin America's political economy has come full circle. The 1980s witnessed a paradigm shift where the goals of democratisation and profound economic reform were pursued simultaneously. Politically, in the early 1980s, the region began its transition from bureaucratic-authoritarianism toward a more open and competitive form of representative democracy. In the economic realm, neo-liberal macroeconomic policies have replaced populism and demand-management policies and import-substitution with a new economic logic that emphasises the market, domestic decentralisation, deregulation, privatisation, trade liberalisation and, generally speaking, the removal of the state from the ownership of production. Latin-American states have embarked on a bold path of reform to achieve the political stability and economic growth and development that has eluded them for so long.

A look at indicators of economic performance shows a picture of the general success of economic reform in Latin America. Inflation has plummeted from an average of 200 per cent annually to around 20 per cent for the region. GDP growth has accelerated from stagnation, or at times contraction, during the 'lost decade' of the 1980s to a healthy average pace of 3 per cent in the 1990s, and exports have increased by more than 35 per cent since trade was liberalised in the late 1980s. Latin-American economic outcomes would thus appear to offer good evidence that neo-liberal policies *can* launch Third-World economies towards development.

While these trends in macroeconomic indicators do portray some very positive results of the reform process, they do not convey some of the serious socioeconomic problems that have arisen during the process that could potentially scuttle the transition. One of the most pressing problems facing Latin-American economic reform is increasing poverty and unequal distribution of wealth. As Mexican scholar and writer Jorge Castañeda pointed out, the region is experiencing the worst period of social and economic deprivation in half a century.[2] Economic liberalisation in Latin America has markedly increased the wealth and living standards of the upper classes, but the positive effects of reforms have not been as apparent to the middle and working classes. In fact, in much of Latin America, living standards for workers and peasants are deteriorating while the aggregate economy grows at a healthy pace. The number of Latin-American billionaires rose from six in 1987 to forty-two in 1994. However, the wealth being generated by economic reform is not trickling down to the mass of society. In short, Latin America is doing fine, but Latin-Americans are not.

While the distribution of wealth is generally not much of a concern for neo-classical economists focusing on the economic transformation of the region, it is of concern to political scientists.[3] Political scientists are concerned with the question of how political and economic reform can be sustained when the majority in society is in fact worse off now than before the liberalisation process began. The increasingly inequitable distribution of wealth seems to be a recipe for political instability, which could reverse the trends toward democracy and neo-liberal macroeconomic growth. Economic reform and growth without equity threatens to undermine the political and economic transformation that began in the 1980s.

A second major problem facing the economic reform process is the growth of corruption and violence. Observers of the Latin-American political economy have noted that with the move towards neo-liberal policies, there has been a concomitant increase in the amount of corruption and violence. Kick-backs and bribes have become standard operating procedure in many Latin-American countries over the years and the trend seems to be worsening. Violence and other criminal activities in the sprawling urban 'shanty towns' of Latin America, such as in the *favelas* in Rio de Janeiro and the *ranchos* of Caracas, are reaching disturbing levels. The retreat or dismantling of state capacity has provided fertile ground for illicit and criminal activities to flourish in a 'survival of the fittest' environment. This corruption has the negative effects of scaring away foreign investment and increasing the public's doubts about the reform process. Corruption and illicit or violent criminal activities are tearing at the confidence and trust required to strengthen and consolidate democratic governance and economic liberalisation. Fury at the human and social costs of neo-liberal economic reform is brewing throughout the region, threatening to destroy everything that has been achieved so far.

A third important problem associated with the economic reform process in Latin America is that many investors, scholars, and even policy-makers, are concerned that Latin-American policy-makers are not securing the long-term success of their economic reforms.[4] The emphasis generally is on the short-term, principally on lowering inflation, lowering government debt, and attracting foreign investment. While privatisation and neo-liberal macroeconomic policies have helped to achieve these goals, the volatility of financial markets (witness the Mexican financial meltdown and the ensuing 'tequila effect' in 1995) and the unevenness of growth in the region, across both time and space, demonstrates that it should not be taken as a given that Latin-American governments' present policies are enough to guarantee steady and sustainable low-inflationary growth into the future. Additionally, the frail and tenuous nature of democratic rule in Latin America, with its many hybrid and, in some cases, autocratic forms, makes democracy a tentative reality.

This chapter looks at these problems and argues that the reason why Latin America faces them is because of the incomplete nature of the economic reform process and the deleterious effect of stabilisation and market-orientated reforms on state capacity and the consolidation of democracy in the region. Neo-liberal macroeconomic reforms were necessary steps for Latin America to overcome the legacy of populist and import substitution policies. Neo-liberal policies have increased the efficiency of Latin-American markets, increased investor confidence, and reduced the burden of a crippling debt. But neo-liberal policies are only one side of the coin of necessary reforms. The other side is the restructuring and strengthening of the state to establish a solid foundation for the continuation of economic reform. The Latin-American state must be modernised and strengthened, not so that it can return to interventionism, but so that it can provide the public goods that every economy needs in order to operate effectively and efficiently. The restructuring and strengthening of the state constitutes the *institutionalisation* of reform that will heighten the credibility of the reform process and guarantee its success in the future.[5] The Latin-American state must strengthen its capabilities to extract taxes from its citizens in order to resolve some of the social problems threatening transformation. Unless the administrative capacity of Latin American governments is increased, social conditions are bound to deteriorate rapidly. This requires a 'second stage of reform'.

Additionally, the Latin-American state must invest in physical capital (infrastructure), create a professional and highly-skilled civil service, and establish an independent and efficient judiciary and central bank that can ensure impartiality, justice, and confidence in the system. In short, as Sebastian Edwards suggests, economic growth, while essential, is insufficient to deal adequately with the problems of poverty, inequality and the long-term consolidation of reform.[6]

On the political front, Latin America also needs to strengthen and restructure other state and non-state institutions, such as legislatures, political parties, and civil society organisations (for example, business associations and labour unions) that can consolidate democratic rule and create the mechanisms and environment needed to instil trust and confidence – critical in any reform process. Democracy and the public institutions that support it, such as parliaments or legislatures and political parties, lose prestige and legitimacy when they are unable to produce answers to the region's growing problems of unemployment and poverty.[7] Latin America has entered an important and deciding phase in its recent political-economic transformation. Reforms will have to move beyond fiscal austerity and elections towards a more comprehensive institutionalisation of reforms, requiring the strengthening and modernisation of state and non-state institutions to ensure its long-term sustainability.

This chapter will begin with an overview of the macroeconomic policies that have been adopted by Latin-American governments. The next section will explore patterns of economic growth, inflation and unemployment that have resulted from the process of market-orientated reforms, and the severe social disparities and dislocations of reform. We then turn to how institutional reform could overcome these problems. This section also examines the challenges to the region's democratic state and non-state institutions from neo-liberal policies and will note the need for political institutionalisation. Finally, the chapter concludes with a discussion of the political viability of a process of institutional reform in the context of macroeconomic liberalisation.

THE DEVELOPMENT OF NEO-LIBERALISM

In the 1930s and 1940s, Latin America, confronted with the disastrous consequences of global depression and the disruption of the Second World War, adopted an inward-looking economic model that would address and limit the region's dependence on the international economic system. Discontent with *laissez-faire* economics and exclusionary political systems contributed to a ground-swell of support for a shift in the political economy of Latin America. As a result, a number of Latin-American governments adopted a hyper-Keynesian, populist economic model along with import-substitution industrialisation (ISI), where governments sought to spur economic growth and development by investing in, and protecting, the industrialisation of these economies. Rudiger Dornbusch and Sebastian Edwards define economic populism as an 'approach to economics that emphasises growth and income redistribution and de-emphasises the risks of inflation and deficit finance, external constraints and the reaction of economic agents to aggressive non-market policies'.[8] Specifically, traditional populist policies included tariff protection and subsidised credits for industry, discrimination against agriculture and exports, wage hikes, deficit spending and proliferation of state planning, employment and welfare agencies.[9] Behind these policies is a political logic characterised by these features: authoritarian, paternalistic often charismatic leadership and mobilisation from the top down; multiclass incorporation of the masses; integrationist, reformist, nationalist development programmes for the state to promote simultaneously ISI and redistributive measures for populist supporters.[10]

Between 1950 and 1980 this economic model produced some positive results. ISI generated average annual growth rates of 5.5 per cent, per capita income grew by 2.7 per cent and from 1960 to 1980 life expectancy increased by ten years, in a context of very rapid population growth. Overall, Latin America experienced an unprecedented degree of economic growth and development. However, by the late 1970s the populist model had run its course and had begun to exhibit flaws and vulnerabilities. Bottlenecks developed, prompting unsustainable economic pressures that, in the end, resulted in the plummeting of real wages and severe balance-of-payments difficulties. The final outcome was the collapse of the economic system. This was exacerbated by the world-wide recession of the early 1980s that drove down the demand for Latin-American exports and cut off the supply of credit as higher interest rates raised the cost of foreign debt. The so-called 'scissors effect' of high interest costs and falling export demand explained the region's balance-of-payment problems.[11] In short, the post-war development model, based on industrialisation, statist/populist modes of regulation and demand-management policies, not only failed to deliver promised goods but was central to the macroeconomic and social disaster of the 1980s. Authoritarianism (populist or bureaucratic) and economic populism were exhausted and delegitimated, quickly displaced by liberalisation of economics and politics.

In the 1980s, a number of countries began the process of democratic transition, and post-authoritarian governments were forced to implement economic stabilisation and adjustment policies. Moreover, with international credit in retreat and a new free-market ideology on the upsurge, global forces and trends were requiring a re-evaluation and transformation of the failed populist economic model. A growing convergence emerged in the early 1980s among newly-elected conservative governments in Europe and North America and international financial institutions (the IMF and World Bank) on the appropriate set of structural policies needed to streamline and reform inefficient economies in the Third World.[12] These structural adjustment policies (the preferred development recipe of the so-called 'Washington Consensus') sought to make both state and market more efficient in such a way as to accelerate growth and eliminate waste. Specifically, the Washington Consensus revolved around ten key reforms needed to streamline the economy and institute a strong market-orientated economic system: fiscal discipline, elimination of government intervention, deregulation, privatisation, trade liberalisation, financial liberalisation, promotion of foreign direct investment, flexibilisation of labour markets, severe retrenchment of public spending, and, generally speaking, 'getting the prices right', with a priority given to the maintenance of a free market.[13]

In the early 1980s, under considerable pressure from domestic and foreign monetarist economists and the IMF, Latin-American governments implemented a series of orthodox stabilisation programmes to control inflation and correct macroeconomic distortions. These included some combination of currency devaluation, reduction of import controls, credit restrictions, higher prices for utilities, wage repression, and a reduction of subsidies. The aggressive manner in which these orthodox policies were implemented constituted 'shock therapy'.[14] Chile and Mexico in 1982 and Bolivia in 1985 implemented the most severe and comprehensive stabilisation programmes during the first half of the 1980s, resulting in successful macroeconomic consequences.

As may be expected, these adjustment policies required considerable economic sacrifice from much of the population. As a result, such policies were politically unpopular and destabilising for governments seeking to strengthen fragile democratic institutions. Several governments, such as those in Argentina, Brazil and Peru, not wishing to unleash political unrest, turned to less severe, heterodox policies (embodied in the Austral, Cruzado and Inti Plans) that addressed balance-of-payments deficits and inflation through such measures as import restrictions, foreign exchange controls, and wage and price controls.[15] These policies fell well short of the reforms and austerity measures needed to restore equilibrium, and economies fell back into inflationary disarray.

Short-term balance-of-payments and stabilisation measures were not sufficient to spark investment and growth. In the late 1980s, governments not only adopted orthodoxy but also extended the reforms to broader structural measures aimed at strengthening the export sector by way of tariff reductions, deregulation of financial markets and the privatisation of state-owned enterprises. Even presidential candidates and political parties known for their populist backgrounds (Carlos Menem in Argentina, Rodrigo Borja in Ecuador, Alberto Fujimori in Peru, and Carlos Andres Perez in Venezuela) embraced neo-liberalism once elected. Apart from Brazil, by 1991 Latin America was well ensconced in liberal orthodoxy and structural adjustment.

ECONOMIC AND SOCIAL CONSEQUENCES

The record of Latin-American economic performance since the inception of the neo-liberal reform programmes in the 1980s has been largely positive. Inflation has been drastically reduced; economic growth, while uneven, has generally increased at a healthy

pace; and foreign capital has returned in increasing amounts, fuel-
ling sectoral diversification and industrial development. The greatest achievement of the economic liberalisation process has been
the decrease in the average inflation rate, which by 1993 had declined to 20 per cent.[16]

Increases in economic growth have been moderate. The 1980s, a
decade dominated by the debt crisis and stabilisation policies, saw
a 1.1 per cent average annual increase in GDP. In the 1990s, on
the other hand, growth has averaged 3.1 per cent annually. Such
modest rates are not keeping up very well with population growth,
however. Whereas GDP per capita rose by a regional annual average of 3.4 per cent in the 1970s, it fell by 1.2 per cent during the
1980s. The same average only rose by 1.8 per cent during the years
1990 to 1994. This means that Latin America's economic growth is
barely outpacing population growth, which implies that growth will
have to be accelerated for Latin-American societies to raise the
standard of living of the population.

The picture for unemployment in the decades of the 1980s and
1990s has also been less positive. Unemployment rose during the
mid-1980s because of the economic crisis associated with the debt
crisis and then fell during the late 1980s as the crisis tapered off in
some countries. But unemployment rose again in the 1990s as Latin-
American governments privatised firms and rationalised labour and
production. At the decade's halfway point, the average unemployment rate was nearly 8 per cent and is expected to rise steadily.
Five countries have official unemployment rates above 15 per cent,
led most significantly by Nicaragua's 21 per cent and Argentina's
17 per cent.[17]

Thus, as firms sought improved competitiveness, unneeded workers
were let go. As a result, a growing segment of the labour force has
been pushed towards the informal sector where an increasing number
of the region's employment and economic activity is generated. In
1995 the informal sector constituted about 57 per cent of the region's economy and generated about 80 per cent of all new jobs.[18]
Investment and economic growth has not made much of a dent in
this growing unemployment. Foreign direct investment (FDI) has
not helped much because most of it is directed towards buying
privatised firms (existing production) and not towards establishing
new production.

The record of foreign investment in Latin America is mixed.[19]
While the aggregate amount of foreign investment in the region

increased substantially during the 1990s, the nature of foreign investment gives cause for concern. First, investment has been very concentrated. In 1995, nearly 70 per cent of foreign investment went to only four countries: Mexico, Brazil, Argentina and Chile. The reason why these four countries have attracted so much foreign investment is because they have privatised large government enterprises, mainly bought by foreigners. Other countries, without large state enterprises to sell off, are struggling to attract foreign capital.

While the selling off of state enterprises is helpful in reducing government debt, it is problematical in that it does not necessarily raise the aggregate amount of capital in Latin American economies. The lack of 'greenfield' (new production site) investment means that foreign direct investment may be only a minor stimulus to economic growth. New plants must be established in Latin America for economic growth to really take off. Another troubling aspect of foreign investment is the ratio of portfolio investment to foreign direct investment. Portfolio investment, which in 1990 accounted for only 3.7 per cent of all foreign investment in Latin America, in 1996 amounted to over 50 per cent. While this investment aids firms in modernising and increasing production, this type of capital allows the investor to make profits while not being tied to the investment. This means that portfolio investment tends to flee when there are signs of economic instability or impending crisis.[20] The great amount of portfolio investment can be seen as a sign that investors in Latin-American economies lack confidence and want to have the option of withdrawing their money at the first sign of trouble. In essence, this implies a lack of faith in the efficacy of the reform process in Latin America. The huge capital flight out of Mexico and Argentina in 1995 was a prime example of how portfolio investors abandoned those economies when signs of economic instability appeared. To a large extent, this lack of confidence in the investment environment is because of the institutional weakness of the regulatory and legal mechanisms of these states, making institutions such as the judiciary, the financial system and property rights vulnerable to corruption and delegitimation.

One of the most disturbing consequences of economic reform in Latin America is the widening gap between rich and poor.[21] The richest 10 per cent of the population receives about 70 times what the poorest 10 per cent does in Brazil, and about 50 times more in Mexico.[22] These countries have the most inequitable distribution of wealth in the world, and the situation is getting worse. There are several sources for the growing chasm between rich and poor. The unequal distribution of land in Brazil, Colombia, Ecuador, Honduras, Mexico and Paraguay is one traditional and continuing cause, recently leading to a number of protests and land invasions.[23] The 'lost decade' of the 1980s led to a cumulative change in GDP per capita of –7.9 per cent and to an increase in the incidence of poverty among Latin-American households, from 33 per cent in 1980 to 40 per cent in 1986.[24] By the late 1980s, as a number of countries implemented heterodox and orthodox stabilisation policies, social indicators declined further as these 'belt tightening' measures tended to place the burden of austerity on the working and middle classes.[25] The elimination of subsidies on food, fuel and transportation, along with the rationalisation of labour, had negative consequences for the poor. Expenditures on social services also declined in absolute and relative terms.

Another reason for income inequality is that economic adjustment and reforms, including privatisation and financial-market reforms, have provided new opportunities and even windfalls for upper-income groups, exacerbating concentration of wealth. Unlike privatisation in several transition economies in Eastern Europe, where vouchers were distributed to the populace, Latin-American privatisation has not been designed and implemented in a transparent and impartial fashion, and economic elites are reaping the benefits of new income opportunities, whereas the wages of workers have in fact been suppressed by flexible labour markets. Public firms were often sold cheaply and frequently for political reasons, in order to solidify the support of powerful economic elites; this encouraged rent-seekers while at the same time worsening income distribution and social deprivation.[26] Paradoxically, traditional patronage requirements have been served well by the modern drive toward Latin-American privatisation.

A final factor accounting for the growing income inequality in Latin America is the general decrease in education spending in Latin America. In an attempt to rectify the dismal fiscal situation, governments cut back on most aspects of social spending. A World Bank internal paper indicates that education spending in Latin America dropped from 3.5 per cent of the region's GDP in 1980s to 2.9 per cent in 1993.[27] This has meant that many workers are not acquiring the skills needed to make them competitive in the job market. Without the training to find new jobs in a scarce job market, workers are either left idle or, at best, *informalised*.

We would argue that there is every reason to be concerned about the inequality of income distribution in Latin America. One reason to worry is that a very poor distribution of income can be interpreted to mean that the economy is not operating in an efficient manner. A large portion of the population is not enjoying the benefits of wealth creation and accumulation, which could indicate that economic activity is limited to a narrow range of sectors in the economy. If the entire economy were operating efficiently it would tend to balance wages, as labour and capital would have relatively equal bargaining power. Another reason to worry about the growth of income inequality in Latin America is that it represents a serious threat to popular support, both for economic reform and for democratisation.[28] It is not surprising that as unemployment and the income gap between rich and poor increases, the less wealthy portion of society has begun to question the benefits of reform. Reform has meant lower inflation for workers and peasants but it has not brought them the promised increases in standard of living. In fact, workers and peasants in most of Latin America would seem worse off in the late 1990s than they were before the 1980s. There are now nearly 200 million people living below the poverty line.[29] Recently, workers and peasants have begun to show their disapproval of the reform process through demonstrations, strikes, roadblocks and violence. The Chiapas Rebellion in Mexico; food riots in Venezuela; strikes by teachers in Argentina, Ecuador, and Venezuela; and peasant marches in Bolivia, Brazil, Ecuador and Honduras must be seen as evidence that the manner in which economic liberalisation is being carried has led the losers from the reform process to demand recourse from the government.

The erosion of state capacity and the social crisis sparked by economic restructuring are central to understanding the rise of violence and feelings of insecurity felt by many in Latin America. Douglas Kincaid and Eduardo Gamarra suggest that neo-liberal reforms have not only led to a rise in illicit activities, but have also contributed to an *informalisation* of security functions that undermines state authority and responsibilities, while threatening to exacerbate public insecurity and disorder.[30]

Thus, the lack of a 'trickling down' of the benefits of reform could destabilise governments, as workers and peasants fight against a process that increases their socioeconomic marginalisation. Striking increases in inequality have occurred concurrently with market-orientated policy in several countries, including Argentina, Brazil,

Chile, the Dominican Republic, Ecuador and Mexico.[31] So far, a return to growth under the new, more open, economic regime has failed to bring about a reduction of the poverty and inequality that characterise the region.[32] Combined with increasing levels of corruption and violence, this is endangering the consolidation of the region's new political economy.[33] Uncertainty, frustration and, in many cases, indignation, is spreading as people cry out for 'justice, accountability, equity and an end to impunity'.[34]

Economic reform is, therefore, at a crossroads; it has achieved some goals such as curbing inflation and bringing debt levels under control, but other aspects of economic performance such as economic growth and employment remain disappointing. Increases in foreign investment are encouraging but still show a lack of confidence in the reform process. There are also definite signs of trouble on the horizon: growing income inequality and corruption. If negative trends are not reversed, the reform process could be abandoned by a public that has had enough of paying for the increased wealth of political and economic elites. Additional reforms must be implemented or economic neo-liberalism in Latin America may turn out to be yet another failed strategy in achieving economic development.

THE SECOND PHASE: THE IMPORTANCE OF INSTITUTIONAL REFORM

Most observers of the reform process in Latin America acknowledge that it is not yet complete. While the reforms so far undertaken have been profound, policy elites face a public that demands, in an increasingly vociferous manner, better employment and earning opportunities, and an end to social inequity, corruption and impunity. Here we look at potential next steps and their importance.

Sluggishness in creating and restructuring new institutions and public agencies that are critical for the functioning of an open, market-based economy is undermining economic performance. As former Venezuelan Finance Minister and noted scholar, Moises Naim, states: 'Bringing the state back in ways that support and reinforce recent progress – without restoring the state previously displayed penchant for inflicting economic, social, and moral havoc – will be the central challenge facing governments throughout the region.[35] We argue that the main task that Latin-American states must undertake is the restructuring of the state to create the institutional basis for improved economic performance and political stability. The key measure is to create institutions that increase the efficiency of the market, increase the credibility of policies, and give the state the capacity to enforce those institutions. The increasing informalisation of Latin America's economy is because, in large part, of a lack of strong and modern institutions that can give the state the necessary legal and regulatory mechanisms to ensure the stability, equity and overall success of the economic neoliberal model.[36] Without these institutional reforms, Latin America will continue to be beset by corruption, insecurity, a lack of capital necessary for solid economic growth, equity problems, and political instability.

When the institutions of the populist, import-substitution era were dismantled they were not replaced with a new set of institutions appropriate for the new economic model, leaving an enormous vacuum that has been filled by predatory forces not interested in the long-term development of Latin America. In other words, in the rush to reform, Latin America neglected to build the institutions needed to deepen these reforms and ensure long-term growth and development. Unfortunately, in the absence of institutions, corruption, violence, insecurity and a lack of confidence on the part of investors has taken hold over a society characterised by its 'extreme Darwinian attributes'.[37]

The case of Chile is usually offered by monetarists as an example of how a successful reform process should occur; shock therapy or a 'big-bang' process of deregulation in which populist macroeconomic institutions and policies were dismantled, invigorating the market and sparking growth. However, a closer examination of the Chilean case demonstrates that the initial phase of shock liberalisation, from 1974 to 1981, yielded poor results. When Chile altered its strategy in 1982, maintaining liberalisation within a context of building appropriate regulatory institutions, the real success began.[38]

The importance of institutional reform lies in their creation of a stable structure for political, social and economic interactions, lowering the information costs of those interactions.[39] In other words, institutions allow individuals to develop expectations about what other individuals will do in a given situation; it brings a degree of predictability needed to ensure trust, confidence and stability. Without institutions, individuals must search for an understanding of what others are likely to do; that costs time and energy. Institutions, or the rules of the market, reduce uncertainty and allow investors to calculate their future returns. In an economic market, nothing dampens investment like uncertainty about the future value of transactions.

Institutions are important; not just for reducing uncertainty, however – they are also important in determining distributional outcomes.[40] In other words, the rules of the market help to decide who gets what. Some institutional arrangements help certain individuals and groups, others produce different distributional outcomes. This is very important to economic performance. Institutions may be created by a powerful group in a way that gives that group a disproportionate share of the benefits from economic exchange, but may in fact hamper the overall efficiency of the market. In short, an institutional overhaul is needed.

Take, for example, the process of privatisation in Latin America. Privatisation was judged to be the solution to all the region's fiscal and socioeconomic problems: it would make production and markets more efficient. However, governments, in their rush to liberalise, failed to create the institutional or regulatory mechanisms necessary for this process to produce expected results through competition. As a result, the predatory nature of liberalisation resulted in higher levels of corruption. An unholy union between powerful economic groups and the government has impeded true competition and ignited unprecedented levels of corruption, thus making the consumer the ultimate casualty of the process.[41]

In another important area, the structure of institutions in Latin-American political economies, combined with policies of fiscal austerity, are suppressing a very important input of production: human and social capital. The need to reduce the size of government not only resulted in privatisation of state-owned companies but also in the reduction of social spending on education, health services and social security.[42] Those most affected by the retrenchment have been the poor. Spending on education has dropped substantially since the beginning of reform; one can surmise that this decrease in the amount of skilled workers in the labour pool is hurting the ability of technology-intensive firms to find the workers they need. Health-care expenditure has also declined dramatically, leading to increases in infant mortality and epidemics in the region. Since human capital is such an important factor in raising productivity, the most important variable in determining economic growth rates, an educated and healthy workforce is crucial in sustaining a vibrant economy.[43]

While a decision to decrease aggregate social spending is part of the reason for the drop in education spending, another reason for the drop can be found in the nature of Latin-American taxation institutions. Historically, Latin America has had problems developing an effective tax collection system. With no viable income tax system, and a sharp decrease in revenues because of fiscal austerity and reductions in tariffs, there simply is no money for spending on education. So, for governments to increase education spending, which they must if they want to sustain economic growth, they must change the nature of tax institutions. A viable and effective income tax system must be created so that the state can extract resources from society to provide the public good of educational opportunity. A more effective tax system is also needed to finance targeted social programmes and needs to help those that have been hurt the most by structural economic reform.[44] Targeted human capital investments, consistent with sound macroeconomic management and financed by a more efficient tax system, will not only help to increase the standard of living of the most disenfranchised but will also assist in building popular support for economic reform.

In addition to financing human capital, an efficient tax collection system will allow the state to accrue the revenue needed to invest in physical capital (infrastructure), which has deteriorated significantly since the mid-1980s.[45] The Latin-American state desperately needs to increase spending on indispensable public goods and services that the private sector cannot provide, but that are so important in 'crowding in' potential foreign and domestic investors.[46] Enrique Iglesias, Inter-American Development Bank president, estimates that to support a 5 per cent growth rate in Latin America, the annual investment requirements in infrastructure are of the order of US$65 billion. This is an indication of how handicapped trade and development are by a poor infrastructure.

Finally, reforming Latin America's regressive tax system is also designed to make tax collection more equitable so that the middle class does not carry a disproportionate share of the tax burden. The simplification and enforcement of tax laws to ensure that the wealthy in fact pay their taxes could not only increase revenue but also reduce the anger of the poor, in particular the urban formal sector and middle strata, who are likely to suffer the steepest relative losses from economic liberalisation, and are especially likely to feel resentment over unfairness.[47] In short, increasing state capacity in key areas by restructuring, strengthening and modernising institutions is a critical condition of development and stability. The institutions that must be reformed in order to increase investors' sense of security are property rights, central bank independence, the judiciary, and banking sector regulation. The development of the state's legal and regulatory capacity are central components of all market-orientated reforms. These institutions have done the most to repel investors from Latin-American markets. The institutions have raised questions of how investors can calculate the future value of their investments, how their investments will be protected if claimed by others, and how the investors will be treated if they need to take legal action. Property rights institutions must be changed so that the right to own property is guaranteed. Investors must be made to know that their property cannot be claimed by the host government or by a native claimant. Foreign property owners must have the same property rights as locals. This must be codified, and not merely stated by the host government. Codification of property rights represents a more substantial constraint on governments and others who might make claims on foreign investors' property. In Latin America, the most egregious violation of property rights has been in the area of intellectual property and patents. Foreign investors have complained of piracy and weak enforcement of patent laws. European and US governments have particularly noted Argentina, Brazil and Paraguay as the most flagrant violators. Not only does it discourage further investments, it can also lead to reprisals such as trade sanctions.

The institutional status of the central bank is another important factor in investor confidence. Investors are concerned about central banks that are under the control of the government because those central banks can be used for political purposes, such as stimulating the economy before an election. This practice is typical of many countries in the region, particularly Argentina, Brazil, Mexico, Venezuela, and several Central American republics. Such measures threaten monetary stability and the value of investments. Central banks can also be used to devalue the currency if a government wants to increase exports by making them cheaper. This can breed inflation and threaten the value of investors' assets. The Mexican financial crisis of 1995 was in large part a result of the Mexican government's politicisation of the central bank. Thus, the best way to ensure investors' confidence in monetary policy and the stability of the currency and financial climate in the country is to make the central bank independent. As of 1997, only Chile has a truly independent central bank, though some governments, such as those of Bolivia, Chile, and Mexico, have recently taken steps in that direction. In fact, Latin America continues to have some of the least independent central banks in the world.[48] Considering its poor track record of fiscal and monetary discipline, central bank autonomy would do a great deal to increase the credibility of stability-orientated policies.

The judiciary is one of the bleakest aspects of the institutional landscape of Latin America. Judiciaries in Latin America have traditionally not been independent of government control and that pattern has persisted into the 1990s. In addition to autonomy, Latin-American judiciaries lack professionalism, training and financing, leaving them vulnerable to corruption and intimidation. The general public in Latin America has a profound mistrust of the judiciaries because of their belief that political leaders manipulate judicial decisions freely and often openly. There is a general sense of 'institutionalised impunity' where the main culprits of corruption and violence are agents of the state, who usually go unpunished. In Mexico, only 22 per cent of the population has any faith that the judiciary is fair, while the highest rate of trust is in Uruguay, where 53 per cent of the public trusts the professionalism and impartiality of the judiciary.[49]

This government-controlled judiciary is a major reason why corruption is able to persist. If a government official is brought to count on corruption charges, there is a good chance that the charges will not result in conviction, because of a tainted judiciary. Making the judiciary truly independent would lower the incidence of corruption and increase investor confidence that they will be treated fairly in the legal system, thus increasing their propensity to invest. In short, the security of capital and of any democratic political system are best entrenched by a strong rule of law, protected by an independent judiciary. Institutional reform in Latin-American political economies must include the creation of banking regulations. An absence of banking regulations leads to frequent bank failures and a constant sense of financial crisis. The lack of viable legal and regulatory institutions is the principal cause for the banking crisis that has plagued Latin America since 1994,[50] producing the greatest number of financial bankruptcies since the 1930s. Unless the banking system is given a stable institutional foundation, the

financial system in Latin America will be liable to panic and capital flight. This will dissuade investors from investing anything that
is not liquid, if they decide to risk the investment at all. Thus,
banking rules that clearly state the rights, obligations and liabili-
ties of banks will restore confidence in the system.

In the political arena, the success and consolidation of economic
reform will depend on the ability of governments to stabilise and
consolidate democratic rule. In turn, consolidation is not possible
unless it is deepened and made more genuine for all citizens, and
this requires *political institutionalisation*.[51] The process of deepening or institutionalising democracy implies strengthening and de-
mocratising political parties and local government, strengthening
the legislative and judicial branches (state institutions), developing
grass-roots civic movements (civil society), punishing corruption and
human rights abuses, and subjecting the military to civilian control.[52] In other words, as Peter Evans suggests, effective economic
adjustment demands stronger political institutions and a more capable state that can mitigate the negative and deleterious effects
of structural adjustment: corruption, rent-seeking and predation.[53]
As Larry Diamond also aptly describes the situation:

> Democracies with more coherent political institutions are more
> likely to produce, over the long run, workable, sustainable, and
> effective economic and social policies, because they have more
> effective and stable structures for representing interests and be-
> cause they are more likely to produce working congressional
> majorities or coalitions that can adopt and sustain policies.[54]

Latin America finds itself in the midst of attempting to institu-
tionalise its democracies while advancing economic reforms. Many
scholars have suggested that an inherent tension, if not a contradiction, exists between pursuing simultaneously democratisation and
economic reform. The issue of sequencing and timing of reforms,
along with which regime type was most appropriate in implementing economic adjustment, has dominated the political economy debate
in the 1980s and 1990s.[55] It was thought that either reform would
undermine democracy by placing undue strains on fragile polities,
or democratic politics would undermine the coherence of policy,
generating a downward economic spiral.[56] Except for Chile and
Mexico, Latin America has pursued both simultaneously, possibly
endangering the prospects for democratic consolidation and suc-

cessful socioeconomic restructuring in the region.[57] In the mid-1990s, the debate shifted from whether democracies can initiate economic reform to how Latin-American democracies will meet the new social and political challenges likely to arise as economies are stabilised. Latin-American democracies remain institutionally weak and democratically incomplete. During stabilisation, many young democracies sought to take advantage of their 'honeymoon period' (enjoying greater freedom and policy manoeuvrability after years of authoritarian rule and economic stagnation) to implement much-needed but politically costly economic reforms. In the process, post-authoritarian governments postponed building democratic institutions in favour of implementing 'shock therapy' economic reforms in a rather undemocratic fashion. Paradoxically, economic neo-liberalism has weakened the democratic institutions it now needs to extend and consolidate itself. The initiation of reform required a substantial concentration of discretionary political power to contain resistance from status quo interests who threatened to undermine economic reform. Governments made every effort to insulate the technocrats and the decision-making process from political pressure.[58] Moreover, proposals for state reform, including reduction of public spending and privatisation, involved decisive, even authoritarian, actions on the part of democratically elected governments. In light of the growing lack of confidence in the institutions of democracy (political parties, legislatures and judiciaries) weakened and delegitimised by fragmentation, corruption and political manipulation, the vacuum has been filled by a concentration of power in the executive. *Decretismo*, or governing by presidential decree, in economic decision-making has reinforced a broader tendency toward what Guillermo O'Donnell has called 'delegative democracy', in which elected executives skirt coalition- and institution-building in favour of an authoritarian style that excludes civil society from the policy arena in order to protect the coherence of the economic reform programme and governs in a manner largely unconstrained by any 'horizontal accountability' to courts or a legislature.[59] This plebiscitarianism is inherently hostile to accountability and the institutionalisation of mechanisms of representation, allowing the executive to chip at the constitutional limits of power. The coincidence of strong presidential styles and neo-liberal reforms in Latin America has sacrificed many of the important institutional formalities of democracy. This has been particularly the case in Argentina under Carlos Menem, Brazil with the administration of Fernando Henrique Cardoso, and

Alberto Fujimori in Peru. O'Donnell asserts that the exclusionary nature of this new political economy, where the concentration of power and the privatisation of parts of the state has led to the atomisation of civil society, or what he specifically calls 'low intensity citizenship', has diminished the ability of society to participate in and strengthen democratic rule.[60]

Therefore, institutionalising and consolidating democracy in Latin America will require improving, extending and restructuring democratic structures and processes that will help make the region's political economy more accountable, transparent, participatory and responsive. If both economic reforms and democracies are to be consolidated, executive authority must eventually be depersonalised and integrated into a broader framework of contestation and accountability. However, this can only be achieved through political strategies that seek consensus, coalition-building and the institutionalisation of strong, representative political parties, legislatures, judiciaries, and state and local governments:[61]

> [These reforms] ... involve a shift from delegative to representative democracy and, ideally, from presidential, closed, top-down styles of politics and governance to forms that emphasise the construction of broad coalitions, the decentralisation of power and policymaking, and the generation of broad and relatively stable bases of support ... they require ... the broad enhancement of the rule of law and a strengthening of civil society.[62]

The future political stability of Latin America hinges on this process of institutionalisation as does the successful consolidation of the region's 'second phase' of economic reform.

CONCLUSIONS

The creation and development of the institutions needed to support new economic policies will be slow, cumbersome and technically difficult, but very important. This second generation of reforms, particularly those related to the modernisation of the state and financial regulations, will determine whether the paradigm shift in Latin America's political economy is successful. An important component of this process is also whether governments are able to consolidate democratic rule in the region. Latin America will need to strengthen those political institutions and coalitions (or social pacts) that are so critical in facilitating the difficult process of economic and institutional reform lying ahead.

If the new market-based policies do not produce positive medium-term results, particularly in the area of growth, employment and social justice, opposition will increase and, in spite of the weakening of the traditional support of populism, a return to populist cycles could occur in at least some countries. Even John Williamson, the intellectual father of the Washington Consensus, warned governments that they had better start aiming money and talent at social programmes, public institutions, the civil service, and public education.[63] Strengthening and modernising states and designing institutions that work, including more reliable legal and regulatory systems and a functioning judiciary is key to the success of economic reform.

Additionally, improving the quality of the lives of Latin-Americans, and not just their macroeconomic situation, by boosting programmes in education, infrastructure, health care and employment opportunities, must become the central feature of economic reform. Building legitimate and viable economic and political institutions is the key to linking neo-liberal reform with tangible improvements in the standard of living of the average citizen. The persistence of poverty and other factors associated with economic exclusion call for a more comprehensive approach to development that, while stimulating economic reforms, will build solid institutions, internal socioeconomic integration, modernisation of the state, and consolidation of democratic institutions. Otherwise, Latin America's impressive gains since the mid-1980s will be placed in danger by the combined forces of irresponsible populism, military coups, guerrilla movements, drug traffickers, lawlessness and social disintegration.

Notes and References

1. For example, A. Przeworski, *Democracy and the Market: Political and Economic Reforms in Eastern Europe and Latin America* (Cambridge: Cambridge University Press, 1991).
2. J. Castañeda, *Utopia Unarmed: The Latin America Left after the Cold War* (New York: Knopf, 1993), pp. 8–19.
3. For example, J. Nelson (ed.), *Economic Crisis and Policy Choice: The Politics of Adjustment in the Third World* (Princeton, NJ: Princeton University Press, 1990).

4. J. Williamson (ed.), *The Political Economy of Policy Reform* (Washington, DC: Institute for International Economics, 1994).
5. C. Bradford (ed.), *Redefining the State in Latin America* (Paris: OECD, 1994). Also, S. Edwards, *Crisis and Reform in Latin America: From Despair to Hope* (New York: Oxford University Press, 1995).
6. Ibid.
7. M. Shifter, 'Tensions and Trade-offs in Latin America', *Journal of Democracy*, vol. 8, no. 2 April (1997), pp. 114–28.
8. R. Dornbusch and S. Edwards, 'The Macroeconomics of Populism', in R. Dornbusch and S. Edwards (eds), *The Macroeconomics of Populism in Latin America* (Chicago: University of Chicago Press, 1991), p. 8.
9. For an excellent analysis of economic populism in Latin America, see R. Dornbusch and S. Edwards (eds), *The Macroeconomics of Populism in Latin America*.
10. M. Coniff, *Latin American Populism in Comparative Perspective* (Albuquerque, New Mexico: University of New Mexico Press, 1982), p. 5.
11. For a review of Latin America's severe macroeconomic situation and foreign debt crisis, see J. Hartlyn and S. Morley (eds), *Latin American Political Economy: Financial Crisis and Political Change* (Boulder, Col.: Westview Press, 1986).
12. B. Stallings, 'International Influence on Economic Policy: Debt, Stabilization and Structural Reform', in S. Haggard and R. Kaufman (eds), *The Politics of Economic Adjustment* (Princeton, NJ: Princeton University Press, 1992), pp. 41–87.
13. For a description and defence of the Consensus see its two most important proponents: J. Williamson, *The Progress of Policy Reform in Latin America* (Washington, DC: Institute of International Economics, 1990), and J. Sachs, *New Approaches to the Latin American Debt Crisis;* (Princeton, NJ: Princeton University Essays in International Finance no. 174, 1989).
14. J. Sachs, 'Life in the Economic Emergency Room', in J. Williamson (ed.), *The Political Economy of Policy Reform* (Washington, DC: Institute of International Economics, 1994), pp. 501–24.
15. For a discussion of the nature and consequences of heterodox policies, see W. C. Smith, 'Heterodox Shocks and the Political Economy of Democratic Transitions in Argentina and Brazil', in W. Canak (ed.), *Lost Promises: Debt, Austerity and Development in Latin America* (Boulder, Col.: Westview Press, 1989), pp. 138–68.
16. Inter-American Development Bank (IDB), *Economic and Social Progress in Latin America: 1995 Report* (Washington, DC: Johns Hopkins University Press, 1995), p. 9.
17. D. Schrieberg, 'Dateline Latin America: The Growing Fury', *Foreign Policy*, vol. 106, Spring (1997), p. 168.
18. O. Altimir, 'Economic Development and Social Equity: A Latin American Perspective', *Journal of Interamerican Studies and World Affairs* vol. 28, no. 2/3, Summer/Fall (1996), p. 53.
19. M. R. Agosin (ed.), *Foreign Direct Investment in Latin America* (Baltimore, Md: Johns Hopkins University Press, 1996).

20. R. Hausmann and L. Rojas-Suarez (eds), *Volatile Capital Flows: Consequences for Latin American Economic Reform* (Baltimore, Md: Johns Hopkins University Press, 1996).
21. O. Altimir, 'Income Distribution and Poverty through Crisis and Adjustment', *CEPAL Review*, no. 52, April (1994), pp. 7–31.
22. L.-F. Jimenez and N. Ruedi, *Rasgos Estilizados de la Distribucion del Ingreso y de sus Determinantes en Algunos Paises de la Region* (Santiago, Chile: Comision Economica para America Latina y el Caribe, 1997).
23. For a review of this continuing problem and its implications for income distribution, see W. C. Thiesenhusen, *Broken Promises: Agrarian Reform and the Latin American Campesino* (Boulder, Col.: Westview Press, 1995).
24. For a review of the increase in poverty and income inequality during this period, see Comision Economica para America Latina (CEPAL) *El Perfil de la Probreza en America Latina a Comienzos de los Anos 90* (Santiago, Chile: CEPAL, 1992).
25. For a review of the negative social outcomes of orthodoxy, see J. Sheahan, *Patterns of Development in Latin America* (Princeton, NJ: Princeton University Press, 1987).
26. See, for example, P. Cook and C. Kirkpatrick, *The Distributional Impact of Privatization in Developing Countries: Who Gets What and Why?* (Development and Project Planning Centre, University of Bradford, 1994).
27. D. Winkler, *Educational Expenditures and Reform in Latin America* (Washington, DC: World Bank, 1994).
28. P. Oxhorn and P. Starr (eds), *The Political Limits to Economic Reform: Economic Change and Democratic Consolidation in Latin America* (Boulder, Col.: Lynne Rienner, 1997).
29. Comision Economica para America Latina (CEPAL), *Panorama Social de America Latina: Edicion 1993* (Santiago, Chile: CEPAL, 1993), p. 100.
30. A. D. Kincaid and E. A. Gamarra, 'Disorderly Democracy: Redefining Public Security in Latin America', in R. P. Korzeniewicz and W. C. Smith (eds), *Latin America in the World Economy* (New York: Praeger, 1996), pp. 211–28.
31. A. Berry, 'The Income Distribution Threat in Latin America', *Latin American Research Review*, vol. 32, no. 2 (1997), pp. 3–40.
32. In describing the 'social disaster' caused by economic neo-liberalism, some have suggested a return to 'a Latin American New Deal that would give equal weight to economic growth and social equity'. See D. Green, *Silent Revolution: The Rise of Market Economics in Latin America* (London: Cassell, 1995).
33. The Argentine Catholic Church recently emphasised that corruption and impunity, set against a backdrop of increasing poverty, are feeding the 'temptation of violence – a result of discouragement and social despair', in 'Church and IMF Provide Contrasting Views of Unrest in Argentina', *Latin American Weekly Report*, 27 May (1994), p. 241.

34. F. Rosen and D. McFadyen (eds), *Free Trade and Economic Restructuring in Latin America* (New York: Monthly Review Press, 1995), p. 5.
35. M. Naim, 'Latin America: The Second Stage of Reform', L. Diamond and M. Plattner (eds), *Economic Reform and Democracy* (Baltimore, Md: Johns Hopkins University Press, 1995), p. 29.
36. V. Tokman (ed.), *Beyond Regulation: The Informal Economy in Latin America* (Boulder, Col.: Lynne Rienner, 1993).
37. S. Halebsky and R. L. Harris, *Capital, Power and Inequality in Latin America* (Boulder, Col.: Westview Press, 1995), p. 3.
38. S. Edwards and A. Edwards, *Monetarism and Liberalisation: The Chilean Experiment* (Cambridge, Mass.: Ballinger, 1987), pp. 213–16.
39. D. North, *Institutions, Institutional Change, and Economic Performance* (Cambridge University Press, 1990).
40. J. Knight, *Institutions and Social Conflict* (Cambridge: Cambridge University Press, 1992).
41. L. Manzetti, 'Economic Reform and Corruption in Latin America', *North–South Issues*, vol. 3, no. 1 (1994).
42. For a review of the social costs of reform and the need for a stronger institutional base, see, C. Mesa-Lago, *Changing Social Security in Latin America: Toward Alleviating the Social Costs of Economic Reform* (Boulder, Col.: Lynne Rienner, 1994).
43. W. Glade, 'Institutions and Inequality in Latin America: Text and Subtext', *Journal of Interamerican Studies and World Affairs*, vol. 28, no. 2/3, Summer/Fall (1996), pp. 159–79
44. S. Berensztein, 'Rebuilding State Capacity in Contemporary Latin America: The Politics of Taxation in Argentina and Mexico', in R. P. Korzeniewicz and W. C. Smith (eds), *Latin America in the World Economy*, pp. 229–48.
45. For a discussion of the decline in the quality of, and expenditure on, infrastructure, see World Bank, *Meeting the Infrastructure Challenge in Latin America and the Caribbean* (Washington, DC: World Bank, 1995).
46. E. Cardoso, 'Private Investment in Latin America', *Economic Development and Cultural Change*, no. 41 (1993), pp. 849–64.
47. J. M. Nelson, 'Poverty, Equity and the Politics of Adjustment' in S. Haggard and R. Kaufman (eds), *The Politics of Economic Adjustment*, pp. 231–63.
48. A. Cukierman, *Central Bank Strategy, Credibility, and Independence* (Cambridge, Mass.: MIT Press, 1992).
49. See 'Slow Judicial Reform', in *Latin American Weekly Report*, 22 April (1997).
50. R. Hausmann and L. Rojas-Suarez (eds), *Volatile Capital Flows*.
51. S. Haggard and R. Kaufman, *The Political Economy of Democratic Transitions* (Princeton, NJ: Princeton University Press, 1995).
52. S. Mainwaring, G. O'Donnell, and J. S. Valenzuela (eds), *Issues in Democratic Consolidation: The New South American Democracies in Comparative Perspective* (Notre Dame, Ind.: University of Notre Dame Press, 1992); and L. Diamond, 'Democracy in Latin America: Degrees, Illusions, and Directions for Consolidation', in T. Farer (ed.), *Beyond*

Sovereignty: Collectively Defending Democracy in the Americas (Baltimore, Md: Johns Hopkins University Press, 1996), p. 54.

53. P. Evans, 'The State as Problem and Solution: Predation, Embedded Autonomy and Structural Change', in S. Haggard and R. Kaufman (eds), *The Politics of Economic Adjustment*, pp. 139–81.
54. L. Diamond, 'Democracy in Latin America', p. 78.
55. J. Hartlyn and S. Morley (eds), *Latin-American Political Economy*.
56. J. Nelson (ed.), *Economic Crisis and Policy Choice*, Recent evidence suggests no correlation between economic reform and degree of political liberalism; see R. Bates and A. Krueger, *Political and Economic Interactions in Economic Policy Reform* (Oxford: Basil Blackwell, 1993).
57. C. Acuna and W. C. Smith, 'The Political Economy of Structural Adjustment: The Logic of Support and Opposition to Neoliberal Reform', in W. C. Smith, C. Acuna and E. Gamarra (eds), *Latin American Political Economy in the Age of Neoliberal Reform* (Coral Gables, New York: North–South Center, 1994), pp. 17–66.
58. S. Haggard and R. Kaufman (eds), *The Politics of Economic Adjustments*.
59. G. O'Donnell, 'Delegative Democracy', *Journal of Democracy*, vol. 5, January (1994), pp. 55–69. The term *decretismo* is taken from L.-C. Bresser Pereira, J-M. Maravall and A. Przeworksi, *Economic Reforms in New Democracies: A Social-Democratic Approach* (New York: Cambridge University Press, 1993), p. 208.
60. G. O'Donnell, 'The State, Democratization and Some Conceptual Problems', in W. C. Smith, C. Acuna and E. Gamarra, *Latin American Political Economy*, pp. 157–80.
61. For a discussion of the need for political strategies in building a broader institutional framework, see L.-C. Bresser Pereira, J.-M. Maravall and A. Przeworksi, *Economic Reforms in New Democracies*.
62. L. Diamond, *'Democracy in Latin America'*, p. 94.
63. Williamson's comments on the need for targeted social expenditures were taken from D. Schrieberg, 'Dateline Latin America', p. 173.

10 Southeast Asia in the Twenty-First Century: Human Security and Regional Development
Fahimul Quadir and Timothy M. Shaw

In the post-bipolar period, the notion of 'human security' captures the growing range of 'new' security threats and responses, both state and non-state. We explore the relevance of this concept to understanding and containing the proliferating set of strategic challenges in contemporary Southeast Asia, a region of high growth and resilient states. Such a reconception of security has relevance for several fields of analysis, from development studies to international political economy, especially 'new' regionalisms/multilateralisms and governance, both local and global. However, it has to be set within current contexts of 'new' international divisions of labour (NIDL) and power (NIDP), characterised by the continuing hegemony of neo-liberalism.

Indeed, any plausible explanation of security, development and foreign did policies in the late 1990s has to begin by recognising and evaluating transformations in the global political economy (and political culture), especially in the Third World. These are now largely a function of a trio of mega-trends in the NIDL and NIDP:

1. *Transformed states, especially state-economy/society relations*, after more than a decade marked by the hegemony of neo-liberalism in ideology and practice, with profound implications for civil societies, class forces, gender relations, ethnic and religious identities.[1]
2. *Transformed capitalisms*, now centred around the Pacific as well as the Atlantic rim, including novel features such as flexibilisation, feminisation, growth of service sectors, post-Fordism[2] and so on.
3. *Transformed strategic context*, from bipolar interstate nuclear stalemate to multiple 'new security' threats, such as drugs, crime,

ecology, migration, proliferation, smuggling, fundamentalisms, and disease.³

In particular, at the global level, any situating of the Third World has to take into account the following sets of novel factors:

1. *New states*, from the regions of the Baltic, and Turkic states in the former Soviet Union (FSU) and Yugoslavia, to Eritrea and Somalia.
2. *New relations*, particularly globalisation, regionalisation, transnationalisation (such as private corporations and civil societies), and differentiation, especially between and within states.
3. *New institutions*, including the diversity of intergovernmental (for example G7, G15, G24 and G77), transnational and regional organisations, along with semi-official (such as 'track two' arrangements).⁴
4. *New issues* from environment, gender and informal sectors to crime, democracy, drugs, emergencies, feminisation, flexibilisation, global warming, migration, oceans management, ozone-depletion, viruses and so on.
5. *New approaches* at the levels of both analysis and praxis, which stretch all the way from resilient neo-classicalism to unsettling post-modernism.⁵

Thus far, the orthodox post-bipolar and triumphalist literatures have displayed greater confidence over their perspectives on strategic (especially their new focus on peace-making and confidence-building measures (CBMs)) than economic relations. In part, this may just reflect the position of nuclear hegemony which the USA occupies in the current unipolar moment. By contrast, its economic dominance is clearly problematical. US economic (especially financial and technological) supremacy is challenged increasingly by Germany (notwithstanding the difficulties and expenses of digesting the old East) and Japan (despite its own structural crisis). These states represent the new *First World*.

The rest of the old First is now the *Second World* (most of the EU and Australasia). Meanwhile, the content of the *Third World* is no longer all the G77, but rather the Asian tigers and cubs, large Latin economies, China and India, plus the more industrialised parts of Eastern Europe.⁶ The *Fourth World* of less developed countries (LDCs) now includes the six Southern Turkic states of the FSU and the poorer, still-fragmenting ex-Eastern European countries in the Balkans. And the *Fifth World* of least developed countries (LLDCs) is a growing group as crises and contingencies impact and the downwardly-mobile seek the 'privilege' of access to International Development Association (IDA) funds.[7]

While the voices of these emerging worlds remain tentative,[8] the location of international capital, communication, consumption, innovation and production, quite apart from accumulation, is apparent; in China rather than Chad, Singapore rather than Somalia. Clearly there is a *regional dimension* to any conceivable hierarchy, with Southeast Asia the most expansive and Africa the most vulnerable of the Southern (former Third World) regions.[9] This divergence is perhaps most tellingly captured by the expansion of the middle classes in the Third World and contraction in the rest. The presence or absence of such a vibrant petty bourgeoisie is crucial for political stability as well as economic vitality.[10]

This conceptual, overview chapter is structured as follows. First, we offer an introduction to relevant definitions and debates about 'security' in the contemporary period and, second, an examination of alternative formulations about security, both formal and informal, economic, political and strategic. Third, we focus particularly on the emerging nexus between burgeoning civil society and a resilient military while, fourth, also concentrating on the central place of ocean issues for the region. We conclude by highlighting a set of future scenarios and options with policy relevance in the remainder of the century for both Southeast Asian state and non-state interests alike.

LINKING SECURITY AND DEVELOPMENT: TAKING THE AGENDA BEYOND WEAPONS AND EXTERNAL THREATS

Until recently, the study of national security was largely dominated by the 'realist' paradigm, where states are viewed as the key actors in international relations. With the absence of any authority to enforce agreements among states, each individual state confronts a 'self-help' situation, where it is responsible for the maintenance of its geographical sovereignty. In other words, the pursuit of 'national interests' becomes the single most important issue in the anarchic structure of the international system. The immediate aim of all nation-states is to maximise their (military) power[11] in order to protect territorial sovereignty. In the realist perspective, national security, is therefore perceived in terms of territorial sovereignty from external threats. According to Harold Brown, national security refers to 'the ability to preserve the nation's physical integrity and territory; to maintain its economic relations with the rest of the world on reasonable terms; to protect its nature, institutions and governance from disruption from outside; and to control its borders'.[12] Threats to national security come primarily from other states, and the absence of mutual trust in the anarchic international system prompts heavy reliance on military power.[13] Each state pursues its own courses of action in order to strengthen its relative power position.

Such an understanding of national security not only accelerated the arms race but also triggered interstate conflicts at both regional and international levels. With the end of the Cold War, however, it is increasingly becoming apparent that the realist conception of national security provides a false image of reality as it fails to capture the non-military and internal dimensions of national security.[14] Although a few authors from the Third World have consistently challenged the validity of such notions of security, it was not until the end of the bipolar rivalry that attacks on the orthodox notions of security have truly drawn the attention of mainstream authors. Identifying the 'need' to broaden the agenda of security studies, a number of authors – notably Barry Buzan, Mohammed Ayoob, Richard Ullman and Caroline Thomas – have made a series of attempts to emphasise the fact that insecurity stems from both internal and external sources.

In the case of the Third World, internal non-state as well as state threats are just as important as external threats, if not more so. In much of the Third World, the very existence of national sovereignty has been threatened by the failure of nation-building processes.[15] Sources of insecurity are inadequate provision of basic human needs, a widening gap between rich and poor, and the consequent crisis of government legitimacy. Third-World states rarely represent one single nation within the political boundary of the state; most countries are divided along the lines of ethnicity, religion and class. The state is not seen as the expression of the society as a whole, making it almost impossible to equate individual security with national and/or regime security.[16]

Internal fragility, then, rather than external threat, poses a considerable challenge to the national security of most Third-World states. Kamel Abu-Jaber provides an excellent description of how internal sources of insecurity have threatened the national security of many Arab countries. Internally, regime and national insecurity often emanate, not from the military branch, but from the demands for change, for participation and political liberalisation, as well as from the demands for development.[17] If such non-military and internal threats to national security largely remained hidden during the Cold War, following the end of the bipolar rivalry, the imperative in redefining national security has gained unprecedented attention. A number of authors have begun to demonstrate the importance of broadening the agenda of security studies in the post-Cold War era,[18] reflecting both the need to find new tools of analysis and the inherent attractiveness of this 'new' concept to accommodate more nuanced approaches.

Whereas the aim of previous terms and academic endeavours have the same goal as the newly broadened definition of security, the latter builds upon a longer tradition of seemingly more systematic and concrete analysis, connecting security with a number of development-related concerns. This new approach promises a more encompassing, analytically rigorous and compelling approach to issues that require global attention if they are to be managed successfully. In particular, this approach makes efforts to outline the indisputable links between security and development, thus making 'new' security studies one of the most complementary and promising new approaches to the challenges facing humankind at the turn of the century.

The emerging literature began to identify the sources of insecurity from a broader developmental perspective. Instead of looking at threats to territorial sovereignty, it focuses on a variety of development related issues such as population, environment, gender, human rights and participation. Challenging the assumption that national or state security translates into security for people living *in* the state, the literature identifies the state and/or the regime in power as a source of threat to security of individuals and/or sustainable democratic development. The Palme and Brandt Commission Reports in the early 1980s, the first official reports that identify the linkage between security and development, underscore the need to work towards *common security* that rests on a commitment to joint survival, and a programme for arms control and disarmament as well as transformation of the international system to make it capable of peaceful and orderly change, suitable for trade and travel, and conducive to the intercultural exchange of ideas and experience.[19] This was language fundamentally different from the excessively military idiom that had been articulated in the mid-1960s. The Brandt Report emphasised the interdependent nature of the global economy and the necessity of taking drastic action to avert a breakdown in the international system. More particularly, Brandt underlined the significance of the state as a purposive intervener for development.

However, it was not until the end of the Cold War that attempts to redefine security drew widespread attention from scholars, policy-makers and development activists. With the sudden realisation that non-military threats to security are as important as military threats, the realist perspective has virtually lost its analytical ability to explain the changing dynamics of both international and national security, giving rise to the literature that broadens the agenda of security studies. Taking the agenda beyond military threats, it examines a variety of non-military sources of insecurity, such as poverty, disease, environmental degradation, migration, drugs, and authoritarianism within and between nations that appear to have endangered the future of democratic development in many parts of the world. In his Plenary Address to the British International Studies Association in 1990, for example, Ken Booth defined it as emancipation:

'Security' means the absence of threats. Emancipation is the freeing of people (as individuals and groups) from those physical and human constraints which stop them carrying out what they freely chose to do. War and the threat of war is one of those constraints together with poverty, poor education, political oppression and so on. Security and emancipation are two sides of the same coin. Emancipation, *not power or order*, produces true security. Emancipation, theoretically, is security.[20]

Drawing upon similar arguments, attempts are made to shift the focus of security from traditional geo-military to human and global security. Such efforts are reflected in the coinage of new terms/ ideas, notably *comprehensive security, cooperative security, human security and global human security*. Comprehensive security, for example, refers to the process of forming a regional non-military alliance, or alliances, in order to promote mutual co-operation among the people of a region. The term is designed to broaden the scope for traditional CBMs in regions by managing common security problems collectively.[21] Also, it underscores the need to undertake collective measures for advancing the goals of disarmament and demilitarisation.

However, what changes the orthodox definitions of security dramatically is the concept known as 'human security'. Identifying the threats that are more or less common to all people, human security seeks to protect and promote the interests of ordinary citizens. Unlike the traditional concern of national security, it is only interested in the security of people through human development. Given recent changes in the global political economy, it suggests that conflicts within nations are the primary sources of insecurity for most people. Human security therefore refers to a process of protecting people from, as outlined in the *Human Development Report*, 'the threat of disease, hunger, unemployment, crime, social conflict, political repression and environmental hazards'.[22] The report identifies seven major threats to human security: economic, food, health, environmental, personal, community and political.

While many of these threats arise from internal sources, they are appearing as global challenges to human security, creating common concerns for security and development that are almost impossible to manage effectively by one single nation or actor. The emphasis is therefore placed on collective actions to ensure security of people. The concept of 'global human security' recognises that the international community has an obligation to take action against the threats to human security. Also, it calls for the building of a 'new human world order'[23] based on the ideals of justice, equality and democracy. It seeks to promote a new development partnership between North and South, and it relies heavily upon a global civil society for the advancement of popular interests. According to Mahbub ul-Haq, architect of the concepts of human development and human security, 'Future changes will not depend exclusively on governments. Instead, they will come primarily from the actions of people at the grassroots – people who will hold their leaders increasingly accountable for all their actions'.[24] This has represented no more than an introduction to an increasingly sophisticated and complex debate linking security and development. Our primary aim is to set this debate in the context of Southeast Asia as it reaches the new millennium.

NON-TRADITIONAL SOURCES OF INSECURITY IN SOUTHEAST ASIA

Much of the writing on the security of Southeast Asia is predominantly orthodox in nature, primarily concerned with military power, the prospect of war in the region and the role of great powers in maintaining the balance of power. Unlike many other parts of the world, the end of the Cold War and the collapse of communism have hardly affected the concerns over military issues as the security matrix of the region remains largely unchanged. The region is still regarded as one of the most volatile in terms of interstate rivalry, arms races and potential wars.

Most significantly, many states in this region are concerned with China's increasing military and economic strength and feel it is unlikely that the country would adopt a conciliatory approach to regional security in the near future. Tension has remained high recently over both Taiwan and Hong Kong. North Korea also represents a threat to stability in Southeast Asia, particularly in the context of its efforts to acquire nuclear weapons, and has refused, despite tremendous international pressure, to sign the Nuclear Non-Proliferation Treaty.[25]

Accordingly, military issues have dominated debates over Southeast Asia's security and limited focus on the non-military and internal dimensions of security. However, things have begun to change, albeit slowly, with the emergence of civil society groups across the region. The traditional approach to security is gradually losing its hegemony and is yielding to an environment in which non-traditional and non-military issues are considered to be equally important. The following section attempts to identify the region's major sources of non-traditional insecurity.

Conflicts Between Growth and Development

Since around the late 1960s, Southeast Asian states have focused on outward-looking economic policies designed to achieve higher levels of growth. The amazing success of these macroeconomic policies has been reflected in the total transformation of the economies of South Korea, Taiwan, Singapore, Indonesia and Malaysia. The success is so astonishing that the World Bank regards it as a 'miracle' and is currently involved in replicating the model elsewhere.[26] However, a closer look at the model reveals that the rural

poor and other marginalised groups have paid a high price for the
so-called miracle. Benefits of growth have been spread very un-
equally. Southeast Asian economic policies have always been directed towards the people with financial and monetary resources,
assuming that the involvement of such wealthy people in export-
orientated industrialisation programmes would eventually benefit
the society as a whole via 'trickle-down'. In reality, the process of
economic growth has fostered the geometric expansion of a group
of financial and economic elites at the expense of the poor.

A bias against agriculture has had a negative effect on the lives
of the vast majority who still depend on agricultural production
for their living. The percentage of people engaged in agriculture
varies between 34 per cent (in Malaysia) and 66 per cent (in Thailand).[27] Many of the people either own no agricultural land or have
inadequate land to support their families. A sense of hopelessness
is rising as these people become increasingly aware of the fact that
the state is simply is not on their side in their struggles for survival. In sum, what we have experienced in Southeast Asia is sectoral
growth that has benefited certain sectors, a few countries and a
distinct group of financial and economic elites instead of benefiting the entire region. Even this selective miracle is now under threat,
as Southeast Asia has begun to experience economic downturns
and the future of economic growth does not appear to be as certain as it was. Part of the reason is the diminishing demand for
export goods in North America and Europe.

The problem is aggravated further by sharp and sudden increases
in current account deficits. Countries such as Indonesia, Malaysia
and Thailand are running alarming current-account deficits. In 1996,
the rates of these deficits varied between 4 and 10 per cent of
GDP. In an effort to reduce the deficits, a number of countries,
including Malaysia, South Korea and Thailand, have announced
measures to control imports, especially of luxury goods. The region's economy has also been badly affected by a continued rise in
the US dollar, endangering the competitive status of many Asian
economies. While most Southeast Asian states are committed to
keeping their exchange rates low to help their export sector grow,
massive inflows of foreign capital have caused inflation and, more
importantly, have accelerated investments that are basically imprud-
ent.[28] Unless the region finds another 'miracle' to grapple with these
complex issues, it may be extremely difficult for Southeast Asia to
avoid a real economic crisis.

Environmental Threats to the Region's Security and Development

Until recently, the region's preoccupation with economic growth focused only on those macroeconomic policies driven by the goals of 'maximising growth'. Such 'growth-only' policies have consistently encouraged both the state and the private sector to engage in an aggressive capital generation process which has, in effect, overlooked the importance of integrating more sustainable environmental and developmental objectives. The absence of environmental awareness among policy-makers has let profit-seeking entrepreneurs over-exploit natural resources. Accordingly, the so-called 'developmental states' in Southeast Asia have allowed environmental degradation to occur as part of their development strategies. The region is now in danger of environmental catastrophe, as excessive focus on growth has destroyed the region's ecological balance.

Major environmental problems facing Southeast Asia include deforestation, soil erosion, industrial pollution, urbanisation, water pollution, destruction of wildlife, oil spills and coastal degradation.[29] Annual rates of deforestation are high; between 1981 and 1990, the region lost more than three million hectares of tropical forest.[30] Unplanned commercial logging, both legal and illegal, has primarily been responsible. The implementation of the Green Revolution strategy has had a negative impact on ecosystems through the use of toxic chemicals, fertilisers and pesticides, all extremely harmful to human and other species. Pollution of rivers and coastal areas by industries, particularly textile factories, is threatening the region's water and making navigation extremely difficult. Most large-scale industries in the region are located in coastal areas and are the major sources of marine pollution as industrial plants discharge huge amount of waste into the sea; the Indonesian province of East Java discharges 129 700 tons of organic waste per year.[31]

The AIDS Epidemic: a New Sense of Insecurity

AIDS is spreading faster in the region than anywhere else in the world,[32] forcing many countries and communities to change their traditional priorities. By one estimate, about 3.5 million people in Asia are already infected with the HIV virus. The number will stand at over 10 million by the year 2000. In Thailand, the centre of the so-called sex industry, some 750 000 people are reported to be

infected with HIV.[33] If the present trend continues, it is estimated
that another 1.5 million people will be carrying the virus by the
turn of the century.[34] The epidemic is spreading even more rapidly
in countries such as Cambodia, Myanmar, Vietnam, China (southern and eastern) and Malaysia where the 'sex trade' is booming.[35]
Estimates may be conservative; a variety of socioeconomic factors
such as religious conservatism, lack of awareness about the disease
on the part of ordinary citizens, and the fear of losing jobs prevent
many men and women from admitting that they are infected with
HIV. Furthermore, it is hard to rely on government statistics as
they often mask the real figures in order to protect the ever-growing
tourism industry in the region; it was not until the late 1980s that
public officials began even to acknowledge the emergence of the
AIDS crisis in Southeast Asia.[36]

AIDS has serious economic implications. Direct economic loss,
however, is just part of the story, with potentially devastating long-
term effects acting as a multiplier of short-term losses. Severe short-
ages of labour and an influx of foreign workers may also bring its
own problems.

Drugs: A Challenge for Regional Stability

Another major security concern of the region is the ever-growing
problem of production, consumption and trafficking of narcotics.
Since the beginning of the 1960s drugs have represented a mount-
ing problem. Growing demand for narcotics in the informal global
market has seen the production of opium and high quality heroin
more than double between 1987 and 1990 in the Golden Triangle
that includes countries such as Myanmar, Thailand, Cambodia and
Vietnam.[37] Other countries in the region have witnessed a slow
but steady growth in drug consumption domestically. It is, however, worthwhile to mention that while the consumption of drugs
by local consumers has been increasing at an alarming rate, narcotics are grown primarily for export to the USA and Western
Europe, where both the price and demand for quality drugs is high.[38]

The production, consumption and trade of drugs in Southeast
Asia is a developmental problem. In most cases, growers have been
the victims of the existing sociopolitical system which continues to
frustrate legitimate socioeconomic hopes: 'Growers have become
involved in narcotics cropping because they face a set of circumstances that has blocked their chances of finding a more secure

place in their national societies – or even of surviving.'[39] In Myanmar, Laos, Pakistan and Thailand, narcotics growers are mainly ethnic minorities, excluded from the formal systems of governance and development. By directing nation-building programmes towards the promotion of monoculture, most countries in the region have literally forced ethnic minorities to give up their distinctiveness and, more importantly, have compelled them to find alternative livelihoods.

Piracy: A Threat to the Region's Economic Future

The Asian 'miracle' not only attracts foreign investors but also invites pirates to its waters. One study notes that about 76 per cent of the world's total piracy recorded in 1994 occurred in East Asia. An International Maritime Bureau report identifies three major types of piracy taking place in Southeast Asia. Robbery is the primary motive of pirates in most cases. Locally-based pirates, many of them fishermen and small traders, often attack ships with their simple weapons to rob the crew. Once the crime is committed, the pirates rapidly disappear without doing any physical damage to the vessel. In these cases, the average loss is about US$7000. In other instances, using lethal weapons and modern techniques, organised criminals steal the cargo, causing losses of several million dollars. In the third category, the pirates steal the entire ship, change its name and re-register it for semi-commercial use.[40] This type of piracy is believed to be done by a group of highly organised criminals with professional military backgrounds and/or experience.

While such activity presents a substantial threat to the economic stability of the entire region, very little has so far been done to control piracy. Nations affected by rising piracy are not equipped to deal with the problem. The long coastlines of the littoral and archipelagic states demand resource-intensive surveillance efforts beyond the ability of any single nation. The problem is compounded by the overlapping and complex boundaries of the region. Thus, in order for Southeast Asia to deal effectively with the problem, the region needs to devise an integrated approach involving all the nations. Obviously, this will require that the member states arrive at a consensus on the question of sharing the cost and benefit of effective enforcement, which is undoubtedly a complex political task.

Summary

Clearly, Southeast Asia faces a broadened and complex security agenda. How these problems will be dealt with by the region may be determined in large part by how civil society relates to the military, who have long occupied a dominant position within the state. It is to this relationship, entering a period of dynamism and change, that our attention now turns.

CIVIL SOCIETIES, AUTHORITARIANISM AND THE MILITARY

Notwithstanding the overt and covert roles of orthodox and non-traditional military agencies in the Third World in recent decades, relatively little attention has been paid, even within contemporary democratisation discourses, to their relations with more formal multi-party or less formal civil society organisations. Although many liberalisation negotiations now include formal caps on military expenditure and personnel, praetorian pressures continue. Indeed, given the continued primacy of the state in Southeast Asia's political economies by contrast to its relative decline elsewhere, the place of the military is central almost everywhere for regime security. This tends to bring it into confrontation with burgeoning elements of civil society. Yet, if formal parties and national institutions, along with international organisations, cannot constrain the soldiers, why should modest, pacific, heterogeneous elements within national or global civil society?

Southeast Asia: Civil–Military Relations and the Prospect for Democratisation

Responding to both the current 'global democratic revolution'[41] and the internal demand and aspiration for democracy, Southeast Asian states have begun to move away from their authoritarian past. Since the 1970s, this region, like others, has witnessed a slow but steady movement towards democratic transition. After exerting authoritarian control over society for about half a century, hitherto repressive regimes have started to introduce some kind of political liberalisation designed to widen the scope of political participation in decision-making. However, such transitions from authoritarian-

ism have, despite widespread optimism, hardly created the much
needed political environment under which civilian authority could
exercise its control over the military and the 'formulation of national security policy.'[42] In other words, the current global and regional process of democratisation has rarely changed the established
pattern of praetorian civil–military relations in Southeast Asia.[43]
Similarly, the region's movement towards the creation of a system
of democratic governance has not really brought any noticeable
changes in what is called 'Asian modes of paternalistic authority'.[44]

Like many other developing nations, most, if not all, Southeast
Asian countries saw the ascendancy of the military over civilians in
the 1950s and 1960s. Claiming that the former would do better in
protecting national sovereignty, promoting stability and order and
achieving targeted economic growth, the military seized power and
emerged as an assertive political institution in countries such as
Indonesia, the Philippines, South Korea, Thailand and Taiwan.
Following ascension to power, the armed forces deliberately undermined the nation- and state-building potential of civilian political institutions and, more significantly, constructed political coalitions
with bureaucratic elites and the business community. Southeast Asia
therefore experienced the emergence of what Harold Laswell called
the 'garrison state', meaning the advent of the military regimes as
the dominant actors in decision-making.[45]

Within a short span of time, the authoritarian state expanded its
hegemony beyond national security and began to establish effective control over politics, economy and society. In most cases, especially Singapore, South Korea and Taiwan, the civil–military
bureaucratic oligarchy became interwoven with the national economy
and favoured a small group of entrepreneurs who were primarily
involved in export-orientated economic and financial activity.[46] The
authoritarian state actively controlled the mobilisation of different
sociopolitical forces including political parties, trade unions, peasant
organisations and professional associations, many of which appeared
to be a threat to the domination of civil–military bureaucratic elites.[47]

Thus much of Southeast Asia experienced highly confrontational
civil–military relations after independence. As in Latin America,[48]
neither the military nor the civilian leaders of the region trusted
each other, each blaming the other for the collapse of democratic
institutions. The sharp division between military and civilian leaders widened because they disagreed on almost all fundamental issues, such as what constituted a threat to national security, how to

maintain political stability as well as social order, what should be the focus of macroeconomic policies, and whether or not the military would be allowed to play a role in politics.

Continued Struggles Over Redefining Roles for the Military

Given the distinctive contemporary political history of Southeast Asia, it is obvious that the success of democratic consolidation in the region will depend primarily on the ability of the relevant political forces to transcend such conflicting civil–military relations. Crucial to such a process of democratisation is the development of a consensus among the key actors in political society about the importance of limiting the role of the military in politics. The task involves firm action on the part of the pro-democratic political forces to set up political institutions that would ensure civilian control over the military. In other words, a transition towards democracy requires the identification of new and compatible roles for both the military and civilian leaders in any transformed political system. In doing so, given the complex nature of the problem, it is important to include the military in the negotiation process that would eventually promote mutual trust and co-operation between these two contending forces.

Unfortunately, recent transitions towards democracy have rarely succeeded in eliminating the hegemonic control of the armed forces over politics, economy and national security in the region. Countries that have undergone political changes, if not transformations, are still struggling with defining new roles for the military. As with Latin-American experiences,[49] although the military have formally accepted their institutional subordination to civilian political institutions, they have not yet given up their 'veto' power over the whole democratisation process in Southeast Asia. In the Philippines, for example, the successive regimes of Corazon Aquino and Fidel Ramos have found it difficult to reduce the power and influence of the armed forces over the decision-making arena. In order to avoid a direct confrontation with the highly politicised military,[50] both regimes have carefully avoided the adoption of any reform programme designed to dismantle its 'veto' power.[51]

South Korean democratic experiments have also encountered a similar predicament. The assumption of power by democratic regimes and the promulgation of a new constitution have not led to the construction of co-operative civil–military relations in the country.[52] In Thailand, the military still remains the key political actor in decision-making, despite the fact that the armed forces maintained a somewhat neutral role in the peaceful transfer of power from one civilian regime to another in 1995.[53] Similarly, the current wave of democratisation has failed to limit the power of the Indonesian armed forces; indeed, the command of the military in the country has remained almost unchanged since 1965, when General Suharto seized power and institutionalised the political role of the armed forces by creating a framework for governance that gave the military a clear overriding power in policy formation.[54]

Contrary to what the world has experienced since the 1970s, structural economic reforms have hardly challenged the traditional power and functions of the military in Southeast Asia. The conventional role of the armed forces as both protector and promoter of capitalism in the region partly explains why the restructuring of the economy has not yet hurt the military. In fact, the military has constituted an expression of capitalism in the region, playing a central role in providing physical law and order in favour of the rights of markets and private entrepreneurship. Political leaders have always relied upon the military to suppress popular movements for greater sociopolitical reforms.[55] In other words, the armed forces of this region have never appeared as a challenge to the expansion of national and global forces of production and finance. Most of the authoritarian or quasi-authoritarian regimes still need unequivocal support from the military to keep the growth-first development model alive in Southeast Asia.

What appears to be the real obstacle towards limiting the role of military is the political coalition of the armed forces with different civilian groups, including bureaucracy, big business and the emerging urban and rural middle classes.[56] In the process of what is often called 'regime consolidation', the military leaders went on to develop a new form of partnership with these key sociopolitical groups by offering them a wide range of financial and political benefits.[57] Needless to say, these groups now have a vested interest in the maintenance of a military-dominated coalition obstructing the ongoing process of democratisation in the region.

The future of democratisation will depend on the military's acceptance of a less direct social, rather than a political, role in the national decision-making process. As in many Western nations, the military needs to operate as a pressure group in the political system, pursuing its own institutional interest.[58] In particular, the military is expected to find its place within the realm of civil society. Given the history of militarism in the region, however, it is unlikely that the armed forces will encourage the establishment of a democratic political culture in which the military will simply become a part of a broader civil society.

Any attempt to depoliticise the armed forces might appear as a direct threat to the institutional interests of the military. It is likely that such depoliticisation efforts would dramatically cut down their historical role in national decision-making. This might also be translated into an attempt to deconstruct the traditional security agendas, meaning significant reductions in military expenditure. Although there is no reason to believe that the armed forces in Southeast Asia would give way to civilian political institutions, under twin pressure from the international financial community and pro-democratic forces they will find it increasingly difficult to hold the power to dictate to civilian institutions. What seems to be the only reasonable option for the military is to accept a key position within civil society.

It seems quite likely that military officers, both retired and in service, will operate as a distinct civil society group for the maintenance and promotion of their organisational interests. However, in terms of political ideology and social objectives, they share very little with other civil society associations involved in democratisation and development. More importantly, they might create obstacles towards the smooth operation of civil society associations in areas such as democratisation, development and empowerment. This was exactly the case in Thailand when the country went to the polls in July 1995. Thai police and bureaucrats did everything possible to discourage, if not prevent, civil society groups from playing a key role in the election campaign.[59]

SINGLE-PARTY DOMINANT STATE: THE LIMITS OF DEMOCRATISATION IN SOUTHEAST ASIA

Apart from military authoritarianism, the region also witnessed the growth of single-party dominant systems that fostered the logic of limited and/or controlled democracy. Countries such as Malaysia, Singapore and Taiwan (until very recently) adopted and successfully implemented quite similar political development strategies that encouraged the ruling party(ies)/coalitions to determine the rules of political competition. In the name of economic modernisation and political stability, the People's Action Party (PAP) of Singapore, the United Malays National Organisation (UMNO) of Malaysia, and the *Kuomintang* (KMT) of Taiwan have always insisted on the principles of limited opposition and discipline'. While these dominant parties have tolerated a certain amount of political opposition, their policies have largely aimed at co-opting the key sociopolitical groups, leading to the emergence of strong, quasi-authoritarian states. By making the civil bureaucracy an essential partner of the ruling coalitions, the state has become the key player in 'structuring politics and social life'[60] in these three countries, thus constraining the process of democratisation.

Emerging Civil Societies: Hopes for Human Security in the Next Millennium?

While the hegemonic role of the state in the region has impeded the growth of autonomous civil society associations, the ongoing processes of political democratisation and economic liberalisation have begun to create some political space for the operation of non-state actors. With something of a decline of the authoritarian state, a variety of civil society organisations including trade unions, professional associations, farmers' unions, women's associations and NGOs have started functioning at the grass-roots, national, regional and global levels.[61]

The NGO sector is growing fast in Thailand, where some 10 000 registered NGOs are engaged, to varying degrees, in promoting the ideals of democratic development. NGOs emerged as a direct challenge to military authoritarianism, which partly explains why the country has moved to a more democratic environment since the 1970s. In association with other civil society groups, the NGO sector has led the country's democratic movement, forcing the military to establish constitutional rule. The involvement of NGOs was critical in ousting the military-dominated government in 1992.[62] They have played an important role in mobilising popular support in favour of democracy in the last two general elections, making it crystal clear that they represent a force for democracy and development in the country.

NGOs and diverse civil society groups are increasingly becoming the agenda setters in other parts of the region and are becoming a genuine channel through which popular interests are both represented and expressed. However, they face political conditions that are less than favourable for their smooth operation. NGOs are only allowed to work within the existing laws and regulations set up by the government. Most of these laws are designed to control and restrict their operation. NGOs are required to obtain a legal status before they undertake any project; in particular, the existing laws demand that NGOs must be registered with the government and will operate within the parameters set up by the state. Even in Thailand, where the political environment is relatively relaxed, NGOs must be registered and monitored, and work within a tightly-controlled framework. The situation is much more unfavourable in countries such as Indonesia, Malaysia and Myanmar. NGOs are denied both organisational freedom and political autonomy. They have been compelled to work in co-operation with governments and are encouraged to maintain a non-political character. The fear of co-option by the state also prevents them from getting involved in projects that are politically sensitive. Many NGOs therefore prefer to remain indifferent to questions of political mobilisation which might give people an impression that NGOs are very much involved in reproducing state ideology.[63]

While such a complex political climate remains basically unchanged, a number of NGOs and civil society groups have begun to challenge regulatory laws and rules enacted by governments. Rejecting the policy of co-option, they are undertaking programmes that regard political changes as an essential part of development. For example, the Majelis Rakyat Indonesia, a recently formed coalition of thirty NGOs, has launched a massive political movement for restoring democratic rights to people in the country. Taking advantage of the government's decision to oust Megawati Sukarnoputri as the chairperson of the Indonesian Democratic Party, the NGO network began to lead the country's democratic movement by mobilising popular sentiment against the Suharto regime. The coalition claims to be an umbrella organisation that represents a variety of civil society groups including students, women, workers, journalists and human-rights-abuse victims. It hopes to create a momentum in the country's current struggle for sustainable democracy.[64]

Another fascinating example is South Korea, where emerging civil society groups have not only refused authoritarianism as an acceptable form of governance but have also forced the regime in power to liberalise the political system.[65] In a similar fashion, Taiwan's burgeoning civil society, which includes consumer groups, environmental organisations, professional associations, students unions, women's groups and an alliance of small farmers, compelled the nationalist regime to introduce a series of political liberalisation programmes.[66] Similarly, civil society groups exist in all sectors of Filipino society, ranging from church associations, peasant's unions and women's organisations to fishers' and workers' associations. In addition to challenging the state, these groups are actively involved in outlining alternative routes to democratic development. Following the restoration of democracy in the country, the focus of many of these organisations has shifted to forging issue-based coalitions, bringing together marginalised groups throughout the country.

Recent trends indicate the growing power of civil society to challenge the hegemonic control of the state over national decision-making. They have demonstrated their ability to both articulate and represent popular voices and interests. Their capacity to create political space for greater socioeconomic change is indeed very impressive. What is even more important to note is their interest in constructing collective frameworks for regional security and development. The Southeast Asia Sustainable Agriculture Network, for instance, is a regional NGO forum that brings together academics, NGOs and activists working for sustainable agriculture across the region. Established in 1988, the organisation is promoting agricultural policies that are 'people-oriented and environment friendly'. It facilitates a better understanding about the problems of agriculture facing the region through workshops, training and action research.[67] Similarly, the Council for Security Cooperation in the Asia Pacific (CSCAP), a recently formed regional forum that links up a number of private research organisations in ten countries, is making efforts to identify common threats to regional security.[68] Many of these networks are good examples of 'track two' unofficial diplomacy, ostensibly at the non-state level. Such trends illustrate the growing strength of non-state actors, particularly popular organisations, in much of the region.

SECURITY AND DEVELOPMENT: THE REGION'S OCEANS

Having contextualised our work in terms of the security debate and civil–military relations, we now look specifically at oceans. Southeast Asian communities are linked by regional oceans, which are increasingly recognised to be central to both sustainable development and human security. However, until recently, development, strategic issues and other discourses related to Southeast Asia's seas have occurred largely in isolation from each other. The region's oceans therefore constitute an ideal undiscovered area in which to juxtapose these parallel debates as economic growth and strategic tension have both come to pose profound threats to the sustainability of Southeast Asia's seas. The latter may also constitute non-central arenas for functional, environmental CBMs through which to contain antagonism and escalation among diverse regional actors and interests, including states.[69]

The region's oceans present a distinct subset of emerging issues around the nexus of sustainable development and human security that could lead either to ecological and strategic difficulties or towards relatively enlightened 'regimes':

1. Environmental challenges from fish stock depletion, mangrove destruction, industrial pollution, rain-forest elimination and associated run-offs, rapidly declining biodiversity and so on.
2. Disputes over the development and movement of increasingly salient energy resources, particularly oil and gas reserves.
3. Concern over increased volume of often dangerous, incompatible ocean cargoes, especially large oil and gas tankers and container ships, particularly in international straits such as Lombok, Makassar, Malakka, San Bernardino, Sunda and Sarroa.
4. Impacts on local, often marginal, coastal communities by the above contemporary intrusions, exacerbated by related activities of gangs, drug lords, informal sectors, refugees, migrant labourers, pirates and military barracks. These, in turn, may be aggravated by the new salience of ethnic, diasporic and religious connections around these oceans.
5. Jurisdictional disputes arising from implementation of the Law of the Sea, especially given the above issues of resources, usage, communities and so on, most notably in the South China Sea but also in the Gulf of Thailand and around the archipelagic claims of Indonesia, Philippines and Malaysia.
6. Arms races, particularly naval, from coastal patrol vessels and aircraft after independence, to jet fighters, ship- and plane-delivered missiles, small aircraft carriers, potentially submarines (at present belonging to extra-regional powers such as China and India) and so on.

Such trends point to the desirability of a mix of local, national and regional coastal zone management structures involving a variety of actors to ensure both sustainability and security into the twenty-first century. Already there are a variety of helpful, pragmatic 'two-track' mechanisms in place for such ocean management, but these need to be continually refined and reinforced, given the exponential development of threats. They could also be broadened and made more accountable/transparent to reflect emerging notions of good governance. Finally, they could reinforce concepts of new and more open regionalisms in Southeast Asia, reaching beyond mere inter-state, economic concerns towards developmental, environmental and common/human security issues incorporating a flexible, appropriate variety of actors, interests and forums.

CONCLUSIONS

Given the above reformulations of interrelated notions of development and human security what range of scenarios might be foreseen at the turn of the millennium? The following five are informed by a range of theoretical and empirical materials and derive logically from prevailing analytic perspectives. They are not mutually exclusive and might arise together or sequentially, given certain conditions:

1. The prevailing, official, optimistic preview of stability advanced by ASEAN and their extraregional supporters consists of the extrapolation of the NIC model; further growth along with regional co-operation and peaceful foreign relations founded on 'Asian' values/practices;
2. An idealistic 'green' or 'civil society' NGO dream of sustainable, democratic and ecological development in which growth is moderated in the interests of equity, ecology and peace; that is, human development/security.
3. A pessimistic precaution in which a variety of inequalities lead towards inter- and intranational conflicts, ethnic, ideological, personality, racial, regional or religious, around the peripheries of several Southeast Asian states, as the *Economist*[70] has warned. This may lead to the developments outlined in item 4.
4. An authoritarian, corporatist reaction in which more overtly nationalist or fundamentalist groups seize power to contain destabilising liberal reforms, and/or the scenario as in item 5.

5. An 'African' nightmare of anarchy in which some combination,
   of ecological decay, economic decline, exponential corruption,
   and exhaustion following regional wars, fragmentation of military regimes, or over-reliance on imported capital, labour, skills,
   technologies or values lead to suicidal communal/racial clashes
   or genocide/ethnic cleansing which regional and global peace-
   keeping/building interventions are unable to contain.

Clearly, the last trio of possibilities serve as cautions lest some
mix of the first two is not attempted and sustained. If we are to
avoid an 'unpacific Asia'[71] in the twenty-first century, judicious analysis
over the interconnections between development and human security in Southeast Asia, and discourse among a variety of interests
and institutions, including extraregional ones, will increasingly be
necessary.

Notes and References

1. See UNDP, *Human Development Report 1994* (New York: Oxford University Press, 1994); and UNDP, *Human Development Report 1995* (New
   York: Oxford University Press, 1995).
2. J. H. Mittelman (ed.), *Globalization: Critical Reflections* (Boulder, Col.:
   Lynne Rienner, 1997).
3. P. Bennis and M. Moushabeck (eds), *Altered States: A Reader in the
   New World Order* (New York: Olive Branch Press, 1993).
4. P. M. Evans (ed.), *Studying Asia Pacific Security: The Future of Research and Training Activities* (Toronto: Joint Centre for Asia Pacific
   Studies, 1994).
5. R. W. Cox (ed.), *The New Realism: Perspectives on Multilateralism and
   World Order* (London: Macmillan, 1996); and B. Hettne, *Development
   Theory and the Three Worlds: Towards an International Political Economy
   of Development* (Harlow: Longman, 1995).
6. See P. Agrawal *et al.*, *Economic Restructuring in East Asia and India:
   Lessons in Policy Reform* (London: Macmillan, 1995).
7. See, R. D. Kaplan, 'The Coming Anarchy', *Atlantic Monthly*, vol. 273,
   February (1994).
8. A. Acharaya and L. A. Swatuk, *Reordering the Periphery: The Third
   World and North-South Relations after the Cold War* (London: Macmillan,
   1999).
9. T. M. Callaghy and John Ravenhill (eds), *Hemmed In: Responses to
   Africa's Economic Decline* (New York: Columbia University Press, 1994);
   and T. M. Shaw and B. Korany, 'The South in the New World
   (Dis)Order', *Third World Quarterly*, vol. 15, no. 1, March (1994).

10. See J. A. Widner, *Economic Change and Political Liberalization in Sub-Saharan Africa* (Baltimore, Md: Johns Hopkins University Press, 1994).
11. See H. J. Morgenthau, *Politics Among Nations: The Struggle for Power and Peace*, 4th edn (New York: Alfred A. Knopf, 1966), p. 25.
12. H. Brown, *Thinking About National Security* (Boulder, Col.: Westview Press, 1983), p. 4; and A. Wolfers, *Discord and Collaboration: Essays on International Politics* (Baltimore, Md: Johns Hopkins University Press, 1962), p. 150.
13. J. H. Hertz, 'Idealist Internationalism and the Security Dilemma', *World Politics*, vol. 5, no. 2, January (1950), pp. 157–80.
14. B. Korany, P. Noble and R. Brynen (eds), *The Many Faces of National Security in the Arab World* (London: Macmillan, 1993), p. xviii.
15. C. Thomas, *In Search of Security: The Third World in International Relations* (Boulder, Col.: Lynne Rienner, 1987), p. 10.
16. B. Buzan, *People, States and Fear* (Brighton: Wheatsheaf, 1983), pp. 19–20; and D. Baldwin, 'The Concept of Security', *Review of International Studies*, vol. 23, no. 1, January (1997), pp. 5–26.
17. Cited in B. Korany, P. Noble and R. Brynen (eds), *The Many Faces of National Security in the Arab World*, p. 11.
18. K. Krause and M. C. Williams, 'Broadening the Agenda of Security Studies', *Mershon International Studies Review*, vol. 40, no. 2, October (1996), pp. 229–54.
19. H. Haftendorn, 'The Security Puzzle: Theory-building and Discipline-building in International Security', *International Studies Quarterly*, vol. 35 (1991), p. 11.
20. K. Booth, 'Security and Emancipation', *Review of International Studies*, vol. 17, no. 1 (1991), p. 317.
21. J. Macintosh and I. Griffith, *Confidence Building: Managing Caribbean Security Concerns* (Ottawa: Department of Foreign Affairs, 1996), p. 1.
22. UNDP, *Human Development Report 1994*, p. 22.
23. M. ul Haq, *Reflections on Human Development* (New York: Oxford University Press, 1995), p. 117.
24. Ibid., p. 124.
25. K. P. Clements, 'North-East Asian Regional Security and the Role of International Institutions: An Australian Perspective', in T. Inoguchi and G. B. Stillman (eds), *North-East Asian Regional Security: The Role of International Institutions* (New York: UN University Press, 1997), pp. 13–14.
26. World Bank, *The East Asian Miracle: Economic Growth and Public Policy* (New York: Oxford University Press, 1993).
27. J. Durno *et al.* (eds), *Sustainable Agriculture for the Landless* (Bangkok: SEA Sustainable Agriculture Network, 1992), p. x.
28. See 'Wobbly Tigers: East Asia's Economies are Experiencing Growing Pains', in *Economist*, vol. 340, 24 August (1996), pp. 13–14.
29. J. Clad and A. M. Siy, The Emergence of Ecological Issues in Southeast Asia', in D. Wurfel and B. Burton (eds), *Southeast Asia in the New World Order: The Political Economy of a Dynamic Region* (London: Macmillan, 1996), pp. 56–7.
30. UNDP, *Human Development Report 1995*, p. 39.

31. A. B. Jafar and M. J. Valencia, 'Marine Pollution: National Responses and Transnational Issues', in G. Kent and M. J. Valencia (eds), *Marine Policy in Southeast Asia* (Berkeley, Calif.: University of California Press, 1985), pp. 269–70.
32. The lack of epidemiological sophistication makes it very difficult to determine the precise number of people carrying the AIDS virus.
33. G. Fairclough, 'A Gathering Storm', *Far Eastern Economic Review*, vol. 158, 21 September (1995), pp. 26–30.
34. A. D. Usher, 'After the Forest: AIDS as Ecological Collapse in Thailand', in V. Shiva (ed.), *Close to Home: Women Reconnect Ecology, Health and Development Worldwide* (Philadelphia, Pa: New Society Publishers, 1994), p. 10.
35. J. Friedland, 'The Coming Holocaust', *Far Eastern Economic Review*, vol. 157, 18 August (1994), p. 16.
36. M. A. Bonacci, *The Legacy of Colonialism: Health Care in Southeast Asia* (Washington, DC: Asian Resource Centre, 1990).
37. M. L. Smith, *Why People Grow Drugs: Narcotics and Development in the Third World* (London: Panos Publications, 1992), p. 11.
38. A. W. McCoy, *The Politics of Heroin: CIA Complicity in the Global Drug Trade* (New York: Lawrence Hill Books, 1991), pp. 285–7.
39. M. L. Smith, *Why People Grow Drugs*, p. 18.
40. M. Hiebert and M. Lee, 'Pirates or Police?', *Far Eastern Economic Review*, vol. 158, 13 July (1995), p. 25.
41. L. Diamond, 'The Globalization of Democracy: Trends, Types, Causes and Prospects', in R. Slater *et al.*, *Global Transformation and the Third World* (Boulder, Col.: Lynne Rienner, 1992).
42. K. W. Crane *et al.*, *Civil–Military Relations in a Multiparty Democracy* (Santa Monica, Calif.: Rand, 1990), p. 1.
43. For a discussion on the praetorian model of civil–military relations, see, for example, S. P. Huntington, *Political Order in Changing Societies* (New Haven, Conn.: Yale University Press, 1968).
44. M. Tanji and S. Lawson, 'Democratic Peace and Asian Democracy: A Universalist–Particularist Tension', *Alternatives*, vol. 22, no. 1, January–March (1997), pp. 135–55.
45. H. D. Laswell, 'The Garrison State', *American Journal of Sociology*, vol. xliv, January (1941), pp. 455–68.
46. S. Haggard, *Pathways from the Periphery: The Politics of Growth in the Newly Industrializing Countries* (Ithaca, NY: Cornell University Press, 1990), pp. 9–22.
47. T. Shiraishi, 'The Military in Thailand, Burma and Indonesia', in R. A. Scalapino (eds), *Asian Political Institutionalization* (Berkeley, Calif.: Institute of East Asian Studies, 1986), p. 162.
48. L. W. Goodman, 'The Military and Democracy: An Introduction', in L. W. Goodman *et al.*, *The Military and Democracy: The Future of Civil–Military Relations in Latin America* (Lexington, Mass.: Lexington Books, 1990), p. xiii.
49. J. Petras and M. Morley, *Latin America in the Time of Cholera: Electoral Politics, Market Economies and Permanent Crisis* (New York: Routledge, 1992), pp. 8–12.

50. F. B. Miranda, *The Politicization of the Army* (Quezon City: University of the Philippines Press, 1992), pp. 10–17.
51. R. G. Simbulan, 'Militarization in Southeast Asia', in Y. Sakamato (ed.), *Militarization and Regional Conflict* (London: Zed Press, 1988), p. 53.
52. N. A. Graham, 'The Role of the Military in the Political and Economic Development of the Republic of Korea', in C. H. Kennedy and D. J. Louscher (eds), *Civil–Military Interaction in Asia and Africa* (New York: E. J. Brill, 1991), pp. 114–31.
53. D. King and J. Logerfo, 'Thailand toward Democratic Stability', *Journal of Democracy*, vol. 7, no. 1, January (1996), pp. 108–110.
54. D. K. Crone, 'Military Regimes and Social Justice in Indonesia and Thailand', in C. H. Kennedy and D. J. Louscher (eds), *Civil–Military Interaction in Asia and Africa*, pp. 96–113.
55. K. D. Jackson, 'Post-colonial Rebellion and Counter-insurgency in Southeast Asia', in C. Jeshurun (ed.), *Governments and Rebellions in Southeast Asia* (Singapore: Institute of Southeast Asian Studies, 1985), pp. 3–52.
56. J. V. Jesudason, 'Statist Democracy and the Limits to Civil Society in Malaysia', *Journal of Commonwealth and Comparative Politics*, vol. 33, no. 3, November (1995), p. 353.
57. T. Shiraishi, 'The Military in Thailand, Burma and Indonesia', pp. 177–8.
58. C. E. Welch Jr and A. K. Smith, *Military Role and Rule: Perspectives on Civil–Military Relations* (Boston, Mass.: Duxbury Press, 1974), pp. 44–8.
59. D. King and J. Logerfo, 'Thailand toward Democratic Stability', p. 111.
60. J. V. Jesudason, 'Stalist Democracy', p. 336.
61. In the Philippines alone, for example, about 18 000 NGOs are registered with the government.
62. R. Mawer, 'Mice Among the Tigers: Adding Value in NGO–Government Relations in Southeast Asia', in D. Hulme and M. Edwards (eds), *NGOs, States and Donors: Too Close for Comfort?* (London: Macmillan, 1997), p. 244.
63. P. Eldridge, 'NGOs and the State in Indonesia', in A. Budiman (ed.), *State and Civil Society in Indonesia* (Victoria: Centre for Southeast Asian Studies, 1990), pp. 503–38.
64. M. Cohen, 'New Zeal: NGOs Rally Round Opposition Leader Megawati', *Far Eastern Economic Review*, vol. 159, 11 July (1996), pp. 19–20.
65. S. J. Han, 'South Korea: Politics in Transition', in L. Diamond *et al.* (eds), *Politics in Developing Countries: Comparing Experiences with Democracy* (Boulder, Col.: Lynne Rienner, 1990), pp. 313–50.
66. H.-H. M. Hsiao, 'Political Liberalization and the Farmers' Movement in Taiwan', in E. Friedman (ed.), *The Politics of Democratization: Generalizing East Asian Experiences* (Boulder, Col.: Westview Press, 1994), pp. 202–18.
67. J. Durno, *et al.* (eds), *Sustainable Agriculture for the Landless*, p. 280.
68. F. Ching, 'NGOs and Regional Security', *Far Eastern Economic Review*, vol. 157, 30 June (1994), p. 29.

69. See, L. T. Ghee and M. J. Valencia (eds), *Conflict Over Natural Resources in Southeast Asia and the Pacific* (Singapore: Oxford University Press, 1990).
70. EIU, *The World in 1995* (London: EIU, 1995), p. 77.
71. Ibid., p. 71.

11 Security and Development in Africa: Cold War and Beyond
Nana Poku

In *The End of History and The Last Man*, Francis Fukuyama presented a vision of a world based on his reading of Alexandre Kojève's interpretation of Hegelian philosophy. From Kojèvian Hegelianism, Fukuyama derives the notion that history is driven by competing ideologies, in the twentieth century mainly liberal democracy, Fascism and communism. At the current historical juncture, liberal democracy has won the battle between ideologies. As a result, the future can consist only of the continued spread of liberal democracy, albeit with the occasional temporary regression to one or other of the discarded and discredited alternatives.[1] Fukuyama is careful to state that he distinguishes between the claim that there is no other viable model on offer, from the claim that its consolidation in all countries is imminent or even plausible. But, in the (undefined) longer term, there is a fundamental process at work which dictates a common evolutionary pattern for all human societies; something like a 'universal history of mankind in the direction of liberal democracy'.[2] In his words, 'what we may be witnessing is not just the end of the Cold War, or the passing of a particular period of post-war history, but the end of history as such: that is, the end point of mankind's ideological evolution and the universalisation of Western liberal democracy as the final form of human government'.[3]

Over five years have passed since this thesis was first published, and academic commentators have either dismissed it or found themselves in broad sympathy with its internal logic concerning the expansion of liberal democratic ideals to countries with non-democratic traditions. In truth, there is much about this thesis that is questionable or unresolved, yet, in explaining the post-Cold War order, Fukuyama raises a number of interesting questions. For our purposes, one is particularly relevant and merits critical attention – namely,

199

the role of Africa at the end of the Cold War. Fukuyama suggests that we have entered a post-historical period in which the ideological struggle will cease, global peace will prevail, and all that remains is 'the perpetual caretaking of the museum of human history'.[4] Certainly, the superpowers are no longer poised to launch mutually destructive nuclear attacks on each other's territory; nor do Russia and the United States now seek to undermine each other through surrogates in the Third World. But does this imply that there will be a peace dividend for the world at large, let alone for Africa? Indeed, can the continent avert a future Somalia, Sudan, Liberia or Rwanda (as examples)? More fundamentally, where does Africa stand at the end of the Cold War?

These are powerful and difficult questions that cannot be fully answered without first engaging with Africa's colonial history. Predicated on the turbulent history of the continent and the bipolar politics that characterised interstate relations for over forty years, this chapter seeks to analyse the implications of the current global transformations for the quest to secure peace and promote development on the African continent. The chapter begins with brief review of colonialism and its enduring legacy, then moves to analyse the impact of the Cold War on Africa. The extent of the continent's economic marginalisation will be outlined and its emerging security problems contextualised. The chapter will conclude by engaging with Fukuyama's thesis in its African context.

Before proceeding, however, it is important to clarify the point that, in referring to Africa, I am primarily concerned with Black Africa. That is, while Africa is geographically a single entity, it is politically and culturally heterogeneous. The normal division of the continent is provided by the Sahara desert, bringing together the Maghreb states of the predominantly Islamic north, and combining the rest to the south (including South Africa) as Sub-Saharan or Black Africa. It must be stated that, historically, this distinction has served more as a bridge than a barrier between north and south. Goods, people and ideas have moved freely across it, and these contacts continue today in such forms as Pan-Africanism, the Organisation of African Unity, and collaboration in addressing Third World concerns in the United Nations. For the purpose of this chapter, however, although references will be made to the Maghreb states, it is within the context of Black Africa that the chapter will largely be constructed.

THE COLONIAL LEGACY

Black Africa seems to have suffered more severely from alien impact than any other part of the world, with the possible exception of island areas that were decimated by disease and bloodshed caused by such contact. First came the slave trade, which took away millions and degraded both the people and the land. In the wake of the slave trade came European imperialism, which led to a total colonialisation of the continent. The terms denote a power relationship of one political entity over another. Imperialism describes the process of establishing that power relationship, and colonialism has to do with the pattern of domination and rule once the relationship has been consolidated. Fostered by both was the imposition of the myth of the 'Dark Continent', awaiting the arrival of European culture, technology and religion to lift the people from their 'state of savagery'. Motivated by these factors, in addition to a mix of economic and geopolitical considerations, at the conference of Berlin in 1884, European leaders finally decided the rules for the partitioning of the last great land mass, Africa.

To the colonisers, the strategy was simple: whenever they occupied a piece of land they could legitimately integrate that territory into their empire. The particular motives for declaring a sphere of influence varied, as Europeans, convinced of their 'civilising role', the 'truth' of their religion and their right to trade, strove to exploit Africa and to compete with each other. For the Europeans it did become a gigantic 'Risk' game,[5] played with real people and real land. Zanzibar was traded for Heligoland, parts of Northern Nigeria were exchanged for fishing rights off Newfoundland, Cameroun became Kamerun for a 'free hand in Morocco'. This extension of the European notion of sovereignty brought with it a near total compartmentalisation of political space in which there were very few uncolonised areas on the continent. Only 10 per cent of the continent was under direct European control in 1870, but by the end of the century only 10 per cent remained outside it. From the ownership of a landholding through a hierarchy of political administrative areas such as the community, county, state and nation, all the pieces fit together with neither overlap nor extension. By 1914, the political map of Africa was virtually complete, the resulting pattern containing comparable administrative units and clearly defined boundaries.

202 Security and Development in Africa

Within their colonial boundaries, the colonisers constructed African economies to serve European rather than African interests, and integrated African markets into the global division of labour. As large-scale plantations developed and expanded on the continent in order to service European demands, there was also an influx of a significant number of European settlers. These settlers were concentrated heavily in the eastern and southern parts of the continent as well as in Algeria.[7] Although their numbers were *relatively* small, paradoxically this was a major source of strength; it provided a very effective way of preserving the assumption of white superiority on which the whole edifice of colonial administration depended. The whole system functioned on the conviction that the administrators (the white Europeans) were sovereign; and that their subjects neither understood nor wanted self-government or independence. Indeed, such were the ambiguities in which rulers and the ruled were involved, and of which they were generally only vaguely, if at all, aware. If there was any training and adoption of the native, it was a schooling in the bureaucratic toils of colonial government; a preparation not for independence, but against it. It could not be otherwise. Colonialism was based on authoritarian command; as such, it was incompatible with any preparation for self-government. In that sense, every success of administration was a failure of government. With good reason, then, both Africans and Europeans usually approached problems of governance circumspectly. Such mutual caution was in large measure responsible for the relative political tranquillity of the continent until the Second World War.

War shattered the staid pace of colonial rule.[8] The end of the war left the metropolitan powers exhausted and weak. More fundamentally, and as Basil Davidson rightly noted, 'the war gave a new spur to anti-colonial protest'.[9] It brought a new force to the call for anti-colonial change and the war experience helped to develop a better resistance to colonial rule. By the end of the war, although African colonies were still dependent economically on their colonial powers,[10] the latter's political and social control was weakened beyond repair. Indeed, this pattern was evident across the colonial world. The Dutch tried holding on to Indonesia (as the French also tried in Indo-China, and subsequently in Algeria) by massive force and at disastrous cost. The sporadic troubles of the British Empire, previously put down by punitive expenditure, were tending to grow into prolonged guerrilla wars. In the African case, the result was a cascade of constitutional formulae and bargaining processes that eventually culminated in the emergence of native rule states on the continent.[11]

One of the most important observations to be made about this transition from colonial rule to independent states is the fact that the boundaries of the latter changed remarkably little. That is, post-colonial states were, with very few exceptions, territorially identical to the European colonies they replaced. That this must be so was stipulated at the 1964 meeting of the Organisation for African Unity (OAU). As a result, far more than in any other parts of the former colonial world, the identities of African states are a direct product of European colonialism. Its boundaries are the lines drawn on maps by colonial governments, generally with startling unconcern for the people whom they casually allocated to one territory or another. Note, for example, all the straight line boundaries on a map of Africa. These were usually drawn from divides between the coastal nodes of competing powers and extended inland until they conflicted with another colonial power. Thus, every boundary on the continent cuts through at least one cultural area. The Nigeria–Cameroon boundary divides fourteen, while the boundaries of Burkina Faso cross twenty-one cultural areas. At the micro level such boundaries sometimes divided town from hinterland, village from traditional fields and even families from their communities.

This, in short, was the tyranny of African borders. Although it is naïve to suppose that the realities of any environment can, or should, dictate the configuration of a state, it is equally foolish to overlook the impact of predetermined shapes on future defence, communications and governance, and on the shaping of political identities. Whereas the reality of a straight line drawn across the Sahara or the Kalahari may be of little consequence, the impact of similar delimitations across populated areas, such as between Kenya and Tanzania, Angola and Zambia, and Ethiopia and the Somali Republic, obviously have sociopolitical implications. What resulted from this was a compartmentalisation of each country into so-called tribal areas that were supposedly different from one another. In some cases, one, or at most two or three, very large groups were dominant (Dahomey, Upper Volta and Swaziland). In others, several large groups were interspersed among more numerous smaller ones (Kenya, the Congo (Zaire) and Nigeria).[12] This was particularly true in British-governed areas under the policy of indirect rule, where locating indigenous leaders and specifying the prevailing social-political traditions were essential. What resulted was the creation of many new self-conscious identities.[13] A typical example of this would be the Sandawe of Tanzania who, despite their unique language and many customs that set them apart from surrounding ethnic groups, never seem to have possessed a sense of solidarity and separate identity until they were organised into an administrative subchiefdom and virtually told who they were.[14]

The Manyika people of Zimbabwe provide a further example of how colonialism created ethnic identities, and the manner in which these identities, have been manipulated to serve political and economic interests. Before 1890 the Manyika shared a common Shona language and cultural traits with other Shona groups. They were conscious neither of a cultural nor a political identity. Colonial manipulation of territory and, more importantly, the language work of mission stations that privileged a written language based on the Manyika dialect, led to the creation of an ethnic identity around this sub-unit of Shona-speakers. The Manyika migrants further benefited from literacy skills that gave them access to jobs in domestic service and they came to be seen as 'natural' domestic servants in towns in Southern Rhodesia and South Africa. Even migrants from areas where Manyika ethnicity was resisted had to capitulate in the urban areas and claim to belong to this ethnic identity in order to gain employment.

This colonial legacy has been inherited, and indeed accepted, by the present independent African governments. Politicians in Kenya play off Kikuyu against Luo and Kambo and the various minority groups. Sierra Leone must contend with a Creole–indigenous split, with the indigenous peoples being fragmented by a Temne–Mende conflict. Nigeria worked to bring the Ibo back into national life, and Zaire, despite several proclamations declaring all its citizens to be equal, regularly has to play politics with over 250 recognised ethnic groups. Indeed, throughout the continent, states preside over divided societies containing widely divergent ethnic groups, making it particularly difficult for post-colonial states to generate a moral basis for government, which in turn has endowed rulers with legitimacy or authority, rather than with the mere control of the state machinery. Though the notion of government is accepted on the continent, the political institutions through which its powers are exercised are fiercely contested by all the ethnic groups. This has produced a situation on the continent where states preside over fractured societies with a multiplicity of ethnic identities and loyalties. Unlike the colonial state which managed to supervise the disparate elements over which it ruled (usually with unrivalled force), post-colonial states have, in general, failed to resolve intra-ethnic disputes and the result has been the proliferation of violence we have come to associate with the African continent. This, of course, proved to be fertile grounds for Cold War politics.

COLD WAR AFRICA

The world in which Africans achieved their independence contained two opposing visions of the ideal society, under the protection of two creators of purpose and power, the USA and the Soviet Union. Competing anti-colonialist demagogues, they set themselves up as models of political, economic and social developers in the global ideological market-place. At the time of decolonisation there was a view that the continent would drop out of world affairs and be glad to do so. There were African leaders who hoped for Africa's sake that Africa would side-step the frightening prospect of involvement in the conflict between the superpowers that threatened to repeat the nineteenth-century grab by the European powers. This erroneous view persisted for a time because the superpowers were slow to extend their activities into Africa. But the strategic importance of Africa eventually proved an irresistible lure.

There was an asymmetry in the superpowers' respective stances in that the USA was allied with the former colonial metropoles, whereas the former Soviet Union had neither the advantages nor the drawbacks of partners. The Soviet Union enjoyed the rhetorical advantage of approaching the continent with a clear anti-imperial ideology. The USA, while laying claim to an anti-colonial traditions, was generally content to defer to its European allies so long as the latter could maintain a stable presence in their spheres of influence. When they failed, for example, in the Congo, the USA became much more visibly involved. Whether the USA was seconding or displacing its European ally, the concern was the same – to prevent Soviet influence, just as the Soviets strove to diminish Western influence. By the end of the 1980s both superpowers were engaged in Africa for much the same reasons as the European powers had occupied it a hundred years earlier: 'buried treasure', and fear of each other.

The emphasis of the superpowers on ideological action in building international hierarchies strengthened African leaders in their determination to assert, beyond formal independence, African autonomy and the contribution of African nations to world politics. In reality, however, neither superpower simply allowed post-colonial leaders to follow their dreams for total sovereignty and independence. The Soviets were more open to the notion of African nationalism, not least because it implied some rebellious disengagement from the colonial order, but neither superpower believed in 'Africa for the Africans'. Both tended to become involved in those states where the transition from colonialism to independence was most turbulent. Yet, and as will become apparent, it would be misleading to suggest that the great powers took all the initiatives. On the contrary, competing African leaders often looked abroad for support against internal or external enemies. The exigencies of domestic and regional struggles for power often opened the door to intervention. The Horn of Africa provides a typical example of how the superpowers took advantages of the legacies left by the colonial period.

This is not the place to provide a comprehensive history of the region. Yet, one cannot talk about the region in any meaningful way without first providing a brief historical context. The Horn of Africa region consists of Ethiopia/Eritrea and its immediate neighbours: Somalia, Sudan, Kenya and Djibouti. This region has been the site of one of the most endemic inter- and intrastate conflicts on the African continent since the initial era of independence in the late 1950s and 1960s. As Barry Buzan rightly noted, the many conflicts are interlinked in a regional 'security complex', a group of states whose 'primary security' cannot realistically be considered apart from one another.[15] As one would expect, this security complex had its colonial trajectory. During the 'scramble for Africa', Somaliland was divided between the British and Italian spheres of influence. In 1924, Britain gave Jubaland, an area of 36 740 square miles entirely inhabited by Somalis, to Italy as a 'reward for Italy entering the First World war against Germany'.[16] In 1946, the USA and the Soviet Union, suspicious of British strategic intentions, rejected a plan to create a 'Greater Somalia'. The superpowers, having blocked British plans for Somalia, were not long in establishing themselves in the strategic Horn of Africa. In return for a Red Sea base, the USA provided Haile Selassie with vast quantities of arms to help keep his fragile Ethiopian empire together.

The Soviet Union outbid the West to supply Somalia with weapons in return for a base at Berbera. Between them, the superpowers flooded Ethiopia and Somalia with modern weaponry.

In the process of pursuing what they considered to be their own strategic interests, the superpowers exploited the ethnic legacy left by the colonial boundaries to escalate a regional arms race in the Horn. This was to have monumental consequences for an already tense regional security matrix. Paul Henze shows how, over a fifteen-year period, Soviet military assistance to Ethiopia alone was as high as 11 billion dollars.[17] The size of the Ethiopian armed forces, for example, grew from 54 000 in 1977 to more than 300 000 a decade later; by 1991, the Ethiopian army was estimated to be over 600 000 strong. Somalia's army swelled from about 32 000 in 1977 to 65 000 in 1987.[18] In the same period, Ethiopia's defence budget grew from $103 million to almost $472 million. Between 1977 and 1985, Somalia's defence expenditure rose from $36 million to $134 million, and Sudan's from $237 million to $478 million. This level and pattern of growth in military expenditure could not have taken place without superpower patronage.

This pattern of superpower intervention was not unique or limited to the Horn. At the southern end of the continent, a similar pattern was evident during the Cold War, although here the conflicts took on two new protagonists, in the form of the Republic of South Africa and Cuba. Nowhere in the region was the superpower intervention more evident than in Angola. Angola is potentially one of the richest countries in Africa. It produces 500 000 barrels of oil per day, has reserves of almost 5 billion barrels, and has an annual production of about 1 million carats of diamonds. Other mineral resources are considerable and include iron ore, manganese, copper, nickel, gold and silver. But it is a country that has been wrecked by warfare since the 1960s. Although Angola's independence was assured by the 1974 revolution in Portugal, in March 1975 accord between three rival groups broke down and civil war began. In the north was the Frente Nacional de Libertacao de Angola (FNLA), based among the Bakongo and backed by their cousins across the Zaire border. The Movimento Popular de Libertacao de Angola (MPLA) was a large, urban-based radical group among detribalised *assimilados* and mulattos around Luanda. In the northeast was the Uniao Nacional para a Independencia Total de Angola (UNITA), based among the Ovibundu people. The FLNA and UNITA were backed by the USA, the MPLA by the Soviet Union,

but this backing had changed in the recent past and the factions
had divided loyalties.

Such uncertainties were quickly resolved when the apartheid regime in South Africa, backed by the USA, invaded Angola in support of UNITA in late 1977. The South African interest was to
secure their rule in Namibia by denying the South West African
People's Organisation (SWAPO) guerrillas the use of Angola. Their
advance was halted by the MPLA, equipped by the Soviet Union
and 'advised' by thousands of Cuban special forces. The South Africans retreated to just north of the Namibian border while UNITA
held the south-eastern quadrant of Angola. From there, attacks on
SWAPO tightened South Africa's grip on Namibia, and attacks by
UNITA on Angola's infrustrature crippled the country's economy,
so the country became a scene of human devastation.[19]

While war has been concentrated in Ethiopia and neighbouring
countries of the Horn, and in Southern Africa (particularly Angola
and Mozambique), it has occurred also, in some cases over pro-
tracted periods, in many countries elsewhere on the continent
(Uganda, Chad, Sierra Leone, Zimbabwe, Burundi, Rwanda, Nigeria, Zaire and Liberia among others). The Cold War was a major factor in protracting, and at times instigating, these conflicts
but the end of the superpower rivalry has not ended them. Indeed,
such conflicts have become a form of politics via other means. This
is so because the kind of conflict that has become characteristic of
Africa (guerrilla war and skirmishes difficult to distinguish from
banditry) are particularly difficult to resolve. Parties may agree on
a cease fire, but 'a child with a gun can, for a day, be king'. In
truth, Fanon's notion of renovating violence, that real freedom for
Africans could only be won by destruction, true liberation only
through fire, is one of the great lies of post-colonial Africa. Violence on the continent has begotten violence; not freedom, not liberation, not dignity, and not equality. The result has been the
proliferation of intra- and interstate conflicts that have left the
continent's people economically devastated and politically marginalised in the post-Cold War order. Indeed, the scale of Africa's
economic position is nothing short of depressing.

FROM DECLINE TO MARGINALITY: AFRICA'S ECONOMIC CRISIS

At independence, the former colonies looked firmly towards an opportunistic and optimistic future. To a large extent they regarded their colonial past as at least best forgotten; a history of exploitation and humiliation that had left their people poor and underdeveloped. In the 1990s there is scarcely any disagreement about the depth of Africa's economic crisis, since, whatever indicators are used, it is patently obvious that, taken as a whole (and with few exceptions), Africa's economies today are in a worse state than they were at the time of independence. It is not just that there has been no growth or development, but that in absolute terms both the economies of African countries and the economic prospects of the majority of Africans have been eroded steadily since the late 1980s.

In general, the continent's economic growth has failed to keep up with its population's expansion. Exports have declined in relative and absolute terms; food production has declined; imports of food and other necessities have increased; and import substitution industries have not lived up to expectations. Industrialisation has, with some exceptions, failed to materialise; borrowing and debt have soared; currencies (including the almighty franc) have weakened or collapsed. State revenues have plummeted. State-controlled economic activities have foundered. State-funded services have declined or disintegrated; official economies have shrunk, and parallel economies have grown.

The state of Sub-Saharan economies was not always so bleak. Between the onset of independence and the oil crisis in 1974, African economies benefited from rising commodity prices and increased investment from export earnings, modest external commercial borrowing, and official development assistance. In line with the development orthodoxy of the day, most governments, with donor assistance, introduced five-year comprehensive development plans and regulated exchange rates, domestic prices, and credit in order to strengthen import-substitution industrialisation.[20] The average annual per capita growth rate between 1965 and 1973 was 2.9 per cent, which was not far below the overall figure for low-income countries of 3.3 per cent. It has not exceeded that level since. From the mid-1970s, this trend yielded to a combination of adverse external and domestic factors, leading to a phase of economic stagnation (1973–80), which deteriorated into a decline in the average standard of living that still continues.

Whatever the causes of this economic crisis, about which there is (quite rightly) debate, we cannot ignore or deny the magnitude of the continent's economic predicament. Nevertheless, taking stock of Africa's economic breakdown is no substitute for deep academic analysis. Indeed, any interpretation of the crisis must attempt to unravel what is cause and what is effect, and it is precisely at the level of interpretation that the (implicit or explicit) use of simplistic causalities often reduces Africa's economic crisis to a series of casual or tautological clichés, some of which, such as the 'innate economic inability' of Africans, carry distinct racists connotations. For our purpose, however, it is fair to say that, almost certainly, conflicts on the continent since independence, of which there have been many, have contributed significantly to its state of economic decline and political marginalisation. Today, the continent has no strategic or geopolitical relevance to the major powers or to the wider international community. In the strategic literature, it is not discussed even as a threat. It is under these circumstances that the next section reconsiders the notion of security in the African context. Before embarking on this, however, it is first necessary to contextualise Africa's security within the wider security debate currently evident in the discipline of international relations.

REDEFINING SECURITY: WHAT RELEVANCE FOR AFRICA?

In the security discourse, governments have traditionally been the primary point of reference. This is because traditional political theory sees them as the guardians of their people's security, from external and internal threats. Nowhere in the social sciences is this dominance of the state more prevalent in the analysis of security than in the discipline of international relations (IR). Here the debate about security was unapologetically dominated by the methodological and theoretical insight of the realist school. The ontology of this school posits a notion of highly sovereign states acting in a decentralised system where conflict is endemic and security is managed by power-seeking and self-help. In this realist world, states are anxious to preserve their independence. Thus every action they make is in one way or other directed towards securing their survival in the precarious interstate system. As a direct legacy of social contract theory, this image predicated the emergence of a purposeful sovereign entity out of the structural relations of insecurities characteristic of the state of nature.

The orderly polity resulting from the Hobbesian contract between individuals cannot, however, be replicated internationally by a similar contract between states. In the words of Rob Walker, this is the case because the 'ahistoric moment of utilitarian calculation informed by reason and fear that gave rise to social contract has no counterpart in international relations'.[21] In this sense, domestic order becomes the mirror image and necessary condition of international disorder; thus making anarchy the axiomatic and unalterable principle of global life. The implication here is that, in international politics, security is the most important objective. Only if this is assured can states seek such other goals as tranquillity and profit. Hence, even though states may seek truth, beauty and justice, all these more noble goals will be lost unless they make provisions for their security in the power struggle within the international systems. Indeed, the only stability in this dangerous and uncertain international system comes from the nature of the competition itself. War can be avoided only if there is a general understanding that the threat of war exists; and peace can be perpetuated only through the preparation for war. In this realist world, security came to focus on war, the ability to fight wars and the external threats to the state that might give rise to them.

Since the 1980s we have seen a remarkable 'demilitarisation of security thinking' and a parallel retreat of the state as the principle unit of analysis in security studies. This is partly because the notion of security has become fashionable in fields and disciplines beyond its traditional heartland of Strategic Studies and IR. This expansion of the security debate does not, however, mean that a consensus exists on what a more broadly constructed conception should look like. Less still is there a consensus on how it can be conceptualised or what its most relevant questions are. What most contributors to the debate share is a concern with the question of how to study security. This is a deeply epistemological question that involves a fundamental shift from abstract individualism and contractual sovereignty to a stress on culture, civilisation and identity. More fundamentally, there is emphasis on the role of ideas, norms and values in the constitution of that which is to be secured, and on the historical context within which this process takes place.

Epistemologically, this involves moving away from the objectivist approach of the realist school towards more interpretative modes of analysis. In other words, the debate is centred at the cognitive stage of research.

In Chapter 9, Quadir and Shaw provided an outline of the emerging contours of the critical security debate in contemporary international relations. Without traversing the corpus of their argument, suffice to say that the broader conception of security and its accompanying agenda would seem to be particularly pertinent for considering the concept in its African context. As we have already noted, the enduring legacy of colonialism has been the proliferation of weak states on the continent. To use Robert Jackson's distinction, juridical rather than social entities.[22] As a result, the notion of security on the continent has become a codeword for the privileging of the security of the state's political elite over the rest of its population. In this context, the epistemological move to embrace a broader conception of security is primarily, but not exclusively, a level of analysis debate. In other words, if security is conceived and articulated in terms of a wide variety of threats to human life and wellbeing, then it is necessary to consider not just the threats that are relevant at the state level, but at all levels appropriate for individual and group living. For our purpose, this move raises a wider set of issues, such as poverty, human rights, food security, security of the environment, political freedom, democratisation and accountability. Indeed, of the various indicators of domestic insecurity, perhaps the most telling is political refugees; Africa has recently had the largest number of political refugees in any major world region.

Without wishing to underplay the importance of the economic dimension, it is worth making the point that the deep causes of Africa's refugee problem are political in nature. The principle factors that provoke large movement of people throughout the world are well known; violation of human rights; political and military conflicts within a country; ethnic and religious repression; frontier disputes and armed conflicts between neighbouring states; rivalry between the superpowers and regional powers; natural catastrophes; and economic crises. All these factors are so interwoven in Africa's sociopolitical culture that they result in tragedies of which the drama of the refugees is but a part. To understand this and to appreciate the impact on both the refugees and the host country, it is first necessary to narrow our analysis to a specific region. Bearing in mind that all the following generalisations are applicable to any other part of the continent, in line with our earlier discussions, it seems appropriate to use the case of the Horn.

In the Horn the movement of refugees has always been a unidimensional movement. That is, nearly all the refugees have come from Ethiopia. This brings up the question of why Ethiopia, or more exactly why the military regimes in power in Ethiopia, have created more refugees than anywhere else in the region. Contrary to popular opinion, it was not conventional warfare, nor indeed the devastating economic impact they had on the country that was primarily accountable. It was towards the end of these wars, at least in their 'classical' form, that we can note the beginning of a 'silent disaster'. In retrospect, it appears that the main cause of Ethiopian depopulation was the ruling government's policy of repressing and punishing civilians suspected of sympathising or collaborating with enemies of the regime. For these people, their 'own' government was the primary source of insecurity, not the armed forces of a neighbouring country. Similarly, the pursuit of state security in Ethiopia has, over the years, become a major source of insecurity for its neighbouring countries. The two main host countries, Somalia and Sudan, are among the thirty-one countries classified as least developed countries (LLDCs). Djibouti is a tiny country which has virtually no agriculture or industrial resources at all. The socioeconomic (hence security) problems with which these countries are faced are inevitably made worse by the steady influx of refugees. In other words, the pursuit of securing the state apparatus was at the expense of the people of Ethiopia, while Ethiopia's state security was at the expense of the national security of the other countries of the region. Hence giving credibility to the notion that, one country's or group's national security can be another country's or group's oppression. Similarly, alliances between groupings, within and across increasingly permeable and meaningless national boundaries, circumscribe the role and dominance of the state. In this context, it becomes problematic to equate 'security' exclusively with *state* security.

CONCLUSIONS: AFRICA AT THE END OF THE COLD WAR

A common theme runs through virtually all the predictions made concerning the post-Cold War order, where they deal with Africa. The area appears to be cited in order to stress its transience or even decrepitude, as if some curse of dubious scientific basis had been laid on political analysis of the whole continent. Ignored by theoreticians and discredited by militant attackers of imperialism whose dialectical reasoning proved Africa's impotence in international relations (an anachronism in the era of nuclear deterrence and computer-assisted wars), Africa now appears to exist only as a reminder or as the subject, and never as a genuine actor. As we have seen, the circumstances since the 1970s are irrefutable. The generalised decline in standards of living among African people, and therefore in the material and symbolic capacity of African actors, both internationally and internally, is an established fact of daily life as well as of statistics.

To the extent that international calculations of national poverty indices can be trusted, Africans are not yet the poorest people in the world. Only 15 per cent of the continent's population of 420 million in 1992 could be classified as poor. This proportion is nowhere close to the 40 per cent poverty-afflicted population among South Asia's 1.1 billion people. But Africa's consistently declining rates of economic productivity and surging population growth portend deepening impoverishment, compared with South Asia, where an increase in per capita income is already evident.

It is too early to state with any certainty the full implications of the end of the Cold War for Africa, or indeed to speculate about a possible peace dividend. The contours of the emerging order, however, looks quite promising for Africa. This has had positive effects in that conflicts (such as those in the Horn and Southern Africa), which were sustained by the Cold War, have now either been resolved or are in the process of being resolved. Equally, and in line with Fukuyama's thesis, governments on the African continent are witnessing arguably the most monumental change in state–society relations since the era of independence. Authoritarian regimes are being challenged by individuals and movements in search of more democratic forms of governance. Africans in many countries are showing remarkable persistence in forcing their leaders to comply with popular demands for political pluralism to replace the common one-party regimes. Calls for open and democratic governance, characterised by popular participation, competitive elections and free flow of information can be heard in every country on the continent. As a result, the relationship between government and the governed is being radically redefined across the continent. In this sense, Fukuyama is right in that, the avowal failure of 'socialism' in Africa and the decline in the influence of the former Soviet Union (and its allies) have left the continent to face the growing influence of the West and Western conceptions of development (liberalism). Thus, once again, Africa is left to take its Western-imposed fate. From the beginnings of colonialism Africa has been defined and redefined from the outside; treated like a child, its indigenous ideas have rarely been taken seriously and, as Norman Lewis argued in Chapter 5, when they have, the West has subsequently discredited them. Thus, in the late 1990s, the West assumes the moral high-ground and once again assumes the task of helping to redefine Africa in the context of Fukuyaman certainty. The task, though aspiration rather than certainty, is for Africans to define and redefine themselves. In the context of the security debate (and even as liberalism triumphs) there is always room for amelioration; for local interpretations of global trends and for strategies of resistance to increase individual security. In keeping with the rest of this volume, the idea here is to 'set the scene', to show how the 'Third World' has (or had) been defined and to demonstrate the need for a redefinition.[23]

Notes and References

1. To underline this point, Fukuyama in fact predicted that Peru might lapse into dictatorship, a shrewd guess that President Fujimori's subsequent coup vindicated.
2. F. Fukuyama, *The End of History and the Last Man* (London: Hamish Hamilton, 1992), p. 48.
3. F. Fukuyama, 'The End of History?', *The National Interest*, vol. 16, Summer (1989), pp. 3–18.
4. Ibid., p. 18
5. The popular board game.
6. P. Gifford and W. R. Louis, *France and Britain in Africa: Imperial Rivalry and Colonial Rule* (New Haven, Conn.: Yale University Press, 1971).
7. G. Mare, *Ethnicity and Politics in South Africa* (Johannesburg: Ravan Press, 1992).
8. See B. Davidson, *Modern Africa: A Social and Political History* (London: Longman, 1989).
9. Ibid., p. 65.
10. For a detailed economic analysis of Africa's post-war economic development, see R. Sandbrook, *The Politics of Africa's Economic Stagnation* (Cambridge University Press, 1993).

11. On the issue of African nationalism, see B. Davidson, *Africa in Modern History: The Search for New Society* (Harmondsworth: Penguin, 1978).
12. A good introduction to this subject is A. I. Asiwaju (ed.), *Partitioned Africans: Ethnic Relations Across Africa's International Boundaries* (London: Hurst, 1985).
13. The Ewe in Ghana and Togo, the Ibo in Nigeria, the Kikuyu in Kenya, and the Soga in Uganda are typical of such altered societies.
14. An interesting and informative study of this particular group is provided by J. L. Newman, *The Ecological Basis for Subsistence Change Among the Sandawe of Tanzania* (Washington DC: National Academy of Science, 1970).
15. B. Buzan, *People, States and Fear: The National Security Problem in International Relations* (Chapel Hill, NC: University of North Carolina Press, 1993), p. 106.
16. On the issue of ethnicity and conflict in the Horn of Africa, see K. Fukui and J. Markakis (eds), *Ethnicity and Conflict in the Horn of Africa* (London: James Currey, 1994).
17. P. Henze, 'Ethiopia in Transition', *Ethiopian Review*, July (1992).
18. International Institute for Strategic Studies, *The Military Balance*, vols 1976/1977–1989/1990.
19. For a comprehensive history of the region's conflict, see W. Minter, *Apartheid Contra: An Inquiry into the Roots of War in Angola and Mozambique* (London: Zed Books, 1994).
20. For a detailed economic analysis of Africa's post-war economy, see, among others, D. K. Fieldhouse, *Black Africa 1945–1980: Economic Decolonisation and Arrested Development* (London: Unwin Hyman, 1986); A. Adedeji (ed.), *Africa Within the World: Beyond Disposition and Dependence* (London: Zed Books, 1996); and R. Sandbrook, *The Politics of Africa's Economic Stagnation*.
21. K. Waltz, 'Reflections on Theory of International Politics: A Response to My Critics', in R. Keohane (ed.), *Neo-Realism and Its Critics* (New York: Columbia University Press, 1986).
22. R. Jackson and C. G. Rosenberg, 'Why Africa's Weak State Persists: The Empirical and the Juridical in Statehood', *World Politics*, vol. 35, no. 1 (1985), pp. 1–24.
23. I would like to thank Peter Vale and Lloyd Pettiford for their help with earlier drafts of this chapter. What remains is my own responsibility.

Index

development, 10, 70, 81, 111, 176, 199–215
  capitalist, 56, 107; *see also under* capitalism
  economic, 57, 158
  infrastructural, 57
  national, 132, 151
  planning, 137–8
  regional, 84, 172–94
  studies, 2, 39
  uneven, 100–1, 107, 110, 118
  see also underdevelopment
Diamond, Larry, 164
disease, 172, 176
Djibouti, 50, 206, 213
dollar (US), 96, 180
  see also capital *and* investment
Dominican Republic, 158
Dornbusch, Rudiger, 151
drugs, 91, 167, 172, 176, 182–3, 201

East Asia, *see under* Asia
Eastern Europe, *see under* Europe
ECOMOG (Economic Community of West African States Cease-Fire Monitoring Group), 83
economic,
  growth, *see under* growth
  liberalism, *see under* liberalism *and* neoliberalism
ECOWAS (Economic Community of West African States), 83
Ecuador, 153, 156, 157
Edwards, Sebastian, 151
Egypt, 50, 138
elites, 10, 17, 59, 127, 137, 156, 185
El Salvador, 138
empiricism, 33
  see also under methodology
end of history, 70, 199
  see also Fukuyama, Francis
Enlightenment, 28, 114
environmental problems, 85, 91, 172, 181, 212
EPZs (export processing zones), 138, 139

Eritrea, 22, 50, 172, 206
Ethiopia, 50, 51, 203, 206, 213
ethnicity, 45, 60, 113, 121, 172, 204
Europe, 2, 50, 56, 57, 73, 77, 81, 86, 92, 95–6, 115, 152, 180, 201–2
  Central, 58, 77, 78
  Eastern, 3, 28, 58, 60, 100–1, 112, 156, 173
  Northern, 49
  Southern, 81
  Western, 53, 60, 82
  see also under individual countries
European Union, 73, 77, 80, 83, 173
Evans, Peter, 55, 164

famine, *see under* food
favela, *see under* shanty towns
FDI (foreign direct investment), 59, 98, 99, 152, 154
  see also investment
food, 212
Foucault, Michel, 32
Freire, Paolo, 20
Fromkin, David, 11–12
Fujimori, Alberto, 153, 165
Fujitsu, 95
Fukuyama, Francis, 27, 90, 199, 214

G7 (group of 7), 104, 113, 173
G77 (group of 77), 40, 173
Gadamer, H. G., 19
Gaddis, John Lewis, 92
Gamarra, Eduardo, 157
Gates, Bill, 102
GDP (gross domestic product), 31, 147, 154, 180
  see also GNP (gross national product)
gender, 104, 113, 121, 172, 176
  see also under conflict
genealogy, 32–3
  see also under methodologies
General Motors, 101
Germany, 57, 89, 96, 173

United Nations, 72, 83, 104
Development Programme
(UNDP), 6
see also conferences
United States of America, 1, 10,
26–7, 56, 57, 78, 82, 92, 95,
123, 173, 182, 200
see also North America
Upper Volta, 203
urbanisation, 38, 107, 117, 132–43,
181
impacts of, 141–3
pseudo, 133
urbanism, 114
Uruguay, 57

Venezuela, 137, 157, 162
Vernon, Raymond, 90
Vietnam, 80, 82, 137, 182
Volkswagen, 100

Walker, Rob, 211
Wallerstein, Immanuel, 116
war, 76
civil, 82, 207–8
First World, 1, 89

Second World, 6, 70
see also under conflict, *and* Cold
War
Washington consensus, 152, 167
Weber, Max, 6
welfare, 71, 116, 126
West Africa, *see under* Africa
West Asia, *see under* Asia
Western Europe, *see under* Europe
Westphalian system, 70–1, 82
see also under nation-state
Williamson, John, 167
World Bank, 6, 97–8, 100, 103,
152, 178
see also institutions,
international financial
world systems, *see under* theory

Yugoslavia, 173

Zaire, 11, 20, 49, 60, 83, 140, 204,
208
Zambia, 17, 20, 203
Zapatistas, the, 22
Zartman, William, 11
Zimbabwe, 20, 50, 204, 208